How to Do
Everything™

MacBook®

Robin Noelle

McGraw Hill

New York Chicago San Francisco Lisbon
London Madrid Mexico City Milan New Delhi
San Juan Seoul Singapore Sydney Toronto

The **McGraw·Hill** Companies

Cataloging-in-Publication Data is on file with the Library of Congress

McGraw-Hill books are available at special quantity discounts to use as premiums and sales promotions, or for use in corporate training programs. To contact a representative, please e-mail us at bulksales@mcgraw-hill.com.

How to Do Everything™: MacBook®

1 2 3 4 5 6 7 8 9 0   WFR WFR   1 0 9 8 7 6 5 4 3 2 1 0

ISBN   978-0-07-174253-5
MHID   0-07-174253-0

Sponsoring Editor
Roger Stewart

Editorial Supervisor
Janet Walden

Project Editor
Howie Severson, Fortuitous
Publishing Services

Acquisitions Coordinator
Joya Anthony

Technical Editor
Guy Hart-Davis

Copy Editor
William McManus

Proofreader
Paul Tyler

Indexer
Karin Arrigoni

Production Supervisor
Jean Bodeaux

Composition
Glyph International

Illustration
Glyph International

Art Director, Cover
Jeff Weeks

Cover Designer
Jeff Weeks

To my mom for all of her support during the writing of this book

About the Author

Robin Noelle is a professional freelance writer and author of several technology-related books. She has more than 12 years' experience in the fields of high tech marketing and public relations. Having worked for two leading public relations agencies, Noelle has collaborated with a variety of clients, from fledgling Internet startup companies to market leaders such as Microsoft and IBM/Lotus. She spends her recreational time taking art classes, traveling, blogging, and keeping up on the latest video games.

About the Technical Editor

Guy Hart-Davis is the author of more than 60 computer books, including *Mac OS X System Administration, Integrating Macs in Windows Networks*, and *Mac OS X Leopard QuickSteps.*

Contents at a Glance

Contents

Acknowledgments

I'd like to thank my agent, Neil Salkind, for his ongoing support, and Joya Anthony and Roger Stewart at McGraw-Hill for the opportunity to write this book and their patience as I learned the formatting ropes. Also, thanks to Dwight Spivey for his superb book, *How to Do Everything: Mac*, which taught me a lot about the Mac OS and whose humorous writing style made me giggle during the tech editing process.

Introduction

Whether you are new to computers or just new to the MacBook, this book will provide you with valuable information to get the most out of your MacBook. You'll find that you can use your MacBook for much more than just e-mailing and surfing the Internet. You can utilize the easy-to-use Apple software to customize your workspace, edit and share your favorite photos, and create music, movies, and your own DVDs. That's just the tip of the iceberg!

As you move through the book, you'll discover each of the features that your MacBook has to offer and how to use them. Starting at the most simple point, taking your MacBook out of the box, the chapters open with basic information for new and unfamiliar users and gradually increase in complexity. Even seasoned Mac users will learn something from the tips and tricks included in this book.

You can read the book from beginning to end or skip to the chapters and sections that interest you the most. Critical information and convenient tips are highlighted throughout the book and are worth reading, even if you just have time to skim the chapter. Because Apple computers use the same operating system, many of the things you learn in this book can be applied to other Mac computer models, including the desktop versions. Your increased familiarity with the operating system can help you with mobile Apple products like the iPhone and iPad too.

MacBook computers aren't just another offering in the crowded laptop market, but powerful machines capable of handling complex processes with ease. Apple has taken care to create a durable, reliable, and simple-to-use computer that works for users of all levels. I hope you are pleased with your new (or future) MacBook and that this book helps you uncover all of the delightful things your MacBook can do for you. Thanks for buying my book!

What Does This Book Cover?

Chapter 1 explains the different MacBook models and the features included with each model. This chapter will help you choose the right model for your needs, if you haven't already purchased your MacBook, and teaches you how to turn your MacBook on and off, restart it, and put it into hibernation mode.

Chapter 2 covers the various input methods for your MacBook and how to use them, including the trackpad and mouse. You'll find out what Bluetooth technology is and how to add Bluetooth-enabled devices like wireless printers, speakers, and headsets to your laptop. This chapter also covers customizing your keyboard setup and how to use keyboard shortcuts to quickly perform common tasks.

Chapter 3 presents all you ever wanted to know about battery life, including how to best care and maintain your MacBook battery to lengthen the time before it needs to be replaced. If you use your laptop on battery power frequently, you will learn how to maximize your battery's charge and conserve precious mobile computing power.

If you've ever wondered what those slots and holes on the sides and back of your computer are for, Chapter 4 is for you. It explains how to identify and use each port. You'll learn about USB protocols, how to store files on an external flash drive, and how to connect an external display for a cinematic viewing experience.

Chapter 5 gives you tips for organizing your computer and desktop. You'll explore your MacBook's graphical user interface (GUI), including icons and menus, learn the difference between files and folders, and discover how to locate the Finder and Dock. You'll also find detailed information about the programs on your computer and how to access the MacBook and Apple help systems.

In Chapter 6, you'll discover how to search your MacBook for specific files as well as how to create new files and folders. Other file management techniques that are discussed include renaming, deleting, and organizing files. You'll find out how to permanently delete files from your MacBook as well as how to use Spaces and Exposé to keep your workspace and desktop organized.

Chapter 7 explains creating new user accounts for each person in your household and managing user accounts. You'll learn how to set permissions for each user, including how to use parental controls to help your children stay safe online. Parental control topics include how to schedule your child's computer time and how to restrict access to certain websites and adult materials.

In Chapter 8 you'll see how to customize your MacBook by changing user preferences. You can personalize your MacBook with a custom desktop background, screen saver, and icons. You'll discover how to adjust your sound settings, from the volume control to sending output to external speakers. You'll also learn how to add and remove your favorite programs to and from the Dock.

Chapter 9 explores your options for getting online, from dial-up to satellite Internet service. This chapter explains how to connect to wired and wireless networks and adjust your network settings. Network security is also discussed. You'll also find out how to share files and services with other computers.

Chapter 10 covers how to surf the Web with Safari, including how to add and remove your favorite sites from Safari's Top Sites page, create and manage bookmarks, set your browser preferences, and subscribe to RSS feeds. Internet security, including private browsing and choosing passwords, is also covered.

Chapter 11 keeps you in touch with friends and family by explaining e-mail, instant messaging, and video chat. You'll learn how to keep your e-mail inbox organized through the use of mailboxes and labels, set up iChat to communicate instantly with friends and family around the world, and initiate a video chat using your MacBook's iSight camera for real-time video conferencing.

In Chapter 12 you'll learn how to add and organize your contacts for use in other programs like Mail and iCal. This chapter explains how to create new contacts or add them from other programs like Mail, customize your Address Book contacts with photos and personalized information like birthdays and anniversaries, create and share new calendar entries, subscribe to other people's calendars, and sync your contracts and calendar with a mobile device.

If you thought you had to choose between Mac OS X and Windows, think again! Chapter 13 explains why you might want to run dual operating systems, including the advantages and disadvantages. This chapter helps you install Windows on your MacBook so that you can run Windows programs. You'll also learn how to switch between Mac OS X and Windows easily.

Chapter 14 covers all the great applications that are already loaded on your MacBook, providing brief descriptions of the applications so that you know what they do. Shared and common tasks are also discussed, such as how to open, close, save, and print files.

Chapter 15 presents an overview of the iWork productivity suite, including how to perform common tasks in Numbers, Pages, and Keynote. This chapter explains how to perform shared tasks between the applications, such as creating new documents and saving them. You'll also explore the word processing power of Pages, the spreadsheet abilities of Numbers, and how to create exciting presentations in Keynote.

Chapter 16 provides a brief overview of the iLife suite, including how to perform basic tasks in iPhoto, iMovie, GarageBand, iDVD, and iWeb. You'll see how to use iPhoto to edit, share, and archive your digital photos or burn them to a disc that's playable in most DVD players with iDVD. You'll also discover how to add your own digital video clips to iMovie to create and edit your own cinematic masterpiece, and how you can use GargageBand to learn to play instruments and record and mix your own music.

In Chapter 17 you'll discover how to use your MacBook to fill your leisure time. It explains how to find and play games on your MacBook; how to use QuickTime to view movies, and where to find great video content online; how to use iTunes to manage your music library through the use of playlists and ratings; and how to burn your favorite music to CDs so you can take it anywhere.

Chapter 18 covers setting up a new MobileMe account. You can use MobileMe to store information remotely and access it from anywhere, and you can use online MobileMe apps like Mail. You will also learn how to sync your information between multiple computers or mobile devices. This chapter also covers how to find or remotely erase a lost or stolen iPhone, iPad, or iPod Touch.

You can keep your MacBook running smoothly by downloading system and software updates and maintaining your hard drive health, as Chapter 19 explains. It also shows you how to use Disk Utility to identify and solve common problems. You'll also find out how to see the amount of space is available on your hard drive and how to create more when you need it. Time Machine is also covered, which helps protect you from data loss during a system malfunction.

In Chapter 20 you'll learn how to solve common MacBook problems and hardware/software issues. Basic troubleshooting steps are covered for both hardware and software. You'll discover how to reboot and restart your computer if it freezes, or how to turn it off when it isn't responding. This chapter also covers how to get additional technical support by using the Mac OS X and online help systems.

Conventions Used in This Book

In an attempt to be as succinct as possible and to direct you, the reader, to the most important information, a few conventions are used throughout this book.

- Caution, Note, and Tip sections are used to call attention to critical pieces of information throughout the chapters.
- How To and Did You Know boxes highlight important or helpful information and provide clear steps for completing certain tasks.
- The vertical bar (|) is used to link actions together. For example, "choose File | Print" means that you should first click the File menu and then select Print from the menu choices.
- The COMMAND key is referred to throughout the text and appears on your Apple keyboard as the ⌘ symbol. If you see this symbol in the text, it refers to the COMMAND key.

1

The Wonderful World of MacBook

HOW TO...

- Understand the difference between desktop and laptop computing
- Discover the different types of MacBook computers
- Unpack and set up your MacBook
- Power on, shut down, and restart your MacBook

Whether you've just purchased your first MacBook or are considering making the switch to Mac, congratulations! You are about to embark on a journey of discovery! Mac computers have long been lauded for their superior design and ease of use, particularly the MacBook laptop.

It used to be that to use a personal computer, you were tethered to a desk and a hulking, whirring piece of machinery stored beneath it. Since the advent of laptop computers, people have become increasingly mobile, taking their computers and using them wherever they go. The MacBook is the newest incarnation of Apple's popular laptop series. Previous lines included the iBook and PowerBook models. The MacBook is now one of Apple's top-selling products and one of the most popular laptop brands in the United States. Considering the strong sales figures, it seems that computer purchasers agree that Macs are easier and more convenient to use!

Another reason that Mac computers are so popular is that they've made areas that were once mostly the domain of professionals, like graphic arts, video editing, and music recording, accessible to novice users and hobbyists by providing powerful yet easy-to-use software and hardware. Mac computers are now purchased and used by everyone from grandmothers to students. Regardless of the reasons behind your recent (or upcoming) MacBook purchase, you've made the right decision.

This book will give you a wealth of information to get you started with your new computer. You'll find out how to care for your MacBook, both inside and out, as well as gain an overview of the included software and hardware. You'll learn how to perform common system-wide tasks like launching applications, opening files, and saving documents, as well as a few main tasks specific to the various programs. By the end of this book, you'll have mastered your MacBook, and pretty soon people will be turning to you for help!

Desktop vs. Laptop Computing

There are two main types of Mac computers, desktop and laptop, with the primary difference being portability. Even modern desktop computers, many of which come in diminutive sizes and styles, are not made to be transported and used in a variety of settings. With the portability of a laptop, you have everything you need at your fingertips—the screen, your pointing device, and optical drives (unless you purchased a MacBook Air, which doesn't have an optical drive) are contained in one light, streamlined shell, all powered with a rechargeable battery. All you need to do is grab it and go.

 If you plan on taking your MacBook with you frequently, invest in a good computer bag that offers a padded compartment for your laptop. If you do a lot of air travel, see the Transportation Security Administration's (TSA) website for approved laptop bags that can cut down on security hassles: www.tsa.gov/press/ happenings/simplifying_laptop_bag_procedures.shtm.

Choose the Best Laptop for You

There are three models of Apple's laptop computers, all in the MacBook family: the MacBook, MacBook Pro, and MacBook Air. Each offers differing features and capabilities, and the pricing widely varies by the model and the screen size.

The MacBook, shown in Figure 1-1, is the most affordable laptop model and includes the standard MacBook software and hardware. This basic MacBook model is made from a durable polycarbonate shell, unlike the MacBook Pro and Air, which use aluminum. This basic model is only slightly more than an inch thin and weighs only 4.7 pounds. The built-in battery lasts up to seven hours on a single charge. Its viewing area is a 13-inch LED-backlit widescreen display, and it is loaded with the most commonly used software, including programs for e-mail, Internet browsing, photo editing, and movie making. The MacBook currently retails for a suggested price of $999.

The MacBook is a good choice for people who mainly use their computer for word processing, e-mail, surfing the Internet, and using the included software like iTunes and iPhoto. If you are a traveler or student, you may prefer the more lightweight and portable MacBook Air. If you use professional-level software packages or are serious about playing the latest graphics-intensive games, you should look at the MacBook Pro.

Apple recently revamped its MacBook Pro line, adding a longer-lasting, ten-hour battery, more RAM (memory), and faster, more powerful graphics processors. As you can tell, the MacBook Pro was designed with the computer or graphics professional

FIGURE 1-1   The MacBook is the most affordable of the laptop models and is a good choice for most consumers. (Photo by Jared C. Benedict, Creative Commons; used by permission of the creator)

in mind and is all about performance. The MacBook Pro (see Figure 1-2) is available in 13-, 15-, and 17-inch models. The 13-inch MacBook Pro is available in two configurations: one with a 2.4 GHz Intel Core 2 Duo processor and 250GB hard drive, priced at $1199; and one with a 2.66 GHz Intel Core 2 Duo processor and 320GB hard drive, priced at $1499. The 15- and 17-inch MacBook Pro models include two graphics processors—one is used for graphics-intensive programs like games and professional video/photo software, while the other is used when energy-efficient operation is required. Both models also have batteries that last up to eight to nine hours on a single charge. MacBook Pro offers more ports and connections than other models. The new 15-inch MacBook Pro is available in three models (based on configuration) priced between $1799 and $2199. The new 17-inch MacBook Pro features a 2.53 GHz Intel Core i5, NVIDIA GeForce GT 330M, and 500GB hard drive for $2299.

Currently the MacBook models that are available contain one of three processor types: the Core 2 Duo, i5, and i7. In order, those processors go from least powerful to most. If purchasing a new MacBook, most consumers should opt for an i5 processor while power users should opt for the more powerful i7.

FIGURE 1-2   The MacBook Pro is a robust laptop made for top performance even when running resource-intensive applications. (Photo by Andrew Plumb/Clothbot, Creative Commons)

You should consider a MacBook Pro if you run powerful applications, do a lot of computer multitasking, or want to play the latest graphics-heavy games.

The MacBook Air, shown in Figure 1-3, is the thinnest and lightest of the Apple laptops, less than an inch thin and weighing just 3 pounds. The biggest difference between the Air and the other models is that it was designed with portability in mind

FIGURE 1-3   The MacBook Air is focused on portability. It's the perfect travel companion. (Photo by Renato Mitra, Creative Commons; used by permission of the creator)

Processing Speed, Memory, and Screen Resolution

Two of the most important features to take into consideration when choosing a MacBook (or any computer really) are the processing speed of the central processing unit (CPU) and the amount of memory. You will notice that all advertising for computers includes these two figures—CPU is expressed in GHz (gigahertz, such as 2.4 GHz Intel Core i5) and memory in GB (gigabytes; most MacBooks start with 4GB of memory). The CPU is your computer's brain, and the speed refers to how many tasks your computer can execute during a set amount of time (called a cycle). The faster the processor, the more processes your computer can handle. You should opt for models with a faster CPU speed if you need to run many programs simultaneously, are a serious gamer, or use professional-level software (which usually uses more resources than standard-level applications).

When your computer is performing these tasks, it temporarily places information in your computer's memory so that it can quickly access it to complete each process. If the memory on your computer becomes full, it will start writing the information to your hard drive and accessing it from there. This becomes a two-part process and slows everything down. Again, the standard configuration of most laptops is fine for the average computer user, but as you advance to more complex applications or games, you will need more speed and more memory to get the best performance.

One other item to consider, especially in a laptop for which you don't use an external display, is screen resolution. MacBook models come with varying screen resolutions (expressed as 1280×800, 1920×1200, and so on). The higher the resolution, the clearer and more detailed the graphics. The average user probably won't be put off by the lower resolutions of the 13-inch MacBook model, but if you work with graphics and video, a higher-resolution screen like that found on the 17-inch MacBook Pro model is a must.

and not performance. For example, while there is a full-sized screen, keyboard, and trackpad, there's no built-in optical (CD/DVD) drive like that included in the other MacBook models, but you can purchase an external one at an additional cost. The MacBook Air's processing speed is also slightly slower than other models, and it comes with a smaller hard drive. The MacBook Air is only available in the 13-inch screen size, and it also has fewer ports for connecting external peripherals like cameras and microphones. It's priced at $1499 and what you are really paying for is the compact size and low weight.

The MacBook Air is a good choice for people who spend the majority of their computing time traveling and use their computer mostly for e-mail, productivity software, and surfing the Internet. Because of the slower processing speed, lower amount of memory, and less powerful graphics processor, the MacBook Air isn't recommended for gaming or running complex applications.

Explore What's Included

All MacBook computers are ready to go right out of the box. Upon opening the package, you'll find your MacBook computer, power adapter and cord, install/restore DVDs, and the printed and electronic documentation. The Pro and Air models include a cleaning cloth to wipe your screen, and the Air model includes a USB Ethernet adapter for connecting to the Internet.

Basic Features

If you've never used a laptop before or never used an Apple computer before, it's a good idea to familiarize yourself with the basic features (see Figure 1-4) and functions, such as how to turn it on and off, how to connect it to a power source, and how to insert and eject CDs or DVDs. You'll especially want to know what the various ports on the side of the computer are used for and how to attach external components like your digital camera or speakers.

MacBooks come with a built-in iSight camera and microphone, and all but the MacBook Air come with a CD/DVD optical drive. Available ports that vary by model include FireWire 800, Gigabit Ethernet, Mini DisplayPort, audio in/optical digital audio in, headphone out/optical digital audio out, and USB version 2.0 ports.

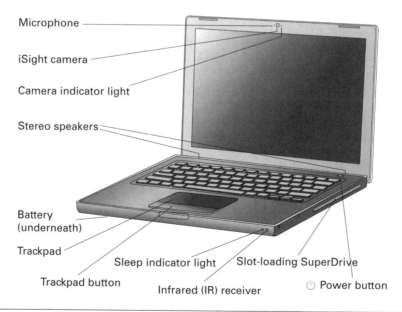

FIGURE 1-4 Locating your MacBook's main external features

Ports

Ports are those little slots that are on the side and sometimes back of your computer (see Figure 1-5). If you take a look, you'll see that these slots vary in size and shape to prevent you from inserting the wrong type of connector into the wrong port.

The most common type of port is the Universal Serial Bus (USB) port. USB ports are used to connect a variety of components to your computer, like a mouse, digital camera, or printer. These ports come in two speeds: 1.1 and 2.0. Version 2.0 is much faster than version 1.1, and is backward compatible. This means that you can have an older, 1.1-version scanner and it will work with a 2.0 port just fine.

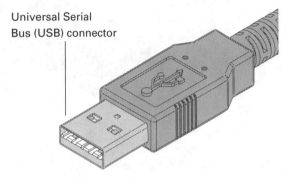

Universal Serial
Bus (USB) connector

USB 3.0, a significantly faster upgrade to USB 2.0 (theoretically ten times faster), was recently announced. No current MacBook models use 3.0 as of this writing but it is coming. Look for USB 3.0 in your next computer purchase, especially if you do a lot of data transfer to external drives or from a video camera to your computer.

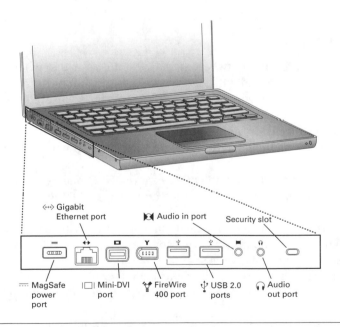

FIGURE 1-5   Ports on the MacBook

Another type of port that you can use to connect peripherals to your computer is the FireWire port. FireWire is an extremely fast connection type used primarily for connecting digital video cameras and external hard drives. There are currently two speeds of FireWire: FireWire 400 and FireWire 800. While the FireWire port may look similar to USB, you'll notice that the shape is slightly different and one will not fit in the other.

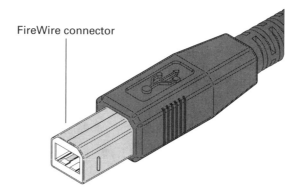

FireWire connector

If you aren't connecting wirelessly, you'll need to use your computer's Ethernet port. This is what you use to connect a Mac to the Internet or your home network. The Ethernet port looks similar to a phone jack but is wider. Ethernet cables have the appropriate connector that will fit, connecting your computer to a modem, switch, hub, or router.

The other ports you'll see are for headphones, external speakers, and a microphone. For more information on ports, please refer to Chapter 4.

Software

There's no difference between models when it comes to what software is included. All versions are loaded with the most recent version of the Snow Leopard operating system (Mac OS X), which includes programs for a variety of uses:

- **Communication** Mail, iChat, Safari, and Address Book are just some of the applications included to help you stay in touch with friends and family around the world.
- **Entertainment** Watch DVDs with the DVD player or surf the Web with Safari. You can play chess, watch video clips in QuickTime, and watch slideshows of your photos in iPhoto.
- **Creativity** Create your own playable DVDs with iDVD. Record and edit your own movies and music with iMovie and GarageBand. Your MacBook will help you become your creative best.
- **Productivity** Use the simple text editor or upgrade to iWork to use Pages, Numbers, and Keynote for your word processing, spreadsheet, and presentation needs.

And a lot more! See Chapter 14 for a list of applications on your MacBook.

Get Your MacBook Ready to Use

As previously stated, MacBooks are ready to go out of the box. With just a few steps, you can be up and surfing the Internet or writing a report in no time at all.

Connect to a Power Source

One thing that isn't usually ready right out of the box is the laptop battery. It must be fully charged before you start whisking your computer away to the local coffee shop. Remove the plastic covering from the AC adapter and locate an available plug near your primary workspace. Apple uses a magnetic power cord, and as you bring the adapter close to the computer's power outlet, you'll feel the pull. Just remember when detaching your computer from the power cord to always remove it from the adapter and not to pull on the cord. Keep your laptop plugged in until the charging light on the MagSafe plug (where you connect it to your computer) turns green and the battery is fully charged.

Surge protectors should be mandatory for your computer or any other expensive piece of electrical equipment. A surge protector keeps your computer safe from power surges that can fry delicate circuitry. The surge protector prevents these spikes from harming your computer by absorbing the excess electricity and, in the end, could save you from having to buy a whole new computer!

Turn It On

You've probably already located the power button on your MacBook. It's located in the right-hand corner of your computer above the keyboard. Once you've connected to your power source, just press the button briefly and wait for the computer to start up. Once it does, the setup wizard will walk you through the basic setup procedures and customizations for your computer.

Follow Setup Assistant

When you turn your Mac on for the very first time, you will automatically get started with Setup Assistant. Apple has provided this wizard to make it easy for you to set up the basic features of your computer. Setup Assistant will lead you through setting up a user account, setting the computer's time, registering your new computer, and even transferring your files from another Mac computer. If you prefer to not go through Setup Assistant, you can quit it at any time by pressing COMMAND-Q (simultaneously pressing the ⌘ and Q keys) and then choosing Skip from the available options.

Identify Desktop Features

Once your Mac has finished booting up, you'll see the Finder and your default desktop picture. You can further customize your MacBook desktop by clicking the Apple symbol on the menu bar and selecting System Preferences (hereafter, Apple | System Preferences). See Chapter 5 for the details on customizing your new MacBook.

Did You Know?

Transferring Files from One Macbook to Another

You can transfer files, applications, and user accounts from one Mac to another by using Setup Assistant. Just follow the prompts to migrate information from another Mac computer. You can do this either with an Ethernet cable connecting both computers directly or by connecting both computers to the same network wirelessly. Just make sure to run your software update on your new computer so that everything is up to date, and then, during the transfer, do not use the other Mac for anything until the download is complete. If you don't use Setup Assistant to transfer information when you first start your computer, you can do it later using Migration Assistant from the Applications | Utilities menu.

The following are the desktop elements:

- **Menu bar** The menu bar at the top of your screen contains several menus: the Apple menu (accessed by clicking the Apple symbol), the Finder or application menu, status menus (such as File, Edit, and View), and the Spotlight menu (the small magnifying glass icon in the upper-right corner).

- **Desktop** The desktop is the main surface area on your computer screen and what you will see every time you boot up your computer. You can change the default picture to anything you like. The desktop will be covered in Chapter 5.
- **Dock** The Dock is the area at the bottom of the screen that contains shortcuts to applications and documents that you use most often. Click an application's icon on the Dock to launch it.

Navigate

MacBooks use a trackpad (see Figure 1-6) for navigation instead of the more traditional mouse used by desktop computers. The trackpad can take some getting used to but operates similarly to the mouse. To use a trackpad, place a finger on the pad and move it around on the surface; you will see the cursor on your screen move in the direction that you move your finger. To select an item, click the trackpad button once; to open the item, double-click the button. More options are available by using the "right-click" function of a mouse; to right-click with the trackpad, hold down the

FIGURE 1-6   A MacBook trackpad. (Photo by Highway of Life, Creative Commons)

CONTROL key on the keyboard while clicking the trackpad button. If you do a lot of mouse-related activities on your computer (like photo editing or gaming), you might want to add a USB mouse instead of always using the trackpad. Also, not all new MacBooks have a trackpad button. Instead, you can tap anywhere on the trackpad and get the same result!

You can also secondary click by tapping the trackpad with two fingers instead. In the Trackpad pane (Apple | System Preferences | Trackpad), check Tap Trackpad Using Two Fingers for Secondary Click. See Chapter 2 for more information on pointing devices.

Power On, Power Off, and Reboot

You already know how to turn on your MacBook—just press the power button and wait for the computer to boot up. It's almost as easy to shut down your computer or put it into energy-saving hibernation.

Restart Your MacBook

Sometimes you may need to restart your MacBook, such as when you've installed some new software or downloaded updates that require a restart. To restart your Mac, choose Apple | Restart. You are asked if you are sure you want to restart. After you

How to... # Check Which Version of Mac OS X You're Using

There are situations where it's important to know what version of the operating system you have installed, such as when you purchase new software or need to troubleshoot a problem. You can easily check which version of Mac OS X your Mac is running by choosing Apple | About This Mac. The resulting dialog box will show you what version of Mac OS X you are running.

click Restart, your screen will go dark as the computer resets; then, after the operating system finishes loading, you will be back at your desktop.

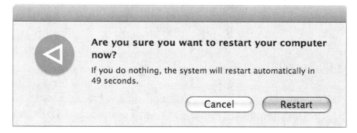

 If you decide you do not want to restart your computer after you've selected Apple | Restart, you must click Cancel within one minute or the operating system will restart automatically. Normally, if you are working in open applications with unsaved data, you will be prompted to save and then close the program before you can restart.

Shut Down Your Mac

To shut down, or turn off, your MacBook, choose Apple | Shut Down. You are again asked if you are sure you want to shut down. Just click Shut Down and your screen will go black.

Make sure that your hard drive and fans have stopped spinning (that's the whirring noise you hear when your computer is starting or rebooting) before you move your computer. Moving a computer while the hard drive is working can cause damage and lost data.

Sleep

Sleep mode is a nice compromise between shutting down your computer every time you use it and just leaving it on. Sleep mode saves energy and allows you to quickly resume your activities without having to wait for the computer to fully load.

To put your Mac in sleep mode, choose Apple | Sleep. The screen on your Mac will go black, but it will not shut down. When your MacBook is in sleep mode, it uses a very low amount of energy and still keeps all of your documents and applications open, just how you left them.

 If you've left your MacBook on while you've stepped away from the desk, you might return to find that your computer has gone to sleep on its own, especially if you are running on battery power and not the AC adapter. To resume where you left off, just push any keyboard button to wake up your MacBook. See Chapter 3 for information on energy saving settings.

Summary

In this chapter you've learned about the various MacBook computers and the differences between them, as well as how to get your MacBook up and running straight out of the box. You've also learned some basic functions, such as putting your MacBook to sleep and restarting and shutting down your computer. Continue on to the next chapter to learn all about using pointing devices.

2

Taming the MacBook: Using the Trackpad, Mouse, Keyboard, and More

HOW TO...

- Customize and use your keyboard
- Use keyboard shortcuts
- Use the trackpad
- Add and use a mouse
- Go wireless: using Bluetooth
- Add and use a drawing tablet

Your computer won't be of much use to you if you can't figure out how to navigate the screens and move your cursor. If you've never used a computer before, using a trackpad or mouse for navigation can take some getting used to. Even experienced desktop users will undergo a learning curve when using a trackpad. Once you've mastered the basics, you will find that there's a variety of input devices that you can easily add to your MacBook to enhance your experience, including wireless keyboards, mice, and even drawing tablets and pens.

This chapter will help you discover how to get around on your MacBook, from using the keyboard shortcuts to avoiding frustration when using the trackpad. You'll learn how to add and remove new input devices and how to customize the ones that you add. Once you complete this chapter, you'll be able to effortlessly navigate your MacBook with a variety of devices.

FIGURE 2-1 The standard QWERTY layout on a Mac keyboard (Photo by roadmr, Creative Commons)

Orient Yourself to the Standard Keyboard

Before there were keyboards, there were typewriters, so you're probably wondering why using a keyboard warrants a place in this book at all. The reason is that using a computer keyboard is a lot different from using a typewriter, thanks to being able to assign multiple functions to each key through the use of the COMMAND, CONTROL, OPTION, SHIFT, FN, and ALT keys. The truth is that even experienced computer users rarely understand the full capabilities of the keyboard when it comes to special functions (like changing the brightness or ejecting a DVD) and using shortcuts.

The layout of the standard computer keyboard (and that old typewriter in the attic) is called the QWERTY layout. This is because QWERTY are the first six letter keys in the top row. In addition to the letter keys, you'll notice a top row of function keys labeled F1 through F12, a row of number keys, and a numerical keypad somewhere on the right side. On your bottom row, in addition to the SPACEBAR, you'll find the special function keys, which include the FN, CONTROL, COMMAND, and OPTION/ALT keys (see Figure 2-1). You can use these in different combinations to access the special features of your keyboard. Consider your keyboard as command central—you can access nearly any function of your computer through just a few keystrokes.

Use Keyboard Shortcuts

Using a keyboard shortcut usually requires pressing one or more keys to access the function. When multiple keys are required, you press the modifier key first, hold it down, and then press the other key or keys. For example, the keyboard shortcut for copying selected text is COMMAND-C. That means you must press the COMMAND key and then the C key, so that they are depressed at the same time. (The COMMAND key occasionally includes a ⌘ symbol, an apple icon, or both. It's also sometimes called the Apple key.) This is true of all key combinations, including COMMAND-X (cut), COMMAND-V (paste), and COMMAND-A (select all). OPTION-COMMAND-W (close all open windows) means that you press and hold OPTION, then COMMAND, and then the w key.

Use the FN Key

The FN (function) key is available on all built-in MacBook keyboards. Pressing this key in conjunction with other keys will give you access to additional key functions. You will notice that the top row of your keyboard has a number of symbols on each key. These will vary depending on your specific model, but most include pictograms that relate to basic tasks like adjusting the brightness of your screen, opening the dashboard, and controlling DVD playback (fast forward, rewind, play, pause, and stop). You'll notice that on some keyboards, the functions that can be controlled with the FN key are a different color than the main key function.

 Customize Your Keyboard

You can customize your keyboard in a few ways to make typing easier.

1. Choose System Preferences from the Apple menu.
2. Click Keyboard in the resulting window.
3. Click the Keyboard tab, as shown in the following illustration. You can set the sensitivity of your keyboard for how fast you type and make other keyboard adjustments:

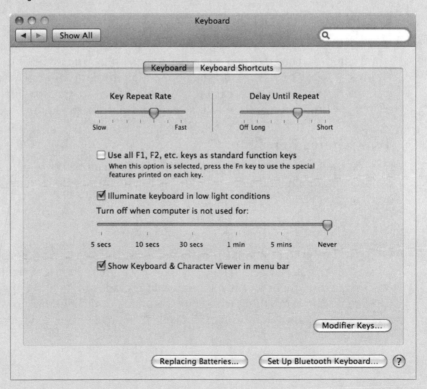

(Continued)

- You can control how quickly a character is repeated when the key is held down by adjusting the Key Repeat Rate slider. Move it to the left to slow down the rate or to the right to increase it.
- You can also adjust how long it takes for a key to start repeating by adjusting the Delay Until Repeat slider.
- Click the check box if you want your keyboard to illuminate in low light conditions for better visibility.
- You can use the slider to alter the setting for when your computer will turn off keyboard illumination when the computer is not in use. Available times range from seconds to minutes to never. Turning off keyboard illumination will save power when running your laptop on battery only.
- To use the F1–F12 keys on your keyboard to control other application features, mark the check box. You'll need to press the FN key along with the F1–F12 key to perform the key's default function.
- Advanced users can reassign the modifier keys (CONTROL, OPTION, COMMAND, and CAPS LOCK) by clicking Modifier Keys. In the menu, you can change which modifier is assigned to what key, or disable a key completely. One reason to use this feature would be if you were adding to your laptop an external keyboard that wasn't made for a Mac.

Use the Trackpad

The trackpad serves as an alternative to a mouse when using a laptop. On many laptop models, the trackpad has a flat surface plus one or two buttons (refer to Figures 1-4 and 1-6). On your MacBook, depending on the model, you'll find that it has one button or no buttons at all. You can use your trackpad in a variety of ways, such as to help you zoom, scroll, select, and minimize windows.

Two-Finger Scrolling

Use the trackpad to move the mouse cursor. You can use two fingers to scroll your window up, down, and sideways. This is a standard use for the trackpad and is turned on as a default.

Secondary Clicking or Right-Clicking

When you use the right-click function of a mouse, you can access a contextual menu for whatever you happen to be doing. For example, you might right-click in your word processing document and see a menu that includes tasks like Copy, Cut, and Paste. You can do the same thing with your trackpad. You can adjust how this works from the Trackpad pane (System Preferences | Trackpad), shown next, and set it up for two-finger or one-finger clicking. You can also access this function by pressing the CONTROL key while clicking.

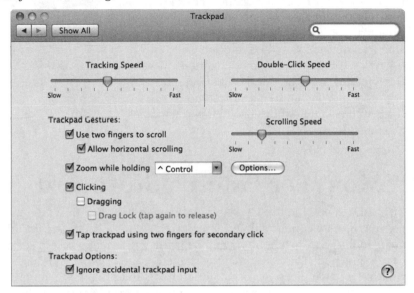

Zooming and Rotating

Some programs allow you to use the two-finger trackpad to zoom in and out and rotate. By pinching your two fingers together on the trackpad, you can zoom into a photo or PDF file. Moving your fingers apart will zoom out.

Place two fingers on the pad and rotate them to the right or left to rotate your photo or PDF document.

Swiping

Brushing three fingers across the trackpad allows you to quickly page through documents or photos. You can move backward or forward using this method to switch to the next or previous item. If you use four fingers, you can swipe left to right to switch between open programs, or you can swipe up and down to access Exposé and either view all open windows or the desktop.

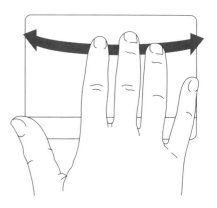

Add a Mouse or External Keyboard

The trackpad and built-in keyboard are ideal for using your laptop while traveling but they may not be comfortable for long-term use. It's a good idea to add a mouse and/or external keyboard when you will be using your MacBook in a stationary area for an extended period. There are many portable yet full-sized keyboards and mice to choose from that you can keep in your computer bag and plug in when you need them.

The most common way to connect these external devices is through the USB port. You can purchase a mouse and simply plug in the USB connector to the port on the side or back of your computer. Your MacBook will automatically install the driver needed to use the mouse. In just a few seconds, you are ready to go!

 Keep a mouse pad in your travel computer bag so that you have a good, smooth surface for using your mouse wherever you end up.

The same is true of using a keyboard. You can purchase a USB keyboard that is full size, such as you would use with a desktop computer, or one that is smaller and thus easier to transport. There are even some that are full size but fold up for easy transport.

 You don't have to purchase your mouse and keyboard from Apple if you don't want to, but there are differences between a Mac keyboard and a PC keyboard (most noticeably the addition of the COMMAND/Apple key). Make sure that whatever you buy connects via USB and is compatible with your MacBook.

Use Bluetooth Devices

Bluetooth is a way to wirelessly share data between two devices over a short distance. Most people are familiar with Bluetooth headsets for their cellular phone, but you can also use Bluetooth to connect a wireless keyboard or mouse to your computer, if your computer has Bluetooth capability.

In order to use Bluetooth, you need to make sure Bluetooth is turned on and your computer is discoverable. To do this, choose Apple | System Preferences and then, under Internet & Wireless, select Bluetooth (see Figure 2-2). You use the Bluetooth Setup Assistant to pair your devices. If you don't see Bluetooth in the menu, your computer does not have a built-in Bluetooth module. In this case, if you still want to use Bluetooth, you can purchase an external Bluetooth adapter and plug it into your USB port like any other device.

Make sure to check that the Bluetooth adapter you want is compatible with Mac before you purchase it!

Follow the manufacturer's directions to insert the batteries into your new mouse (see Figure 2-3).

To continue setting up your Bluetooth mouse on your MacBook, switch on the mouse; the indicator light should begin to flash to show that the mouse is in discovery mode. This will allow you to begin the pairing procedure.

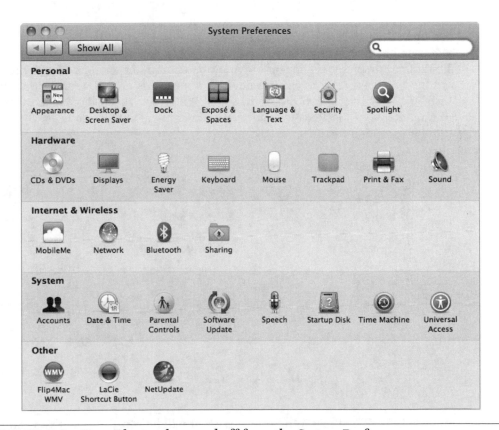

FIGURE 2-2   Turn Bluetooth on and off from the System Preferences pane.

FIGURE 2-3 You can add a wireless mouse or keyboard using Bluetooth technology.
(Photo by Yutaka Tsutano, Creative Commons; used by permission of the creator)

Open System Preferences and then select Mouse. Your MacBook will automatically begin searching for a discoverable Bluetooth mouse (see Figure 2-4). After a few seconds, the mouse cursor should appear on your open computer window. The Setup Assistant will then attempt to pair your two devices. Repeat this procedure to pair a Bluetooth keyboard, only select Keyboard from System Preferences instead of Mouse. Once pairing is complete, your MacBook will automatically connect to these devices when both they and the computer are on.

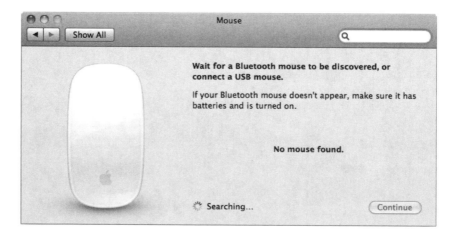

FIGURE 2-4 The Bluetooth Setup Assistant will help you connect your mouse and MacBook.

Add a Graphics Tablet

One thing that Mac computers have always excelled at is graphics. Macs are still very much the computers of choice for serious graphics professionals who work with animation, illustration, animation, and photo editing. Whether you are a budding professional or a dedicated hobbyist, if you are interested in doing graphics work on your MacBook, you might want to consider adding a graphics tablet.

Graphics tablets come with the tablet, which provides a work surface for either drawing freehand or tracing sketched materials, and a stylus that you can use as a mouse or drawing tool. Some graphics tablets also come with a mouse. These tablets come in a variety of sizes and in a range of prices. If you enjoy detailed photo editing or using drawing programs, adding a graphics tablet is a must!

Summary

You now know how to navigate your MacBook computer and how to add new devices to suit your computing style. Now that you've mastered the basics, it's time to start delving into even more ways to make your Mac work for you.

3

Power Struggle: Battery and Power Management

HOW TO...

- Check how much battery power remains
- Prolong the life of your MacBook battery
- Optimize your power management settings
- Calibrate your battery for accurate power readings
- Lengthen the lifespan of your battery
- Store your battery for extended periods
- Replace your battery

If there's one complaint that's almost universal among laptop users, it's battery life—how long the computer will operate on battery power before the battery has to be recharged. As a MacBook user, you'll receive many more hours of use from one charge of your laptop battery than most PC users receive from one charge of theirs. That's because the standard MacBook comes with a battery that lasts for seven or more hours, as opposed to the standard PC battery, which lasts for approximately two to three hours. Still, even the wonderful extended-life battery that came with your MacBook needs proper attention to stay in top condition. With a little time and a few simple steps, you can ensure that your battery maintains its long life and holds a charge even after being recharged again and again.

This chapter will help you discover how to get the most life out of your MacBook battery as well as how to store it properly if you won't be using your computer for a while. You'll find out which power settings will give you the longest portable computing time and how often to calibrate your MacBook so you always know accurately how much battery life you have left.

Understand MacBook Battery Technology

Even the basic MacBook model comes with an extended-life battery that can power your computer for up to seven hours. Other models have even longer-lasting batteries. The technology that Apple uses in its MacBook computers is called lithium-ion. Lithium-ion batteries offer the best performance and hold charges longer than the old nickel-based batteries that used to be common in laptops. Lithium batteries are lighter than nickel batteries, helping to keep the weight down on your super-slim MacBook computer. Also, they pack more power into a smaller space. With the old nickel-based batteries, you had to completely discharge and then recharge the battery to get maximum power, and over time these batteries would hold less and less of a charge until they finally needed to be replaced. That's not to say that your laptop battery will last forever, but with proper care, it will far outlast a nickel-based laptop battery.

Battery life span is measured in charge cycles, and your MacBook battery, depending on the model, is designed to hold up to 80 percent of its charge after 750–1000 charge cycles. But what does that mean? A charge cycle is completed when you use 100 percent of your battery power and then fully recharge it. That completes a single cycle. For example, if you use your laptop down to 50 percent battery power one afternoon and recharge it fully, a charge cycle will not be complete until you've used and recharged another 50 percent of the battery life during a different session. Likewise, you can use 25 percent of your battery power on one day, recharge it, and then use 75 percent battery power on another day and recharge it to complete a single cycle. Supposing that you frequently use battery power and run your computer's battery down and recharge it every day, your battery should maintain its life for at least two to three years.

Did You Know?

Battery Life vs. Battery Life Span

There's a difference between battery life and battery life span. Your MacBook's battery life is how long your MacBook can operate using only battery power before it needs to be recharged, whereas the battery life span is how long your battery will last before it needs to be replaced.

Did You Know? **Resuming from Sleep Mode**

Although your computer goes to sleep when the battery is exhausted, there's still some power left to keep it in sleep mode. Once the battery is completely drained, the computer will shut down, but not before saving its current state so you can resume from exactly where you left off once you've switched to AC power or recharged the battery.

Check Your Battery Power

If you look in the upper-right corner of your display, you'll see a battery icon near the time and date. You can click this icon to see the condition of your battery and how much computing time you have left before you need to recharge it. You can also change the settings so that instead of the icon, your taskbar will show the computing time you have left or the percentage of power remaining.

 Your MacBook will let you know when it is running low on battery power so you can save your work before it goes to sleep. Still, it's a good idea to keep an eye on how much time you have remaining so this warning doesn't come as a complete surprise.

Extend Battery Life

How long your battery lasts during any given computer session depends on how you are using your computer. Watching a DVD on your MacBook will drain the battery much faster than using the photo editor or surfing the Internet. The more features and programs you use, the more power is required in battery mode to keep your computer running.

 Even if your MacBook is your primary computer and you don't travel frequently, don't exclusively run your laptop on AC power. The battery needs to be used at least occasionally to maximize its performance and life span. Make sure you use your MacBook on battery power and complete one full charge cycle at least once per month.

The easiest way to extend the life of your battery is to turn off features that you aren't using. For example, if you do not need to connect to the Internet, turning off the wireless capabilities (AirPort and Bluetooth) will save you significant battery power because, although you aren't connecting to the Internet, your computer is always looking for available network connections when these features are on.

If you aren't using the optical drive on your MacBook, remove any CD or DVD that is in the drive. Every now and then your MacBook will check the drive and read your disc, so removing any media you aren't using will save this small amount of power.

Another easy way to save power when using your computer is to disconnect any peripheral devices that you have connected, such as a digital camera, iPod, or printer. Even when not in use, these devices can draw small amounts of power from your battery's stores. You should also set the screen brightness to the lowest but most comfortable level for your conditions. If you're using your laptop in low light conditions, you won't need the screen brightness turned all the way up. Dimming the screen will save quite a lot of power over time. To change your screen's brightness, press F1 (darker) or F2 (brighter) until you find the right setting that's comfortable for you.

 Close any open programs that you aren't using to conserve even more power.

Optimize Your Power Management Settings

Your MacBook's System Preferences pane has some handy features that let you determine how your battery power is managed. If you frequently use your laptop on battery power, you can access these power management settings and adjust them to conserve power (Figure 3-1).

1. Open the System Preferences pane from the Apple menu.
2. Choose View | Energy Saver.
3. Select Battery or Battery Power from the Settings For menu.

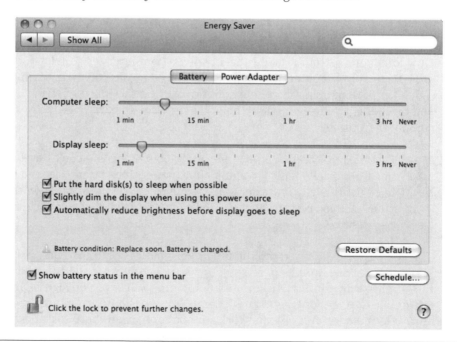

FIGURE 3-1 You can change the Energy Saver options for battery power to lower the power consumption of your MacBook. By clicking on Power Adapter, you can also adjust AC power settings.

How to...

Turn off AirPort and Bluetooth

Turning off AirPort will stop your MacBook from constantly looking for networks to connect to and help conserve your battery. Here are the steps to follow:

1. Open the System Preferences dialog box from the Apple menu.
2. Choose View | Network.
3. Click Turn AirPort Off.

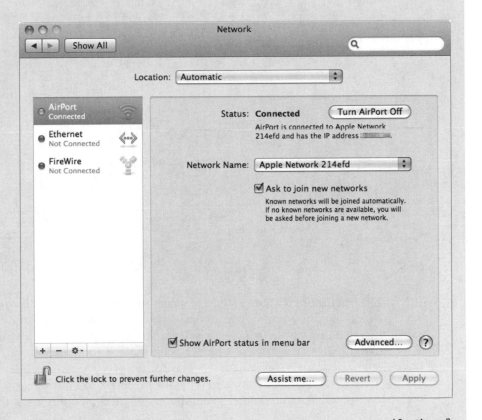

(Continued)

Turning off Bluetooth will also help conserve power when you are running your MacBook on battery power. Here are the steps to turn off Bluetooth, for Mac OS X 10.2 or later:

1. Open the System Preferences dialog box from the Apple menu.
2. Choose View | Bluetooth.
3. Uncheck the On check box.

4. Use the Computer Sleep slider to select the length of time after which you would like the computer to go to sleep when on battery power and not in use.
5. Use the Display Sleep slider to select the length of time after which you would like the display to "sleep" when the computer is unattended.

You can also check the boxes to tell your MacBook to put the hard disk to sleep whenever possible and to keep the computer screen dim when using the battery.

Calibrate Your Battery for Optimal Performance

When using your computer on battery power, you'll notice the battery power indicator in the upper-right corner of your screen. Your computer knows approximately how much power your battery contains and how long it will last by using an internal process that tracks your battery power as it charges and discharges. In order to keep this estimate as accurate as possible, it's occasionally necessary to recalibrate your battery. You should perform this calibration when you first use your computer and then do it again every few months. If you mainly use your computer on AC power, then you should calibrate the battery once a month to ensure accuracy.

How to... **Calibrate Your Battery**

Your MacBook will keep track of how much time you can operate your MacBook while operating on battery power. To keep your computer accurate, you should occasionally calibrate your battery.

1. Use your AC adapter to fully charge your MacBook computer, until the charging light turns green.
2. Keep your computer plugged in and on AC power for a minimum of two hours. You can use your computer during this time as long as it remains plugged in and charging.
3. Unplug your computer from the AC adapter and begin using battery power only. Use your computer until the battery is low enough that the power warning dialog box appears.
4. Save any projects that you are working on and continue to use the computer until the battery is depleted and your MacBook automatically goes into sleep mode.
5. Turn off your MacBook or allow it to remain in sleep mode for five or more hours.
6. Reconnect the power adapter and allow the battery to fully charge once more.

Store Your Battery

There may come a time when you need to put your MacBook away for a while. If you're going to be storing your laptop for six months or more, you should use your battery until it reaches 50 percent power and then remove it and store it in a cool, dry place. If you store it when fully depleted, it's possible that the battery will no longer be able to hold a charge when you want to use it again. Storing it while fully charged can also lead to a decrease in battery life. In many of the new MacBooks, the batteries are not user-accessible. To remove or replace your battery, you will have to take your MacBook to an Apple service provider.

Tip   Using your MacBook in very hot temperatures (above 95 degrees F) can permanently damage your battery's ability to hold a charge. Charging or storing your battery in these high temperatures will also permanently reduce the life and life span of your battery. Conversely, although storing, charging, and using your battery in cold temperatures may cause a temporary decrease in performance, once the battery returns to a normal temperature, you should regain any lost capacity.

Replace Your Battery

Unfortunately, your MacBook battery won't hold its maximum charge forever, and you may want to replace it before you purchase a new MacBook. When you start noticing that your battery life has significantly decreased (Figure 3-2), you'll want to look into having the battery replaced. Older MacBook models have batteries that

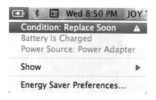

FIGURE 3-2   Your MacBook will let you know when it's time to replace the battery.

can be replaced by the end user, and a number of companies produce compatible after-market batteries. New MacBook models have built-in batteries that need to be replaced by an authorized Apple service provider.

 Your MacBook will let you know when it thinks your battery should be replaced. You can find this information by clicking the Battery icon in your taskbar or from the System Preferences | Energy Saver menu. Your MacBook may not always know what's best, however. If you don't notice a significant decrease in computing time while using battery power, you can probably hold off on buying a new battery until you really need one.

Summary

Now you should be able to get the most life and life span out of your built-in MacBook battery. Proper care, storage, and calibration of your battery will ensure that you get the maximum use out of it before it needs to be replaced.

4

Ports: Where They Are and What They Do

HOW TO...

- Identify the ports on your MacBook
- Install and use USB devices
- Install a USB printer or scanner
- Connect an external display
- Connect external speakers and a microphone
- Connect video and digital cameras
- Use a memory card

All MacBook computers come with at least a few ports so that you can use external devices like printers, speakers, and digital cameras. The types and locations of these ports vary depending on the model of your Apple MacBook. The 17-inch MacBook Pro comes with the most ports while the MacBook Air comes with the fewest. Determining which ports are most important to you and how many you need will help you decide which MacBook to purchase (if you haven't already purchased one).

This chapter will help you identify the types of ports that are available on the various MacBook models and how to connect the devices that use them.

Identify the Ports

As soon as you take your MacBook out of the box, you'll notice a number of ports and slots along the side of your laptop. While some of these ports look the same, they each have their own specific use. Each port is uniquely shaped to only accept connections from the correct cable or card and to only allow them to fit in the proper way. For example, you won't be able to connect a USB cable to a FireWire port, nor will you be able insert your USB cable upside-down. This prevents you from accidentally inserting the wrong device into the wrong slot, which could damage both the slot and the cable. It's a good idea to keep this in mind and never force a cable or card into your MacBook! Now let's look at which MacBook models come with which ports.

MacBook Ports

The MacBook is the basic Apple laptop model and comes with a standard set of input and output ports (see Figure 4-1). The types and number of these ports are probably sufficient for most general computer users. The MacBook includes

- MagSafe power port
- Gigabit Ethernet port
- Mini DisplayPort
- Two USB 2.0 ports (up to 480 Mbps)
- Audio in/out
- Kensington lock slot

The MagSafe power port is pretty self-explanatory. This is where you connect your AC adapter to charge your MacBook's battery or use your MacBook on AC power. It has a magnetic connector so that if your cord becomes snagged or is yanked suddenly, it simply disconnects instead of dumping your laptop on the floor or damaging the power port.

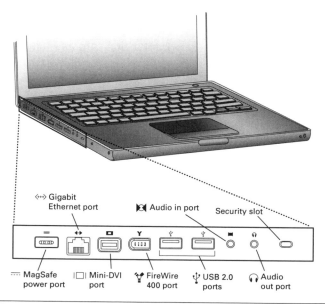

FIGURE 4-1 The placement of ports on a MacBook

The Ethernet port is for connecting to a wired Ethernet network. See Chapter 9 for more information on how to connect to a network and the Internet.

You probably won't be using your Kensington lock slot, but in case you're curious, it's a slot designed for, you guessed it, a Kensington lock! Kensington locks usually come attached to a thick cable that can be looped around something solid and then connected to your computer to prevent sticky-fingered thieves from running off with your expensive computer. In most cases, retailers use these to keep their laptops on the shelves and out of people's backpacks, but if you use your computer a lot in public places, it may be of some use to you as well.

MacBook Pro

The MacBook Pro is the professional laptop model and contains a larger number and wider variety of ports to support external devices (Figure 4-2). There are three MacBook Pro models, each with a different screen size, ranging from 13 to 17 inches. While there is no difference between the 13- and 15-inch models (port-wise), the 17-inch MacBook contains additional ports.

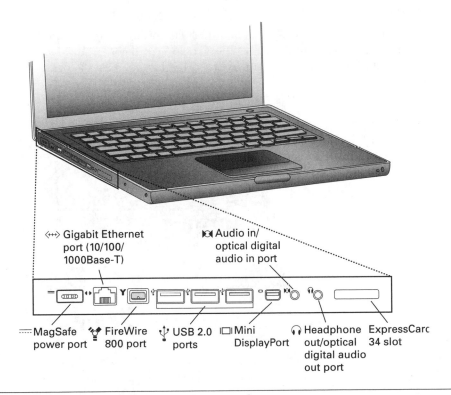

FIGURE 4-2   The port locations on a MacBook Pro

The 13- and 15-inch MacBook Pro models contain the following ports:

- MagSafe power port
- Gigabit Ethernet port
- One FireWire 800 port (up to 800 Mbps)
- Mini DisplayPort
- Two USB 2.0 ports (up to 480 Mbps)
- SD card slot
- Audio in/out
- Kensington lock slot

The 17-inch model includes everything except the SD card slot but adds an additional USB 2.0 port and an ExpressCard/34 slot. The ExpressCard/34 slot is just another way to connect peripherals to your computer, like the USB 2.0 slot. There are a number of devices that use an ExpressCard slot, including external disk drives, wireless network interface cards, cards for attaching multiple displays, and TV tuner cards for watching TV on your computer.

MacBook Air

The MacBook Air is the lightest and most streamlined of all of the MacBook computers. To this end, it contains the fewest ports (see Figure 4-3). Your MacBook Air will come with an audio out jack, a Mini DisplayPort, and one USB 2.0 port.

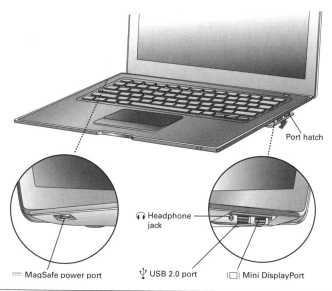

FIGURE 4-3 The port locations on a MacBook Air

Work with USB 2.0

USB stands for Universal Serial Bus and allows peripheral devices like printers and cameras to "talk" to your computer. It used to be that there were very specific ports on the back of a personal computer to connect things like a monitor or printer. Sometimes you needed a special cable or adapter in order to connect a device, and there was a lot of hunting around for compatible connectors. Now that USB is available, manufacturers use this technology to ensure that their devices can be connected to every computer with the use of one standard cable. How convenient!

USB has been around for a while and is a huge improvement over the old connectors used for monitors and printers. The first version of the USB protocol (USB 1.0) only allowed connections of a certain speed; USB 2.0 is faster and handles more data, and thus supports a wider variety of devices. Your MacBook comes with at least one and as many as three USB 2.0 ports, as this is the current standard. You can still use USB 1.0 devices in these ports but you will experience reduced data transfer speeds. USB 3.0 was recently announced but I wouldn't recommend that you run right out and purchase a device with it. You won't receive the benefits of USB 3.0 until MacBooks are available with ports that support it.

USB Mass Storage

One of the more common uses for a USB port is to connect a portable mass storage device, frequently called a flash or jump drive. These drives come in a variety of shapes, sizes, and storage capacities. Flash drives are handy if you want to back up documents, photos, or video or transfer them to other computers. You can store work or school documents on your flash drive and then open them on any computer you happen to be using by plugging in the flash drive. Save your changed document to your flash drive and you've always got the most recent copy available at your fingertips.

Another way to gain more storage by using your USB port is to connect an external hard drive. External hard drives are larger and more expensive than flash drives but they can hold a lot more data. External drives are great if you download or create a lot of music or movies, take tons of photos, or collect other space-intensive files. You can

Did You Know?

It's Important to Properly Eject USB Devices

You always want to properly eject your USB devices instead of just unplugging them from your computer. This is because your MacBook keeps a cache of the information stored on your drive in its memory and only occasionally copies it to the drive. If you yank your device out of the USB port before this syncing happens, you could corrupt the data or your drive could have an earlier version of your files.

also use an external drive to back up your system to transfer to another computer or restore your laptop in the event of a system failure.

Using a USB storage device is easy. If your USB drive requires external power, plug it in and then plug the USB connector into the port; your MacBook will take care of the rest. It installs any drivers that it needs to be able to recognize the device and then formats the drive if necessary. Once it's installed, you can drag and drop your files onto the drive.

After you've loaded onto your USB device the files you want to store on it, do not pull the drive out of the port without first "ejecting" it via software. This ensures that your MacBook has a chance to wrap up any unfinished tasks. If you don't give it this chance, it will warn you that the disk was not ejected properly. There are two ways to eject a USB drive from your Mac:

- Drag your device's icon from the desktop to the trash can.
- CONTROL-click on the device's icon and select Eject from the resulting menu.

USB Printers and Scanners

If you're like most people, you have a printer at home to print out your documents and photos. If your printer was made in the last decade, the chances are that it has a USB connector. Installing your printer is easy. In most cases, you simply need to plug in the USB cable and let your MacBook do the rest. If, for some reason, your printer doesn't then appear in the Printer pop-up menu, you can add it by choosing Apple | System Preferences | Print & Fax to open the Print & Fax pane (see Figure 4-4). Then, follow these steps (follow the same steps to connect a USB scanner to your MacBook):

1. Connect your printer to the computer with the provided USB cable.
2. Open the System Preferences window from the Apple menu.
3. Click the Print & Fax icon to open the Print & Fax pane.
4. Click the + under the Printers box to start the Add a Printer wizard.
5. Select your printer from the available list and click Add.

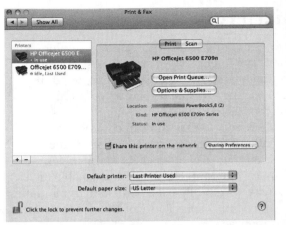 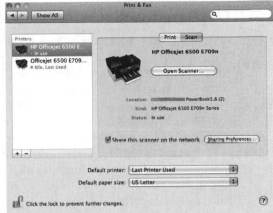

FIGURE 4-4   The Print & Fax preferences window. You can add new printers and set up printer sharing in the Print tab (left). Click the Scan button to add or share a scanner (right).

Other USB Devices

Many other devices come with a USB connector. The most common is probably your printer, but there are lots of other things you can connect to your MacBook too. These include scanners, cameras, speakers, graphics tablets, and wireless mice and keyboards (which usually have a signal receiver that needs to be connected to your computer). To install one of these devices, just plug in its USB connector and wait for your MacBook to load the files it needs to run it; if your MacBook doesn't recognize the device, consult the installation instructions that came with your device.

 If after plugging in your USB device to the port it fails to work properly, run Software Update from the Apple menu and check for important updates to your software from Apple. You should also check the device manufacturer's website to see if it has updated drivers for your device. Look for a Support or Downloads page to find these drivers.

Did You Know?

Choosing Additional Printers

You will be able to see other available printers in the Print & Fax pane, including ones that are connected by USB to an Apple Time Capsule (for automatic wireless data backup) or AirPort base station (for wirelessly connecting to the Internet), a network printer that supports Bonjour (an Apple protocol that allows devices to discover each other), or a printer being shared by another Mac (see Chapter 9 for information on sharing). Just select the one you want to use from the list.

Connect an External Display

If you use your MacBook at home a lot or frequently work with video or graphics, you might want to connect an external display. The larger screen size of most external displays is great for watching movies, editing photos, using art programs, or editing film. You can decide whether you want to use the external display as your only display (mirroring) or as an extension of your desktop.

Your MacBook comes with a video output port so that you can connect your computer to a television, projector, or monitor. The newest models of the MacBook come with a Mini DisplayPort that can use a number of adapters to connect your computer to nearly any kind of video display. The Mini DisplayPort is capable of resolutions of up to 2560×1600, such as those commonly used with 30-inch monitors or televisions. With the correct adapter, your Mini DisplayPort can be used to connect to displays that use a VGA, DVI, or HDMI interface.

One type of adapter that you can use with your Mini DisplayPort is the Dual Link DVI output. DVI stands for Digital Video Interface and is popular in flat-screen displays and high-end graphics cards. All you need to know about the Dual Link aspect of your DVI output is that it doubles the power of the transmission and improves the speed and signal quality of your connection.

In order to connect your computer to any type of display, you simply need to connect the appropriate cable to the corresponding ports on both your computer and the display. What type of cable you use will be determined by what type of connector your display has. Once the display has been connected, you will be able to view your computer screen on the second display (see Figure 4-5). Visit your local Apple store or speak to Apple technical support if you need assistance determining which type of connection your display uses.

How to... Set Up Your External Display Arrangement

You can opt to have your external display mirror what is displayed on your laptop screen or you can use your display as an extension of your desktop. Here's how to set up either option:

1. Open the Apple menu and choose System Preferences.
2. Click Displays and then click Arrangement.
3. Follow the onscreen instructions.

FIGURE 4-5   Some displays from Apple include a power supply and additional USB ports, creating a workstation for your laptop. (Photo by Greg Wagoner; used by permission of the creator)

Connect Speakers and a Microphone

Although your MacBook comes with quite capable speakers and a built-in mic, there are times when you need a little more power behind your sound, especially if you like to watch movies or play computer games. The more powerful computer speakers are those that are powered by a separate AC adapter. Others may be powered by the USB port on your computer or batteries (or both). Regardless, most modern computer speakers connect through a standard USB connector and all you need to do is plug them in!

More rudimentary speakers can be used with your MacBook by inserting the audio jack into the audio out port (which also provides digital output) on the side of your laptop.

Your MacBook also has a built-in microphone to accompany the built-in web camera. If you only occasionally use video chat or Voice over IP (VoIP) services, your built-in mic will probably suffice, but if you plan on participating in a lot of video conferences or making a lot of phone calls, you might want to upgrade to a headset. Most headsets that you can purchase today are also USB devices.

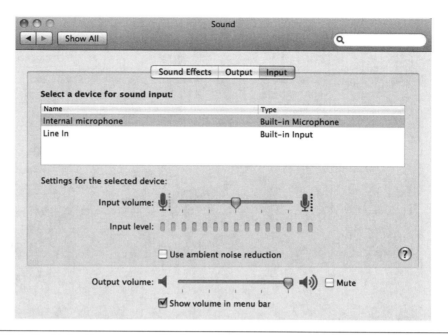

FIGURE 4-6   Selecting your audio input device

You can also use an external microphone for recording music and voice using the programs that are already loaded on your MacBook. You'll need a 1/8-inch stereo mini plug to 1/4-inch phono adapter to make a connection from your computer to a standard microphone, or a 1/8-inch stereo mini plug to XLR connector adapter for professional mics.

 You can use this same adapter to connect your guitar, bass, or other instrument and use your MacBook as a recording studio, although you will get better performance with a USB or FireWire external audio interface.

Once you've got your adapter, just connect it to your computer's audio input port and the other end to your microphone. Open the System Preferences pane from the Apple menu and click Sound. Click the Input tab (see Figure 4-6) and make sure that the audio Line In is the device selected for your sound input.

Connect Digital Still and Video Cameras

Macs have long been used by creative professionals for all types of graphics work, including photo and video editing. With iPhoto and iMovie already installed on your MacBook computer, you can create professional-looking photographs and videos even if you've never done any editing before. Of course, in order to use these great programs, you'll first need to download your video and photos onto your laptop so you can get to work.

Fortunately, downloading video and photos from your digital cameras is pretty easy. The chances are that your digital still camera uses what's called a Mini USB port. Mini USB is similar to a regular USB 2.0 port except that one end of the cable has a much smaller connector that fits into your camera (hence the word mini). Your computer's operating system already has many third-party device drivers installed. All you need to do is plug your USB cable into the camera and the computer, turn the camera on, and start downloading photos. In most cases, iPhoto will open automatically so you can start editing right away. Some cameras come with additional software that needs to be installed in order to use its full functionality, so you should check your camera's operating manual to see if this is the case and if the software is compatible with Mac OS X. For more information on how to use iPhoto to view and edit your photos, see Chapter 13.

Downloading video is similar to downloading photos except that you also usually have the option of using a FireWire cable to download your video. Like USB, FireWire is a protocol that allows a device to talk to a controller. In this case, it allows your video camera to talk to your computer. The difference between FireWire and USB is that FireWire was built for devices that transfer a lot more data than regular USB, like video cameras, DVD players, and external hard drives. The FireWire cable even looks similar to the USB cable, but the connector on the end is a slightly different shape, so you won't get the two cables confused. FireWire ports are only standard in the MacBook Pro model, but most video cameras come with both Mini USB and FireWire ports, so you can use your video camera with whichever MacBook you own.

 If you have a camera that uses a tape to record data, it probably uses a FireWire 400 connection. The MacBook Pro has a FireWire 800 port, so you will need to purchase a 400-to-800 adapter from your local computer/electronics store. Camcorders that use digital storage usually connect via USB.

Unlike downloading photos to your MacBook, a digital video camera requires specific software to transfer video. You can't just drag and drop the files like you can with a digital still camera. Your digital video camera probably came with a disc that contains this software; if not, you can download it from the manufacturer's website. Refer to the manual that came with your camera for specifics on installing the required software. In many cases your MacBook will be able to transfer video using the iMovie, iPhoto, or Image Capture software that is already loaded on your machine. For more information on how to transfer video, see Chapter 13.

SD Card Slot

If you have a 13- or 15-inch MacBook Pro, you will find an SD card slot on the side of your computer for reading Secure Digital media cards. These memory cards come in a variety of capacities; some can store up to 32GB or more of data. Many devices use SD cards, including digital still and video cameras and some cell phones.

The SD card slot can use cards that are Standard SD (Secure Digital), which range from 4MB to 4GB, and SDHC (Secure Digital High Capacity), which range from 4GB to 32GB. You can also use other types of media storage cards in this slot, such as the MMC (MultiMediaCard). MiniSD, MicroSD, and higher-density formats like MiniSDHC and MicroSDHC can also work in this slot with the use of specialized adapters.

Your SD card can only fit in the slot in one direction. Insert the card with the metal contacts facing down and toward the computer. Your card will appear as an icon on your desktop. You can click to open it and explore the contents, dragging the files that you want onto your desktop or into an application like iPhoto. Like your USB devices, you should eject your SD card by dragging its icon to the trash before removing it from the slot to ensure that your data transfer is complete.

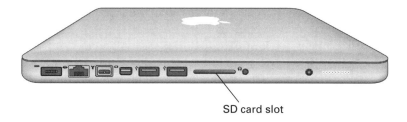

SD card slot

Summary

In this chapter you've learned about all of the ways you can connect peripheral devices to your MacBook. By using the various ports and connectors, you can download photos and video, connect to a wired network, add premium speakers for dynamic sound, and even connect your musical instruments and record your own songs and music.

5

Making Yourself at Home: Getting Comfortable with Your Desktop

HOW TO...

- Identify desktop elements
- Distinguish files from folders
- Locate the Dock
- Find the Finder
- Change views
- Get detailed information on files or applications
- Get more help

Now that you're up to speed on the external properties of your MacBook and how to perform some of the most basic functions, it's time to delve a little bit deeper into how to use it. Your MacBook is loaded with the most recent operating system (OS) that Apple has available. The part of that operating system that allows you to interact with your MacBook is called the graphical user interface (GUI, pronounced "gooey"). Back in the stone age of technology, operating systems were text based. That meant that you had to type in strings of commands in order to perform the most basic tasks on your computer. Now with the GUI, you no longer need to type these commands. You can use a mouse to move around your screen, click icons, drag and drop files, and more. This is one of the advances in technology that opened up computers to the mainstream instead of reserving it for just us geek types.

This chapter will help you find your way around the GUI and learn the terms associated with your operating system. You'll learn about files and folders and how to locate items around your desktop.

Explore Your GUI

The GUI consists of various symbolic elements that you, the user, can manipulate in order to get things done on your MacBook. For example, instead of typing a bunch of words and text symbols into your computer to get it to open the directory where your photos are, you can just click the icon that represents your hard drive, then click the icon that represents the area where your photos are stored. It's a lot easier that way and there's a lot less to remember.

GUI Elements

Your MacBook's GUI is made up of more than just icons and symbols. Let's see what all is included.

Icons

Icons are those cute little pictures and symbols that represent locations or functions. For example, you click a picture of a file folder to open a location on your computer's hard drive and see what files are stored there. You click a picture of a printer when you want to print something, or you click a picture that represents the executable file of iTunes when you want to listen to some music. Figure 5-1 shows some examples of icons on your MacBook.

Menus

Just like the menu at a restaurant, your computer's menus give you multiple options in an ordered list. Most of the time, when you select a menu option, the menu closes and the task you have selected is performed. Other times, you may find that

Front Row   GarageBand

Image Capture   iMovie HD

iSync   iTunes

FIGURE 5-1 These are some of the icons you'll find on your MacBook.

FIGURE 5-2   You'll find similar tasks grouped together in menus.

selecting a menu item leads to another menu, and perhaps additional menus. You'll find generally that menus contain elements that all relate to each other. In your word processing program's File menu, you have the options to open, close, save, and print documents, while in the Edit menu, you typically have the options to cut, copy, and paste text. Figure 5-2 shows how similar actions are grouped together in a menu.

Windows

A window is basically a bordered area that allows you to see what's stored inside your computer, like files, folders, and applications. It's possible to have multiple windows open at the same time, and if you do any multitasking, you most certainly will. You might have iTunes playing your favorite music in one window, be surfing the Web with Safari in another window, and replying to e-mail in yet a third window. You can have many windows open at once. See Chapter 6 for information on Spaces and Exposé, two tools for handling multiple windows. Figure 5-3 shows two open windows (Documents and System Preferences) and the icons they contain.

FIGURE 5-3 It's common to have multiple open windows on your screen.

Files and Folders

Files and folders are how your GUI represents individual items contained in your computer's hard drive and where they are stored. If you think of your computer as an actual file cabinet, the folders would be, well, the folders, and the files would be the paperwork, notes, photos, and such that you keep in those folders. When you open a folder, a window will appear with the files displayed for you to browse through.

Folders are the best way to keep your computer organized. Depending on how detailed you want to get, you can create folders inside folders inside folders. For example, you can create a folder called Photos to store your digital photos in. Inside Photos, you might have multiple folders called Family, Vacation, and Pets. Inside your Vacation folder, you might have even more folders, one for each of the vacations you've taken. Or you can just put all your photos in a single folder and call it good; it's all up to you! Figure 5-4 shows an open folder with more folders and files inside.

The Dock

The Dock is the bar at the bottom of your MacBook screen that contains icons representing programs, files, and folders on your computer (see Figure 5-5). Since the Dock contains shortcuts for the most commonly used programs and folders, you'll probably be using it a lot.

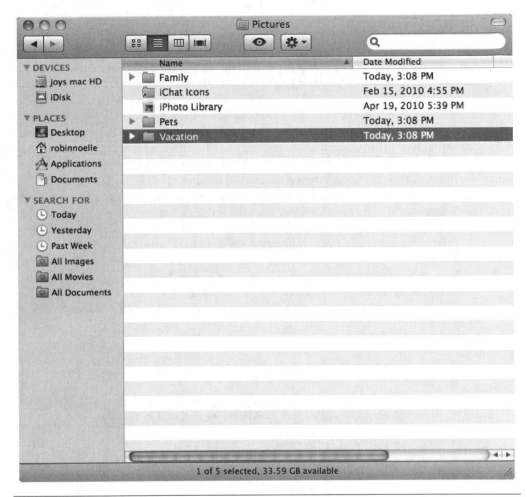

FIGURE 5-4   You can create as many folders as you want for in-depth organization.

The Dock's default position is along the bottom of your screen, but you can move it to the side if you prefer (see Chapter 8). Not everyone uses the same programs or folders with the same frequency, so you'll also learn (in Chapter 6) how to change the contents of the Dock so that it contains only the items that you want it to.

FIGURE 5-5   The Dock contains shortcuts to applications, files, and folders.

The Finder

The Finder does exactly what its name suggests: it helps you search through the contents of your computer and find what you are looking for. By using the Finder, you can navigate the contents of your hard drive or removable storage devices to find files or applications (see Figure 5-6).

The easiest way to access the Finder is by clicking the jolly, smiling fellow on the left side of the Dock. If you have opened other applications since using Finder, you should click on your desktop to activate the application again. If you click the Happy Mac icon, as it is called, when a Finder window is already open, it will bring it to the front of all the other open windows. This is an easy way to get back to the Finder when you have a lot of windows open at once. Yet another way to access the Finder is to click the File menu when Finder is activated and select New Finder Window.

In the Finder window, you'll notice red, yellow, and green buttons in the upper-left corner of the screen (see Figure 5-6). The actions prompted by clicking these buttons are somewhat similar to the actions prescribed by the corresponding colors of a stoplight. Clicking the red button *stops* what you are doing; that is, it closes the window completely. Clicking the yellow button minimizes the window, allowing you

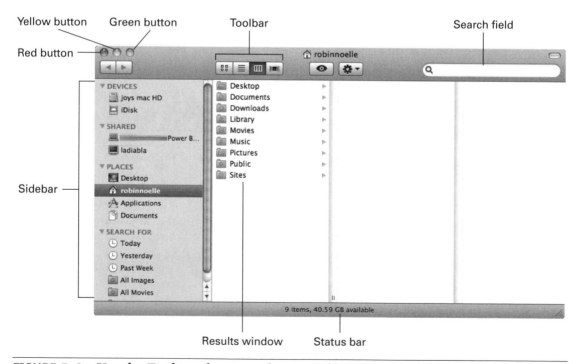

FIGURE 5-6 Use the Finder to locate applications, files, and folders on your MacBook that aren't on the Dock.

to *slow down* (pause, actually) what you were doing. You can click its icon on the Dock to reopen it. Clicking the green button gives you full access by opening the window completely. It's the green light to *go* back to work!

 You can also double-click the title bar of a window to minimize it.

Finder Elements

While the Finder is one element of the MacBook's GUI, the Finder also has multiple elements of its own. Some of these elements can be customized, but the default layout contains the following six areas (refer to Figure 5-6):

- **Toolbar**   The toolbar runs along the top of the Finder window and is where you find options to change how you view the contents of the Finder. More on that in the next section.
- **Search field**   You can type keywords into the search field to search for files and applications on your whole computer or just in specific locations.
- **Sidebar**   The sidebar helps you navigate your computer by giving you access to your hard drive, folders, and network locations.
- **Results window**   The contents of a specific folder or the results from your search will appear in the Results window of the Finder.
- **Status bar**   You can see how many items are contained in a folder and how much space is available on your hard drive in the Status bar.
- **Slider**   Change the size of the icons in the Results window with the slider when in Icon view (not shown in figure).

How to Change Your View

By now, you know that windows display the contents of your computer. But did you know that you can change how those contents are displayed? Well, you can. When you search or click a location in the sidebar, the results are displayed in a window as icons. This might be the way you prefer to see your results, in which case you don't need to change it. However, if you open a folder or location that contains many files, using icons will take up a lot of desktop space, so it might not be the best way to go. Four total views are available, so you can opt for one of the other three that best suits your results. Change your view by clicking the corresponding button on the toolbar. These four views are

- **Icon view**   This is the default view for your windows. Your results will appear as a series of icons that can be rearranged or resized (see Figure 5-7).
- **List view**   In List view, your results appear in the window as an ordered list. You can click the different columns to reorder your list as you see fit. The default is alphabetically ascending order, but if you click where it says Name in the column header, you can change it to descending order. You can also click the Date Modified header to sort your results by date (see Figure 5-8).

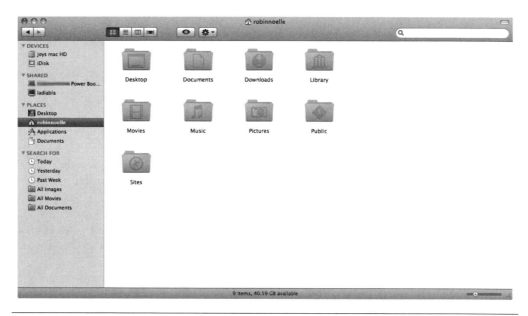

FIGURE 5-7 Icon view is the default for viewing your results.

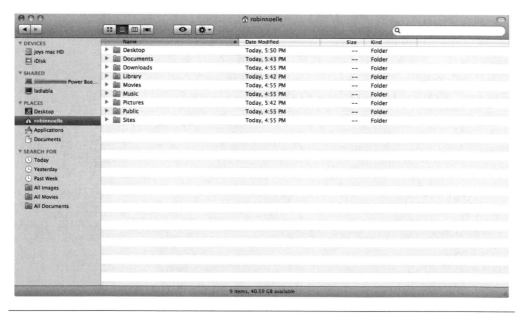

FIGURE 5-8 List view is useful for viewing a lot of information in an ordered list.

- **Column view**   When using Column view, each time you click a drive or folder in the rightmost column, a new column will appear to its right to display the contents. As you move through a file tree, more columns will appear to show more results. If you click on a file instead of a location, a preview of that file will appear in the final column (see Figure 5-9).
- **Cover Flow**   Cover Flow shows your results as a series of large icons that you can scroll through using a slider. Cover Flow is a good choice if you need to browse folders whose contents you are unsure of, as the contents will be easier to see. Otherwise, it's really only good for its "fun factor." It might not be the most efficient way to view results and utilize your space, but it is certainly the coolest (see Figure 5-10).

Tip   When working with multiple pages of results, use the scroll bars and arrows to move through the pages and view the contents.

Check on the Details

From time to time, you may need to delve into the details of a particular application, file, or folder. You can use the Get Info window to find out more than you would ever want to know about the contents of your MacBook. The information contained in the Get Info window could come in handy if you want to know how big or small a file is,

FIGURE 5-9   Column view can show you not only the results, but what path you took to view them.

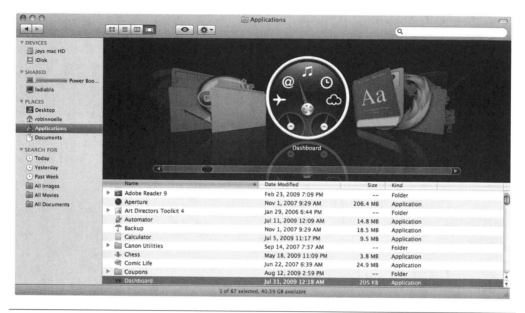

FIGURE 5-10 Cover Flow is just plain cool.

what version of an application you are running, or when the last time a document was modified. You'll also be able to see who has permissions to access the item in question (see Figure 5-11).

You can access this window by CTRL-clicking on the item's icon and selecting Get Info from the shortcut menu or by selecting the item and clicking File | Get Info.

Need Help?

It's normal to feel a little overwhelmed when learning something new, especially if that something has to do with technology. Fortunately, even if you don't have this book handy, you will be able to access help right from your MacBook!

All of the applications contained on your MacBook, whether preinstalled when you bought it or installed by you, have their own Help menu. How you access the Help menu depends on what application you are running. Many applications have their own independent Help menu on the main menu bar, as shown in Figure 5-12. In some applications, the Help menu is contained in the File menu. Some programs have an About menu that offers access to the Help features and gives you the version number and some information about the software manufacturer.

Your MacBook has its own Help menu too. You can access it from the Finder. Just click the Finder icon on the Dock and then select Help from the menu. You can browse the contents or search for a keyword relating to your question (see Figure 5-13). It's really that easy!

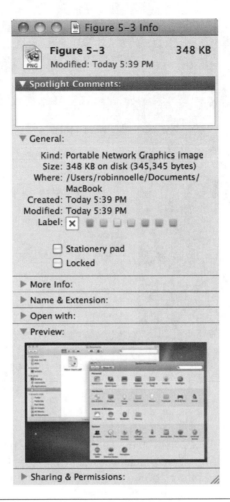

FIGURE 5-11   Get Info gives you a plethora of information about your files and folders.

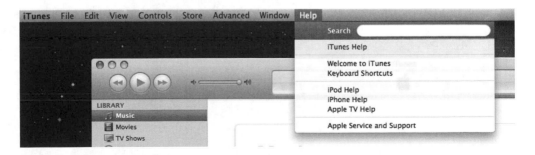

FIGURE 5-12   To get application-specific help, access the Help menu when the application is running.

FIGURE 5-13 Access the Help file from the Finder to get help with using your MacBook.

Do you need more help than your MacBook's Help library can offer? Visit the Support section of the Apple website at www.apple.com/support/ to find even more detailed information on your MacBook and the programs that it contains.

Summary

By now you should be fairly comfortable with the elements that make up the desktop and main work environment on your MacBook. Now that you know what you're looking at, you can learn how to use it! Read on to find out how to navigate your MacBook.

6

Hide and Seek: Navigating Your MacBook

HOW TO...

- Create, rename, and delete files and folders
- Take out the Trash
- Search for files or folders
- Preview a file's contents
- Use the Dock
- Use Exposé
- Use Spaces

In the previous chapter we explored the various elements associated with the GUI of your MacBook. Now we are going to examine how to navigate your MacBook and interact with some of those elements, like folders, files, and windows. We'll explore the Dock a little more, and you'll learn about some cool new ways to organize your desktop when working with multiple windows.

Manage Files

You discovered in the previous chapter that all of the information on your MacBook is stored in files and then filed away into folders, so you've probably already realized that file management is a pretty big deal. A file can be any self-contained item on your computer. Most of the files on your MacBook are system or application files, and you'll never have a reason to interact with them. They are stored to be accessed by the applications that require them to run. As a MacBook end user, the files you will likely work with include items like documents, photos, music files, e-mail messages, movies, and applications.

To get started with managing files, go ahead and open a Finder window by clicking the Finder icon in the Dock. Click on your hard drive icon in the upper portion of the sidebar so that a list of folders that your hard drive contains appears in the Results window. You'll see some of the main folders for your MacBook here.

- **Applications** This is the folder where the information for your installed applications resides. When you're installing new software, this is the default location where your MacBook will want to place the files. All user accounts have access to these applications. Inside the Applications folder is the Utilities folder. You will find some applications in there that will help you perform system tasks on your MacBook, but you probably won't use them very often.
- **Library** The Library folder contains information that your MacBook and its applications use to run, like device drivers that let your computer use an installed printer or mouse. The files in the Library folder can be accessed by all users.

 Because the Library folder is critical to your computer, you shouldn't change or alter the folder or its contents.

- **System** The System folder is where your MacBook stores all of the system files it needs to run the operating system properly. Mucking around in this folder could cause some very serious ramifications, including system instability or a total system meltdown. You may think I am exaggerating, but I assure you, I am not. Unless you know exactly what you are doing, it's best to just ignore this folder.
- **Users** This is where personalized information is stored for user accounts (see Figure 6-1). When you set up a user account, a folder is created just for you with your user account name. In it you will find your documents, e-mails, and personalized settings, like your desktop picture.

FIGURE 6-1 Each user account has its own folder to keep documents and settings separate from other users' documents and settings.

Create, Rename, and Delete Files and Folders

When it comes to file management, the nuts and bolts that you really need to know are how to create new folders and files, rename those that you've created, move or copy them, and delete ones that you no longer need.

Create Folders

If you plan to organize your computer at all, you need to know how to create folders. As you learned in Chapter 5, folders can be created inside one another for some pretty high-level order.

To create a new folder, you can

- ¶⊠ CTRL-click (right-click) on an empty space on your desktop and select New Folder from the shortcut menu.
- Open a Finder window to the folder in which you want to create a folder. Right-click the folder and use the shortcut menu to create a new folder.
- Use the Action button in a Finder window and select New Folder. A new folder will appear called "untitled folder." The name will be highlighted to let you know that you can change the name to whatever you want (almost) (see Figure 6-2).

 Tip   Some characters can't be used to create folder and file names. Colons and slashes are generally forbidden.

Create Files

Creating files varies by the type of application you use to create them. You can create text documents in a word processing application and create photo files in a photo editing application. Once you've created a file, you can save it to your hard drive. When you click the Save button or go to File | Save in whichever application you choose, you will be presented with a dialog box (see Figure 6-3) that prompts you to name your file and browse your drive to select a location to save it to.

The default location for saved documents depends on the type of file. Your MacBook will save document files to the Documents folder associated with your user account (located at *Your Hard Drive Name* | Users | *Your User Account* | Documents). Each user on your computer has their own home folder, so whatever you save in your account won't get mixed up with anyone else's documents.

 Tip   You can create an alias for any file, folder, or application. An alias is a duplicate of the icon that, when clicked, offers a shortcut directly to the original application or file. For example, if you have Photoshop installed, you might normally access it from the Applications menu. Instead, you could create an alias for the application and keep it on your desktop, saving yourself a few steps when you want to launch it. CTRL-click an icon and select Make Alias from the shortcut menu.

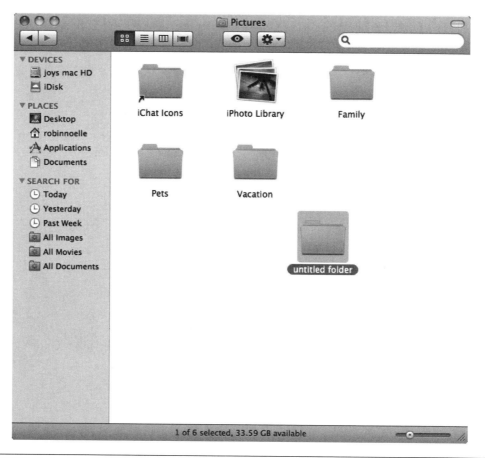

FIGURE 6-2 You'll find folders easier to use if you give them a name relating to their contents.

FIGURE 6-3 Use the Save dialog box to choose where you want to save your document.

Rename Files and Folders

Suppose you've created your new folder but accidentally clicked outside of the text box before naming it. Now you have a folder called Untitled Folder, which isn't very useful. Fortunately, you can easily change the name to anything you want, as many times as you want. All you need to do is click once on the icon, wait a second, and then click again so that the text box is activated (highlighted in blue). Type in a new name and then press ENTER or click somewhere on your desktop to accept the change. You can also edit the name after the text box is activated by using your mouse or arrow keys to place an insertion point and then making your change from there. You can also click the icon to select it and then press ENTER to select the name.

 Although you can't use slashes when naming files or folders, you can use the underscore. You can use this to differentiate between similar versions of files. For example, you could name two photos of the Empire State Building taken at different times of the day Empire_AM.jpg and Empire_PM.jpg. Using the underscore makes a long file name easier to read. You can also use a space instead of an underscore.

Delete Files and Folders

It can be tempting, especially when you get a new computer, to keep every file you create or receive. With the huge capacity of today's modern hard drives, it almost seems impossible that you could ever fill up your hard drive, but it does happen. If you save everything until that time comes, you could end up weeding through thousands and thousands of files! A better solution is to delete the things that you don't need or want as you come across them.

Deleting files on a MacBook is pretty easy. The most common way to do it is to click on the file or folder you want to delete and drag it to the Trash icon. When the Trash is empty, the icon looks like an empty trash bin. When your Trash contains files, it looks like it's holding crumpled paper. In fact, you'll notice a cool crumpling-paper noise when your MacBook empties Trash.

 You can also delete an item by CTRL-clicking on the item and selecting Move to Trash from the shortcut menu or by selecting the item and pressing COMMAND-DELETE.

Unlike your kitchen garbage can, your MacBook's Trash never overflows, but that doesn't mean you don't have to take out the trash. Even though you moved your files to the Trash, they aren't gone yet. You need to empty your Trash from time to time. To empty the Trash, CTRL-click on the Trash icon and select Empty Trash (see Figure 6-4). A dialog box will pop up asking if you are sure. Click OK to go ahead and empty the trash or click Cancel to go back without deleting the Trash files. Once you've emptied the Trash, the icon will return to the empty bin.

You can still access the files you dropped in the Trash until it is emptied. Just click the Trash icon and a window will open to display the files inside. You can drag and drop them to wherever you want on your computer.

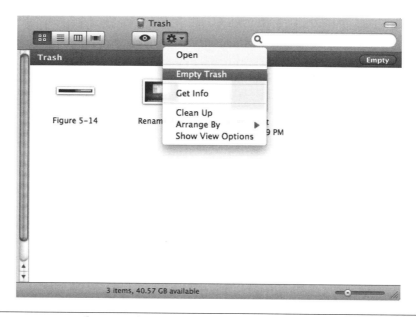

FIGURE 6-4   Remember to take out the Trash if you want to remove your files from your computer!

 Caution Dragging and dropping a folder into the Trash includes all the files located in the folder. Make sure that you want to delete all those files before you drag that folder to the Trash!

Did You Know?

Permanently Deleting Files from Your MacBook

Just because you deleted a file from your computer doesn't mean it's really gone. When you create files on your MacBook, it writes the information to the hard drive. When you delete something, your computer makes a note that whatever space that item was using is now free for something else. However, there's a lot of room on that drive, and until your computer gets around to using that particular space again, your information (or at least parts of it) still lingers on.

By analogy, think of what happens when you erase a word on a piece of paper. Even after you've erased it, you usually can still make out what the word was. If you write another word on top of what you erased, it's harder to read but it can sometimes still be done. If you write 20 words in that space, no one will be able to read the original word. It's the same with computers. Since you wouldn't want someone to be able to pull up private documents like medical or financial information even after you've deleted them, your MacBook comes with a way to permanently delete files.

After you've dragged your files to the Trash, choose Finder and select Secure Empty Trash.

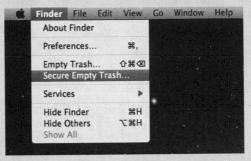

You'll see a security dialog box pop up to confirm that you really want to permanently delete these items. Take a second look because once you click OK, they are for all intents and purposes gone forever!

Search for Files and Folders

Even if you meticulously delete files as soon as you are done with them, your computer still contains thousands of files and folders. Unless you know exactly where you or your MacBook saved a file, you could end up opening folders all day looking for something and still never find it. Fortunately, you don't need to waste all of that time. You can just search for what you want by using one of the two easy options provided by your trusty MacBook.

Use Find

The Find function offers a way to quickly search for files on your computer using a variety of search criteria. This is a great tool if you want to search for a specific file type or if you have a lot of information about the file you want to search for.

To use Find, open a new Finder window by clicking on Happy Mac or going to File | New Finder Window. Click File | Find to open the Finder dialog box. First select the location that you want to search by clicking it in the sidebar. You can select your hard drive and external storage devices, or you can choose a more specific location like a particular folder. You can use the plus (+) and minus (–) buttons to add or remove additional search criteria, such as the file type or date the file was last modified. Once you've filled in as much information as you have about the file, type the name, if you know it, in the text box that contains the magnifying glass icon. Your results will appear in the Results window below the search form. Figure 6-5 shows a Finder window with search fields added.

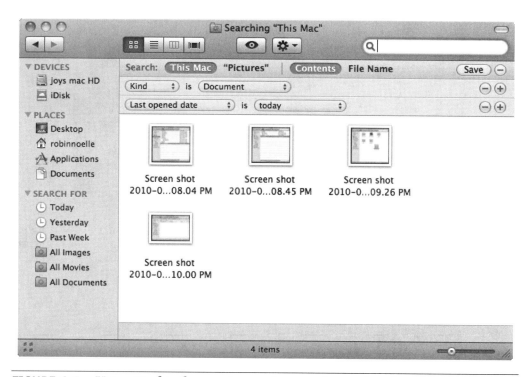

FIGURE 6-5 Using Find is the way to go when you have a lot of information about the file you're looking for or want to search a specific location.

Use Spotlight

Spotlight is a more basic way to search for files. The Spotlight search box is always available in the upper-right corner of your MacBook screen (see Figure 6-6). See the magnifying glass icon? Just click on it, then type in your search term and Spotlight will quickly search your entire computer for files that contain your search terms.

The Spotlight results appear below the text box, helpfully arranged by file type, with the file that your MacBook thinks is the most relevant located at the top and labeled Top Hit. You can double-click a result to open it, or you can place your cursor over the result and see the location of the file.

Tip Try searching for the most unique word you recall being in the target file to receive the most relevant results. If you are searching for a word that is common to many files, your search results could be extensive. If you can't recall a unique word, it's a better idea to use Find instead of Spotlight.

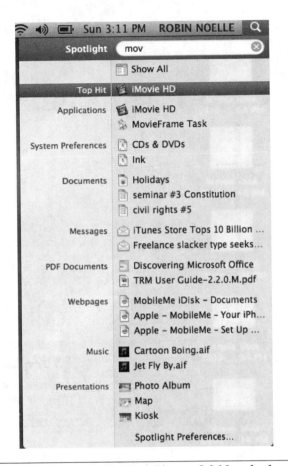

FIGURE 6-6   Use Spotlight to quickly find files and folders by keyword.

Use Quick Look to View File Contents

Sometimes it's hard to tell exactly what a file is by looking at its name. This is especially true of photo files since most digital cameras use a standard naming convention when downloading files. If you want to see what a document contains without having to open the application that it's associated with, you can do this with the Quick Look button on the toolbar.

Open a new Finder window and locate the document you want to preview. Select the file and then click the Quick Look button (it looks like an eye). A preview of the document will be displayed (see Figure 6-7). You can also access Quick Look by selecting the file and pressing the SPACEBAR. Select and view multiple files by COMMAND-clicking each file to select it and then clicking the Quick Look button.

Quick Look button

Full-screen view

FIGURE 6-7 Use Quick Look to quickly preview documents without launching the associated application.

If the document you are previewing in Quick Look contains multiple pages, you will be able to scroll through them using the scroll bar. You can also switch to the full-screen view by clicking the arrows at the bottom of the Quick Look window.

Use the Dock

As you discovered in Chapter 5, the Dock is the bar at the bottom of your MacBook screen that contains icons representing applications, files, and folders on your computer. Later, in Chapter 8, you'll learn how to customize the Dock so that it contains the applications and files that you want to access quickly, but for now take a look at how to use the Dock itself.

FIGURE 6-8   CTRL-click an application icon to see the shortcut menu when available.

The icons on the left side of the Dock are application icons. Use these icons to quickly open an application or to switch between running applications. Some applications have a shortcut menu that is accessible when you CTRL-click on the application's icon. The options on the menu might vary depending on whether the application is running or not. You can try this on the iTunes icon to see what additional commands are available (see Figure 6-8).

If you look closely, you'll see a divider line between the application icons and document icons on the Dock.

The icons on the right side of the Dock represent documents and folders. You can pin specific items to the Dock here so that you can access them instantly without having to open a folder or perform a search. Suppose that you were writing a book about...MacBooks. Instead of opening your user folder, then your Documents folder, and then the MacBook folder, you could just pin the MacBook folder to the Dock so that when you click on its icon, the folder opens and you can access the files inside. To do this, locate the file or folder that you want to pin and then drag it to the right side of the Dock near the Trash icon and drop it.

You can change how you view a particular stack by right-clicking on the icon, selecting View Content As, and choosing the way you want the stack contents displayed, such as Grid or List.

Use Exposé

Exposé is a great tool if you're a multitasker. Multitasking is one of the things that makes modern computers so great. You can have multiple applications running simultaneously with their associated open windows (see Figure 6-9). But what happens when you want to jump to one specific window quickly? It would be too time consuming to scroll and click through to each one, so Apple has provided you with Exposé on your MacBook to help.

Using Stacks

If you drag a folder that contains multiple files or folders, it creates a stack on the Dock. Now you can click the icon representing your folder and the contents will appear in a column.

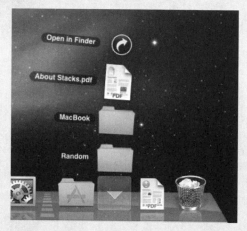

Click the file you want to open. If your folder contains too many files to fit into a column, you'll see the icons arranged in a grid pattern instead.

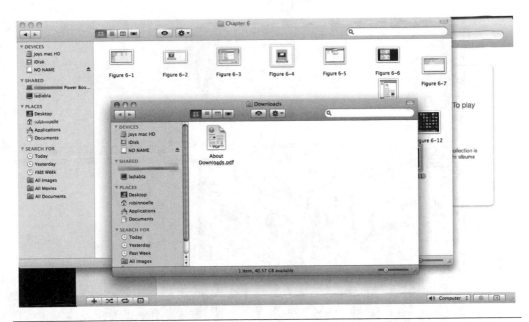

FIGURE 6-9   It's hard to find what you're looking for with all of those open windows.

By using Exposé, you can organize all of those open windows quickly so you can jump right to the window or application that you want to use. Exposé gives you three handy options:

- **Press F3**   Exposé arranges all of your open windows on a single screen so you can see them all at once (see Figure 6-10).
- **Press OPTION-F3**   Exposé arranges the open windows that relate to the application you are running (see Figure 6-11).
- **Press COMMAND-F3**   Exposé clears away all of the open windows so that you can access the desktop. Press it again to bring your open windows back.

 Some MacBooks require that you press FN in conjunction with the preceding keys. Some Mac keyboards also have an Exposé key that you can use instead to access the functions.

Use Spaces

Another way to address the desktop clutter problem is to use Spaces. Spaces divides your desktop into neatly organized and individual workspaces. You can select how many spaces you want to have and assign each one an application. You can assign your web browser to one space, your word processing application to another, a photo editor to a third, and a video player to the fourth. Unlike Exposé, Spaces allows you to see and work in all of your windows from a single screen.

FIGURE 6-10   View all of your open windows at once.

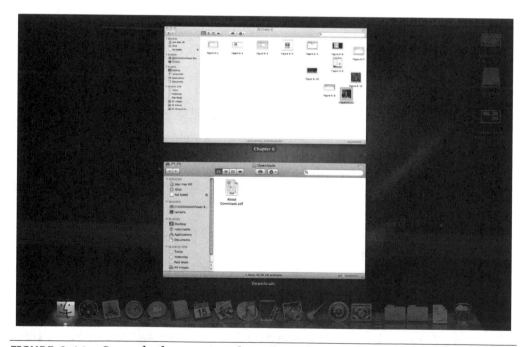

FIGURE 6-11   See only the open windows that relate to your active application.

You can have as few as two spaces or as many as sixteen.

Enable Spaces

Before you can start using Spaces, you need to turn it on. Start by opening the Exposé & Spaces preferences window and clicking the Spaces tab (Apple | System Preferences | Exposé & Spaces). See Figure 6-12.

Click the check box next to Enable Spaces. This turns on Spaces functionality. You can accept the default number of spaces (four) or use the + and – buttons to adjust the number to your liking.

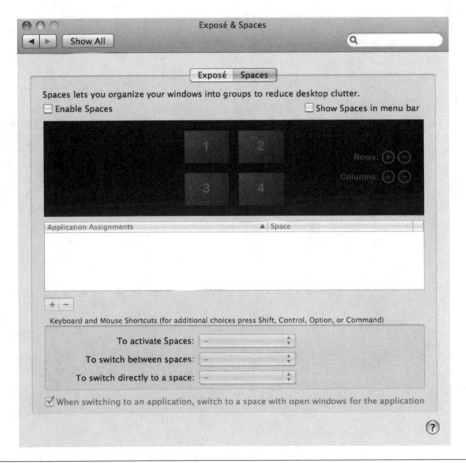

FIGURE 6-12   You need to enable Spaces before you can use it!

If you want Spaces to display the space numbers in your menu bar, click the Show Spaces in Menu Bar check box. Once active, just click the number to jump to another space.

Assign Applications

Once you've created the perfect Spaces layout, you need to tell your MacBook what those spaces will contain. You can do this in the Application Assignments section of the Spaces tab of the Exposé & Spaces preferences pane. Use the + and – buttons to add and remove applications from the list (see Figure 6-13). Once you've added an application, you can assign it to only open in a specific space or to be available in any of the spaces. To assign a new space to an application, click the application name in the Space column. Select the desired space from the list.

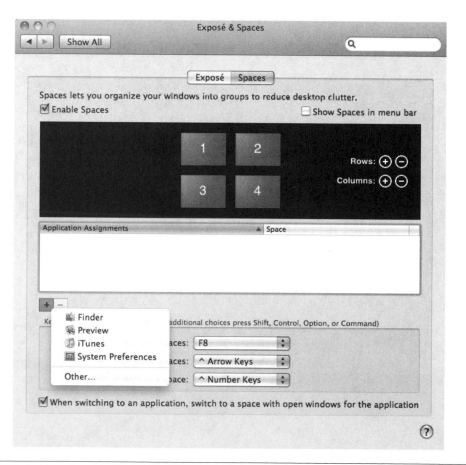

FIGURE 6-13 Assign the applications you use the most to Spaces to access them all at once.

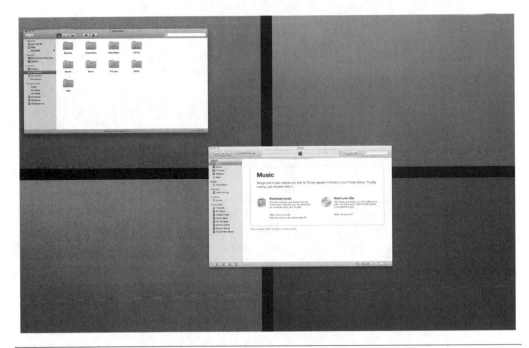

FIGURE 6-14   Moving Spaces content is as easy as dragging and dropping.

    To see the applications or files in spaces, they must be open. Once enabled, use keyboard shortcuts to move between the spaces. Press CTRL and the space number you want to jump to. You can press CTRL and the RIGHT ARROW or LEFT ARROW button to scroll through them instead.

Relocate Spaces

Once you have all of your spaces up and running, you might find that you want to move things around a little. Luckily, it's easy to do so. Just press F8 or click the Spaces icon on the Dock to display the Spaces grid. Drag and drop the contents from one space into another (see Figure 6-14).

Summary

As you can see, your MacBook offers a lot of ways to keep your computer and your desktop organized. You've mastered the basics of file management and learned how to quickly search your laptop for files and folders. You can even get all high-tech and use Exposé and Spaces to multitask!

7

A Home of One's Own: User Accounts

HOW TO...

- Create new user accounts
- Manage user accounts
- Employ parental controls
- Create share-only accounts
- Delete user accounts

While sharing is always nice, sometimes you just need your own space. User accounts are a way to still share a computer while keeping a personalized and separate space just for you.

Privacy is one reason to implement user accounts on your computer. Suppose you have a friend over who wants to check their e-mail on your computer. Well, if you let them use the Guest account instead of your personal account, all of your documents and e-mails will be safely tucked away until you log back into your own account.

Personalization is the other reason to use user accounts. If you've ever lent your car to someone and had to readjust the mirrors and driver's seat after they returned it, then you probably can see the value in having your own personalized settings always available to you. You can have your own desktop picture, Internet home page, and Dock layout, and everyone else can have theirs too.

Select a User Account

There are a few types of user accounts that are available to you. Each type of account has its own set of privileges, allowing you to set restrictions on what other users can and cannot do. This is particularly helpful if you want to limit what your children are doing while using the computer, as you'll see in a moment.

Administrator Accounts

When you were setting up your MacBook for the first time, you automatically created an Administrator account for yourself. This account has the maximum permissions, which is what allowed you to install new software, make changes to the computer, and even create these new user accounts. As the owner of the MacBook, you'll probably want to limit the Administrator account to just yourself to prevent other users from making any system-wide changes or accidentally causing any computer-related chaos.

 You might consider setting up a Standard account for yourself as well. You can log into the Administrator account when you need to install software or make system changes but use your other account for day-to-day computer activities.

Standard Accounts

Standard accounts still have permission to install software for their own use and to personalize their workspace, but they don't have the ability to work with user accounts or to make any system-wide changes. Unless someone else in your household needs to install software or make big changes to your computer, you are probably safe setting everyone else up with a Standard account.

Managed with Parental Controls

As a parent, you can regulate what your kids can and can't do when on the computer. You can restrict certain websites, limit the kids to using specific applications, and even set limits for how much time they spend on the computer. There's a lot more to talk about on this subject, but we'll cover that later in the chapter.

Sharing Only Accounts

A Sharing Only account is for allowing someone to remotely access certain areas of your computer, such as browsing shared documents or folders. Once active, this account can only be logged into remotely.

Activate the Guest Account

Once you have the Guest account active on your MacBook, friends and family will be able to use your computer without having access to your personal documents.

1. Choose Apple | System Preferences and click Accounts (under the System category) to open the Accounts pane.
2. If the lock icon is closed, click it and type an administrator name and password to make account changes.
3. Select Guest Account in the list of accounts.
4. Select the Allow Guests to Log Into This Computer check box.

If you want to set limits on what guest users can do on your MacBook, select the Enable Parental Controls check box. For more information on parental controls, see "Set Parental Controls" later in this chapter.

Add a New User Account

You already created one user account (Administrator) when you first booted up your new MacBook. If you want other people to be able to use your computer with their own accounts, you need to create one account for each of them. You can do this by going to the Apple | System Preferences | Accounts pane (see Figure 7-1).

Look for the lock symbol in the corner of the window, as shown in Figure 7-1. If it is in the locked position, you need to click it and enter your password to make changes.

To create a new account, click the (+) button in the lower-left corner. This opens a new account dialog box (see Figure 7-2) in which you can set a username and password. In the text boxes, choose the type of account you want to create, enter the full name of the user, name the new account, and enter a password. Enter the password again to verify that they match.

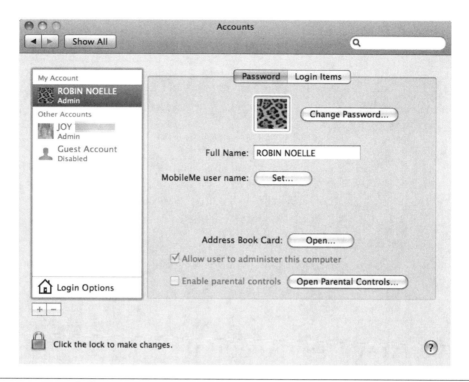

FIGURE 7-1 Click Accounts in System Preferences to create new user accounts.

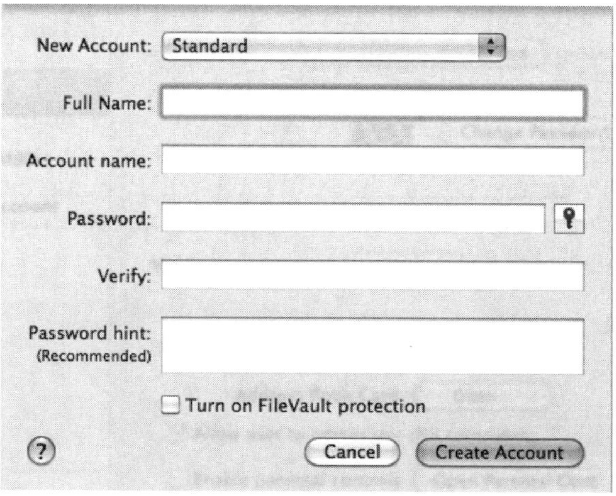

FIGURE 7-2 Choose the type of account to create using the New Account pull-down menu.

How to Select a Strong Password

You should spend some time considering what you want your password to be for your user account. If your laptop is ever stolen, you want to make sure that whoever has it can't access the personal information that's stored inside. You should never use a password that might be easy to figure out, such as any combination of a pet's name, child's name, the date of your birthday, your Social Security number, your ZIP code, or other easily identifiable information. You might think that it's hard for a stranger to figure out this type of information, but all they need to do for many people is visit a social networking website like Facebook or MySpace or rifle through their mail/recycling.

When choosing a password, it should be a minimum of 7–8 characters. Try to use a mixture of upper- and lowercase letters, numbers, and symbols. Of course, it should also be something that you can remember. You'll see in the new account dialog box that you can add a password hint. Feel free to add one, but realize that if it will help you remember your password, it might help someone else figure out what it is. If you want your MacBook to help you select a password, click the key icon next to the Password text box.

Configure a New User Account

Once you click Create Account, your new account will appear in the sidebar on the left side of the Accounts pane. You can click it now to make some additional changes.

User Pictures

You can choose a picture to associate with your account. Click on the small picture to the left of the Change Password button to open a menu of additional photos to choose from (see Figure 7-3). You can select a picture that you like from those listed or you can really go nuts and choose one of your own pictures.

If you want to choose your own picture, click the Edit Picture button to open the photo editing window. Drag a photo from your personal collection into the program or click Choose to browse your computer's directories. If you want, you can click Take Photo Snapshot to use your MacBook's built-in camera to snap a photo. Resize it until you have the image that you want to use, and then assign it to your new account by clicking Set.

Allow User to Administer This Computer

Checking the Allow User to Administer This Computer check box (grayed out in Figure 7-1) turns a previously Standard account into an Administrator account. Before assigning these privileges to another user, make sure you trust them enough not to screw up your computer!

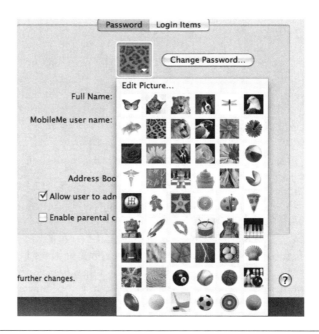

FIGURE 7-3 Use one of the included photos for your user account or make your own.

Enable Parental Controls

Check the Enable Parental Controls check box if you want to set parental controls, such as restricting access to certain applications or websites. See "Set Parental Controls" later in the chapter for more details on this option.

Login Options

Click the Login Items tab of the Accounts pane (see Figure 7-4) to customize which programs start automatically when you log into the computer. You can only access the options for the account that you are currently logged into. If you want your web browser to open as soon as you log in, you can add it to the Login Items list by clicking the + button and finding your browser application on your hard drive. To remove a program, just select it and click –. This will stop the program from running when you log in but won't delete it from your system.

 Like all computers, your MacBook occasionally needs to run applications in the background to get things done like checking your e-mail or reminding you of appointments. You might see that some programs are running that you didn't even know about. Unless you are experiencing a system slowdown or you know that you don't need or want your computer to run a specific application, you should probably leave anything your MacBook added alone.

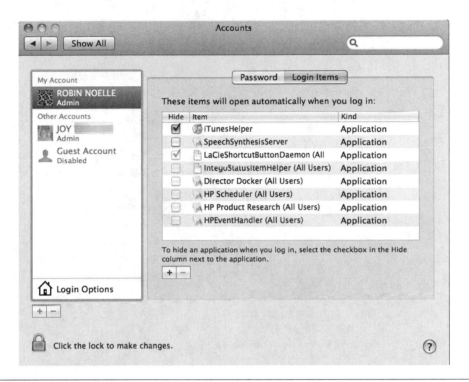

FIGURE 7-4   Use Login Items to select which programs load automatically when you log in.

Configure Login Options

In the main Accounts window, you'll see a little house icon at the bottom of the sidebar that says Login Options next to it. Accessing this dialog box will allow you to configure how you log into your account (see Figure 7-5). The following options are available:

- **Automatic Login**   Select On if you want your MacBook to automatically log you into this account when the computer starts. Remember that if your MacBook gets lost or stolen, activating this feature means that whoever has it will be logged into your account when they turn on the computer.
- **Display Login Window As**   Select whether users select their account from a list or enter their username and password in the login window instead. Opt to have users select their accounts from a list if you share your MacBook with people on a regular basis.
- **Show the Restart, Sleep, and Shut Down Buttons**   Check this box if you want these options to appear in the login window.

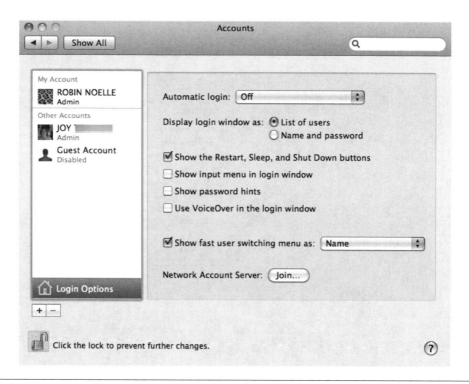

FIGURE 7-5 Use the Login Options to configure how users log into their accounts.

- **Show Input Menu in Login Window** Allows a user to select another language input option when logging into their account.
- **Show Password Hints** When this is checked, a password hint will be shown if a user makes three failed attempts to log into their account.
- **Use VoiceOver in the Login Window** VoiceOver is an accessibility program that speaks commands for visually impaired users. This option allows VoiceOver to be used in the login window.
- **Show Fast User Switching Menu As** You can quickly switch between user accounts by enabling this feature. You can then choose how the accounts will appear (by Name or icon, for example) from the pop-up menu.
- **Network Account Server** You can join a network account by clicking this button.

Set Parental Controls

As discussed, you can set a variety of restrictions to help keep your kids out of trouble when they are on the Internet or just using your computer. Each account has the option to Enable Parental Controls, so go ahead and create a new user account using the steps previously outlined (refer to Figure 7-1) and enable this function. This automatically changes a Standard account into a Managed account.

Now that parental controls are enabled, you can access them by clicking the Open Parental Controls button. You can also access these settings by choosing Apple | System Preferences and then clicking Parental Controls. You'll see the available Managed accounts in the left sidebar (see Figure 7-6). Click the account that you want to set permissions for. You'll notice five tabs along the top of the dialog box: System, Content, Mail & iChat, Time Limits, and Logs.

FIGURE 7-6   Use the Parental Controls pane to manage what your kids can do while using your computer and while online.

You don't have to limit the use of parental controls to children. You can use these tools to help prevent inexperienced computer users from becoming overwhelmed or accidentally making changes to your MacBook. Some settings will help senior citizens use the computer, too, like enabling the Simple Finder, which uses big icons, or limiting the number of items on the Dock.

System

The System tab enables you to set permissions for tasks relating to your MacBook's operating system (see Figure 7-6) through the following check boxes:

- **Use Simple Finder** Creates a streamlined and easy-to-use interface for inexperienced computer users. The icons are larger and there's limited choices available on the Dock. This is a good setting to enable for both Junior and Grandma!
- **Only Allow Selected Applications** Enables you to restrict what applications are available for the user to access when they are logged in. For example, you might want to set access for your middle-school child to use the Internet browser, a word processing application, and an approved game or two, and limit your preschool child to just a few educational games.
- **Can Administer Printers** Allows the user to add and remove printers.
- **Can Change Password** Allows the user to change and create their own passwords (probably not something you want your child to do!).
- **Can Burn CDs and DVDs** Allows the user to use the CD/DVD drive to burn discs.
- **Can Modify the Dock** Allows the user to add and remove items from the Dock.

Content

The Content tab settings relate to the types of content users of Managed accounts are permitted to access (see Figure 7-7):

- **Hide Profanity in Dictionary** Like it or not, the dictionary contains some words that parents would prefer their children not learn at a tender age. Clicking this box prevents them from accessing inappropriate content in the Dictionary application.
- **Website Restrictions** You can choose one of three settings that affect what a Managed account user can view online. Allow Unrestricted Access to Websites doesn't offer any limits to the type of content they can see. Try to Limit Access to Adult Websites Automatically allows your MacBook to decide what is and isn't adult content. Use the Customize button to set up a list of blocked sites. Allow Access to Only These Websites lets you set access for only those websites that you approve of. This is the best setting for very young computer users!

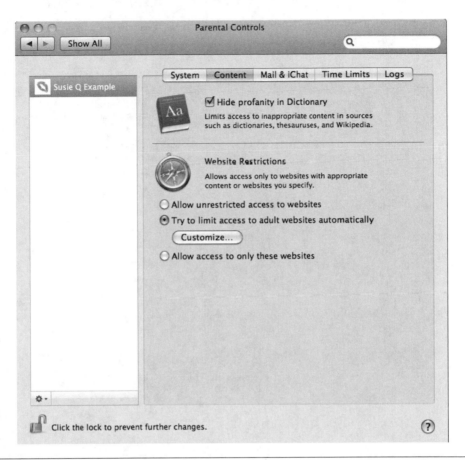

FIGURE 7-7   Limit your child's access to adult Internet content through the Content tab.

Mail & iChat

Probably the number one concern relating to computer use by children is the threat of Internet predators. You can use the Mail & iChat settings to set restrictions on who can and can't reach your child online (see Figure 7-8):

- **Limit Mail**   Check this box to only allow specific people to contact your child via e-mail. You can add and remove contacts at any time by using the + and – buttons.
- **Limit iChat**   Check this box to restrict who your child can have instant message conversations with.
- **Send Permission Requests To**   Check this box and a permission request e-mail will be sent to the address you specify whenever the user attempts to contact someone who isn't on the approved list in Mail.

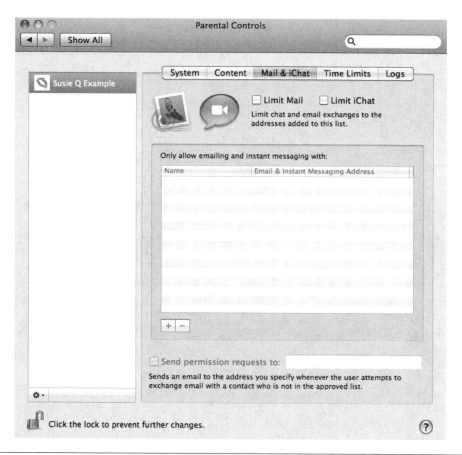

FIGURE 7-8 Protect your children from Internet predators by keeping track of who they contact and who contacts them while online.

Time Limits

You can use the Time Limits tab to set how long your child or other users can be logged into the computer. You can set weekday and weekend limits as well as restrict access completely during certain times of the day (like while you are at work, for example). Click the lock at the bottom of the screen to prevent additional changes to your settings (see Figure 7-9).

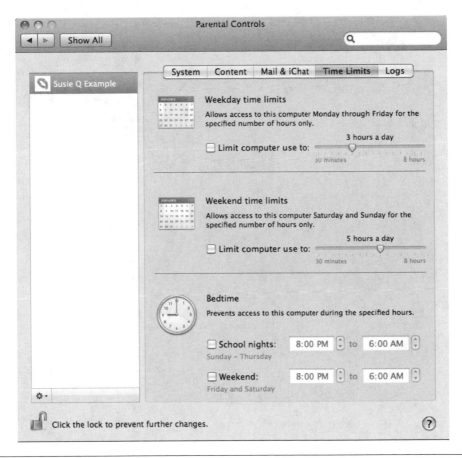

FIGURE 7-9   You can set limits on when your child can use the computer and how long they spend logged in.

Logs

With the Logs feature you can see exactly what your child was up to at any time that they were logged in and using the computer. Check out what websites they've visited (or tried to visit), the applications that they've used, and logs of any instant messaging chats they've had (see Figure 7-10). You can also block unsuitable sites and restrict applications on the Logs tab.

FIGURE 7-10 You will have a detailed history of everything your child has done while logged into their account.

Summary

A MacBook isn't just an expensive piece of technology that lets you type letters and surf the Internet. It contains your photos, videos, e-mails, and any manner of personal and private files and documents. By creating user accounts, you can control who can access certain features and functions of the computer, while protecting your investment and your privacy. Parental controls give you unprecedented control over what your children view while online and who can contact them.

8

Personal Style: Customizing Your MacBook

HOW TO...

- Change your basic settings
- Change your display options
- Add input and output audio devices
- Change your Dock and Finder preferences
- Change your desktop picture
- Choose a new screen saver
- Use custom icons

I'm sure that just using your MacBook is joy enough for some people, but who doesn't like to personalize things a bit? You can change settings that directly affect how you use your computer, or just apply some of the cosmetic options to brighten up your desktop. Add a cool new picture or pick out your favorite screen saver. All of these little changes will help you feel right at home every time you log into your MacBook user account.

Change Basic Settings

You can access the many ways to customize your MacBook from the System Preferences pane (see Figure 8-1), which you can access through the Apple menu. The basic settings of your MacBook mostly relate to the system itself, such as changing the time and date or changing the sound effect that your computer uses to get your attention.

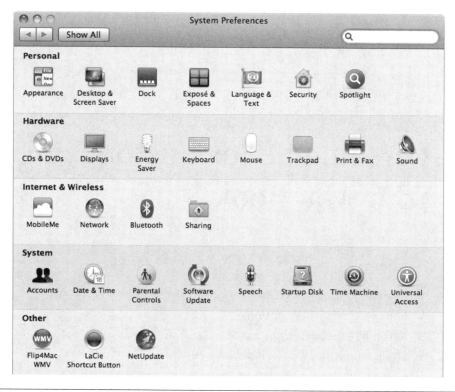

FIGURE 8-1 Create a personalized experience by using the System Preferences pane.

You can also access System Preferences by clicking its icon on the Dock. CTRL-click the icon to access the submenu and select which Preferences pane you want to go to directly.

Set the Date and Time

You probably already set the time and date when you first booted up your MacBook, but if you need or want to change the settings, you can do so by choosing Apple | System Preferences | Date & Time to open the Date & Time pane (see Figure 8-2). If you want your MacBook to automatically set the time and date, click the check box at the top of the screen and select the server nearest to your location from the drop-down list. Your MacBook will periodically check with the server to ensure that the time and date are correct.

To manually set your computer's date and time, you need to use the calendar and clock in the pane. Click on the calendar to set the date (or type it in) and use the clock to set the time. Some countries have a different date format than the United States, so if you prefer to show the date in another way, click the Open Language & Text button to access these options.

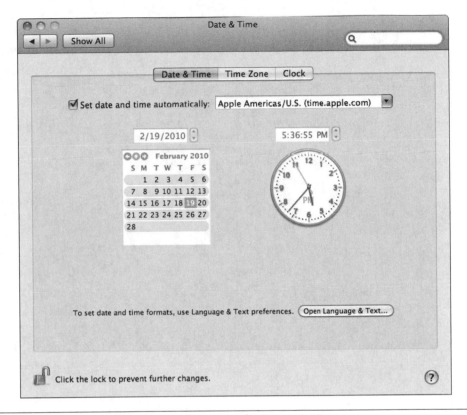

FIGURE 8-2 Change the date and time in the Date & Time pane.

Want to change how the clock looks? Well, you can do that too. Click the Clock tab to access the clock display options (see Figure 8-3). You can choose a 12- or 24-hour clock, digital or analog format, and whether to show or hide the seconds and AM/PM. You can even have your MacBook announce the time with a customizable voice by checking the Announce the Time box.

Click the Time Zone tab to select the time zone that you live in, as shown in Figure 8-4. This will help your MacBook keep the correct time even when seasonal events like Daylight Saving Time take effect. Click the map near your location and then select the nearest city from the pull-down menu.

To keep the time and date automatically, your MacBook needs to connect to outside sources like servers or a Wi-Fi positioning service. These features will only work properly when AirPort is turned on.

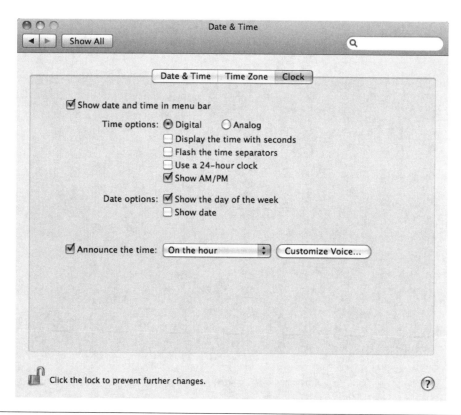

FIGURE 8-3 Click the Clock tab to change the time setting.

Monitor Settings

Monitor settings aren't necessarily something you'll want to customize, but it's helpful to know where they are and what they do, just in case. Open System Preferences and click the Displays icon in the Hardware section. Click the Display tab to access the options shown in Figure 8-5.

Resolution

The default resolution on your MacBook is probably fine for most users. You can opt for a lower resolution if you want the icons on your screen to appear larger. The higher the resolution, the smaller things will appear. If you add an external monitor in the future, you will want to change the resolution of your MacBook to match that which the monitor can support. Some video games also require certain video resolutions. Check the system requirements on your software package for more information.

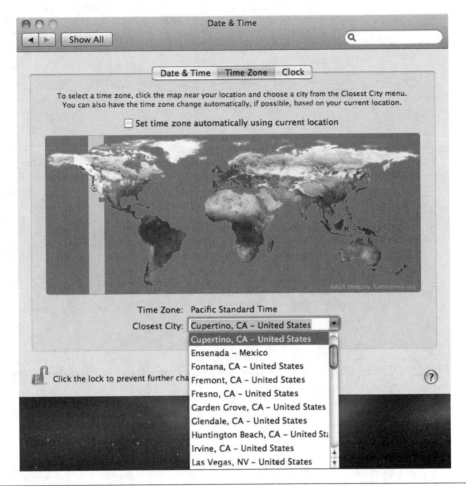

FIGURE 8-4   Select the time zone that you live in.

 If you do attach an external monitor to your laptop, you can detect it and change the settings here.

Color Profiles

Color profiles are used to ensure that colors, as represented on screen, look the same when printed. These profiles are frequently used by professional designers. Various color profiles are available for your MacBook on the Color tab (see Figure 8-6). You can select one from the list or create your own by clicking Calibrate. Generally, you won't need to touch this tab unless you work with print-ready graphics and art.

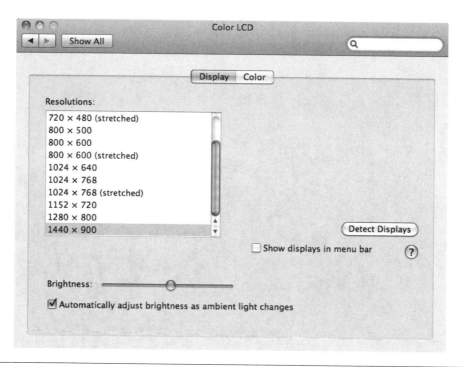

FIGURE 8-5 The Display settings let you connect an external monitor or adjust your screen resolution.

Did You Know?

Native Resolution

Native resolution, as it applies to flat-panel displays, refers to a single fixed resolution. This means that the best picture quality can only be obtained when the input signal matches the native resolution of the monitor or screen. In the past, computers used CRT monitors, which could display images at different resolutions. Now, with LCD and other flat-panel displays, the image must be scaled. This can result in images appearing blocky or distorted at lower resolutions. If you want or need your icons to be larger, you can CTRL-click on your desktop and choose View Options. You can choose a new size for your icons from the resulting pane.

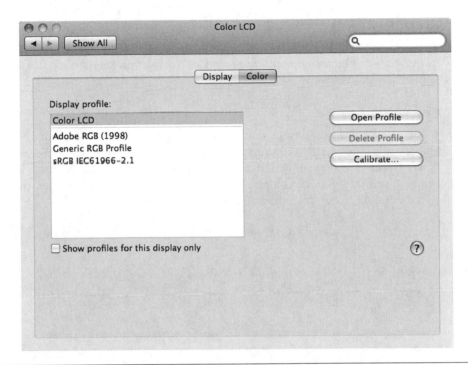

FIGURE 8-6   Use the color profiles when you are working with digital graphics.

Sound Settings

Sound settings let you change more than just the volume and input/output devices. You can also change the sound effect your MacBook uses to alert you when it needs you to take an action, such as approve a system change. To open the Sound panel, choose Sound (in the Hardware category) in System Preferences.

The Output Volume slider runs along the bottom of the Sound pane regardless of which tab you click on. You can adjust or mute the volume here, as well as set the balance. Check Show Volume in Menu Bar to be able to change the volume of your computer without having to open the Sound pane.

The Output Volume is the overall volume of your computer. You can also change the volume on your MacBook by using the volume-control keys on your keyboard. They are F10 for Mute/Unmute, F11 for Volume Down, and F12 for Volume Up.

Sound Effects

The Sound Effects tab is where you can change your MacBook's alert sound, as shown in Figure 8-7. The sounds will be played for you as you select each of the available choices. Select the one you like best.

Output

The Output tab is where you select which device your MacBook will use to play music and sounds (see Figure 8-8). Since your laptop comes with built-in speakers, this is what is selected by default. If and when you decided to attach external speakers (highly recommended if you're a gamer or like to watch movies on your MacBook), you can select those from this tab instead.

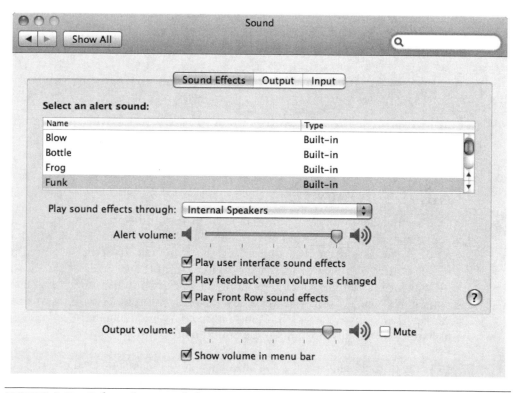

FIGURE 8-7   Select the sound that you want your MacBook to use when it needs to get your attention.

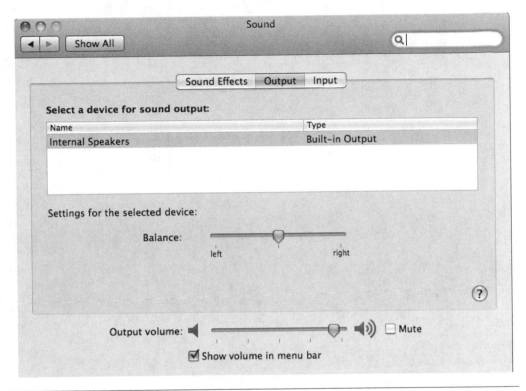

FIGURE 8-8   Connect some external speakers for a powerful audio experience.

Input

Your MacBook also came with a built-in microphone, which is suitable for video chat and voice recording. However, if you want to record music or plan to spend a lot of time making calls from your computer, you'll probably want to use a headset or other external mic. You can select Line In from the Input tab (see Figure 8-9) after you've attached your headset to one of the ports on the side of your laptop.

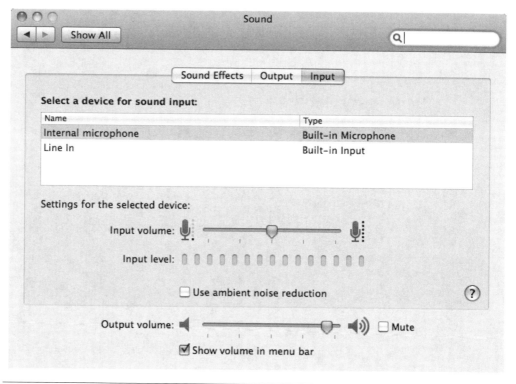

FIGURE 8-9 Use the Input tab to attach an external microphone.

Change Finder and Dock Preferences

You've probably already figured out that as a MacBook user, you'll be using the Finder and Dock a lot. These are two more areas that you can customize to your heart's content.

Finder Preferences

You've discovered by now that the Finder is a pretty useful tool, but by changing your preferences, you can make it even more suited to your specific way of doing things. Open the Finder Preferences pane by opening a Finder window and choosing Finder | Preferences. You'll find a number of tabs that you can use to change your settings.

General

Use the General tab, shown in Figure 8-10, to select which items you'd like to appear on your desktop. You can select hard disks, external storage, iPods, and connected network locations. You can also tell your MacBook whether it should open folders in a new or existing window and which folders you want the Finder to open in new windows.

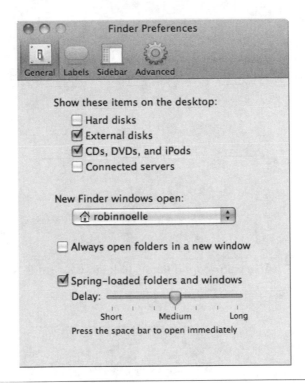

FIGURE 8-10   The General tab lets you select which items you want to appear on your desktop.

Another interesting setting is the Spring-Loaded Folders and Windows setting. When this setting is enabled, you can drag a file to a folder or window and pause for a second to get it to "spring" open. This is helpful when the folder you want to actually place the file in is buried deep within a file tree. Use the slider to adjust the time it takes for the folders and windows to open. Pressing the SPACEBAR will cause the folder to open immediately.

Labels

The Labels tab allows you to assign a color to folders and files. You can edit the label names for each color from this tab. Creating and using labels is just one more way to keep things organized. For example, you could use the blue label to identify folders pertaining to household business and use the red label for work-related files and folders (see Figure 8-11). Right- or CTRL-click on a folder to apply or change a label.

Sidebar

The Sidebar tab lets you select which items appear in the Finder sidebar. Check the boxes of the items you wish to appear and deselect those that you don't want to show (see Figure 8-12).

FIGURE 8-11 Use color-coded labels to keep your folders and files organized.

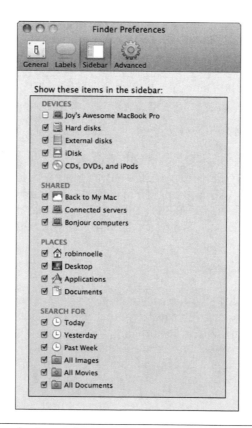

FIGURE 8-12 Choose the items that you want to appear in the Finder sidebar here.

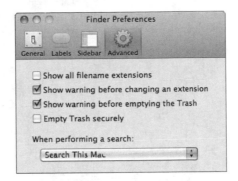

FIGURE 8-13   Change your default Trash settings on the Advanced tab.

Advanced

You can fine-tune some of your MacBook's settings on the Advanced tab (see Figure 8-13). You can tell your MacBook to display file extensions (such a .jpg for photos and .docx for Microsoft Word files) and whether to prompt you when an extension is about to be changed for a file. Showing file extensions is useful for sorting files by type (separating .docx from .doc, or .jpg from .gif, for example). You should leave the prompt for changing a file extension in place, because accidentally changing an extension can prevent the file from being opened, in some cases.

You can also choose whether to receive a warning before emptying the Trash and whether the Trash should always be emptied securely. You can also select a default location for where the Search function should look. You might change this if you regularly have an external drive connected to your MacBook, so that your computer knows to search that as well.

Customize the Finder Toolbar

You can quickly customize the toolbar in your Finder window through the Customize Toolbar options. Just open a new Finder window and then choose View | Customize Toolbar. The Finder customization dialog box shown in Figure 8-14 appears, where you can choose what items you want to be displayed.

 You must have a new Finder window open and active to access the Customize Toolbar options. If the option is grayed out, click the title bar of the Finder window to make sure it is activated.

The following is a quick run-down of the items you can add to the Finder toolbar in the customization dialog box:

- **Back**   You can go back to a previous folder that you were viewing. Clicking the right arrow moves you forward.
- **Path**   See the location of where a file is on your drive.

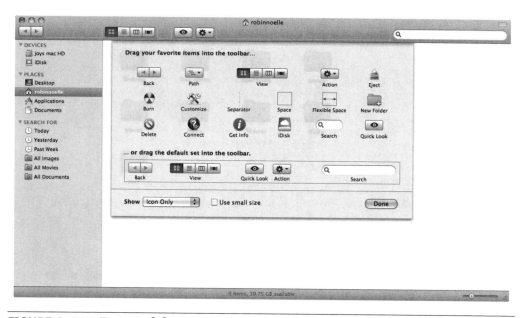

FIGURE 8-14 Drag and drop items from the menu to the toolbar or drag the default set to reset the menu to the default layout.

- **View**   Change how you display files and folders.
- **Action**   Click a file or folder to activate it and then click Action to display a list of available commands for that item.
- **Eject**   Click Eject to remove an external storage device or disk from your optical drive.
- **Burn**   Burn a disc!
- **Customize**   A shortcut to the Finder customization dialog box.
- **Separator, Space, and Flexible Space**   Use these to separate or arrange your toolbar icons.
- **New Folder**   Creates a new folder in whatever directory you are currently viewing in the Finder.
- **Delete**   Select an item and click Delete to deposit it in the Trash. Don't forget to empty it!
- **Connect**   Connect to a server.
- **Get Info**   Get detailed information on applications, folders, and files.
- **iDisk**   If you have a MobileMe account, this will connect you to your iDisk.
- **Search**   Adds the Search text box to the toolbar.
- **Quick Look**   Select a file and click the Quick Look icon to preview it without opening the associated program.

You can drag and drop items onto the toolbar or remove them by dragging them off the toolbar.

You can select how you would like the items in the toolbar to be displayed by clicking the Show button in the bottom-left corner of the customization dialog box. Choose whether you want just the icon, just text, or both displayed on the toolbar. If you want to use small icons, you can check the Use Small Size box. Clicking Done will save your preferences to your user profile so that they will be used whenever you are logged into your account.

Change the Dock Preferences

The Dock is where you will be accessing the majority of your applications, folders, and files. You can customize the Dock to show the applications that you use most often and then, in the Dock pane, you can tweak some of the settings relating to its appearance and location on your desktop.

Add and Remove Icons from the Dock

The Dock already contains the most commonly used applications included with your MacBook. Of course, these could include some programs that you rarely or never use. Why not replace them with applications that you do use?

To add an application to the Dock, just open the folder containing the application and drag the icon to the Dock. The left side of the Dock is for applications and the right side is for files, folders, and documents. Once placed, you can change the location of the icon on the Dock by dragging it to where you want it to appear. To remove an icon, just drag it off the Dock and it will disappear.

 The icons on the Dock are aliases (aka shortcuts), so when you remove an icon, it doesn't affect the actual program.

Dock Preferences

Just like with the Finder, you can change the settings of your Dock to suit your personal style. Open Apple | Dock | Dock Preferences to see those options (see Figure 8-15), described here:

- **Size**   You can use the slider to increase or decrease the size of your Dock.
- **Magnification**   Turning on Magnification magnifies icons when you move your cursor over them. This is a great setting if you have eyesight trouble or if you've made your Dock very small or your monitor resolution very high.
- **Position on Screen**   By default the Dock runs along the bottom of your screen, but you can change its location here. Click the appropriate button to move it to the right or left side of the screen.
- **Minimizing Windows Using**   You can select how windows are minimized from this pull-down menu. The Genie effect is the default. You can slow down the effects by holding the SHIFT key. Pretty cool!

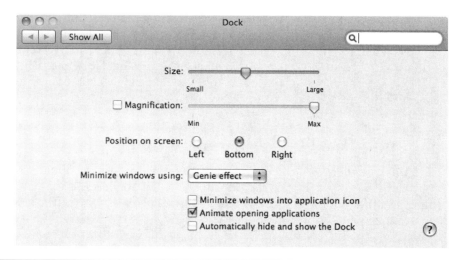

FIGURE 8-15   Use Dock preferences to change the size and location of the Dock.

- **Minimize Windows into Application Icon**   Normally, when you minimize a window it goes onto the Dock so that you can click it to open it again quickly. When this box is checked, the window is instead minimized into the icon of the associated application, saving you Dock space. To view your minimized windows, place your cursor over the application and hold down your trackpad or mouse button (or use your finger if you have no button). All of the windows will be displayed. Just move your cursor over the one you want to activate and release the button. The window will restore to its full size.
- **Animate Opening Applications**   When this box is checked, your icons bounce when you open an application.
- **Automatically Hide and Show the Dock**   Checking this box will cause the Dock to "disappear" when not in use. All you need to do to find it again is move your cursor to the bottom (or side, depending on where you've placed your Dock) of the screen and it will pop up to meet you!

 CTRL-click on an empty space on the Dock to see a shortcut menu where you can change many of these options without opening the Dock preferences pane.

Personalize Your Workspace

Although it serves no functional purpose, everyone likes a workspace that's aesthetically pleasing to look at. You can pick a new desktop photo or screen saver and even customize your icons. Once you've designed the perfect desktop, your settings will be saved to your user profile and available whenever you log in.

Change the Desktop Picture

Choosing a desktop picture is more important than you might initially think. After all, it's going to be one that you see every day! You can select one of the preloaded pictures already on your MacBook (see Figure 8-16) or you can use one of your own.

Open the System Preferences pane and click the Desktop & Screen Saver icon. Click the Desktop tab to access the desktop preferences. Click the folders to see what pictures are available in the various categories and click one to apply it.

 Choose Translucent Menu Bar if you want to see your desktop picture through the menu bar.

Add your own picture by clicking the + sign at the bottom of the pane and browsing your computer for the picture you want. You can also access your photos by clicking on the iPhoto folder in the sidebar.

If the picture you want to use isn't the perfect size for your laptop screen, you can resize it. You can preview your photo on the Desktop tab. If your picture isn't the proper size, a pop-up menu will appear so that you can choose another display option.

FIGURE 8-16   Select a desktop picture from the preloaded graphics, use your own, or let your MacBook surprise you with a random image.

As they say, variety is the spice of life! You can opt to have your MacBook automatically change your desktop picture for you on a regular interval. Check the Change Picture check box and select a frequency from the pull-down menu. When you check the Random Order box, the picture will be changed randomly from the ones contained in the folder that you selected.

Select a Screen Saver

Back before the time of LCD monitors, screen savers were actually very important. When a static image, like your desktop, remained on the screen too long, it could "burn in" to the monitor, leaving a permanent, ghostly impression.

Now a screen saver serves other purposes. You can use it for entertainment, to display a slideshow of your favorite photos, for example. Or you can set your computer to lock when it's been idle for a certain period of time. With this setting, it will display a screen saver, and then you will need to log back into your user account to access your files.

Open System Preferences and click the Desktop & Screen Saver icon to open the options. Click the Screen Saver tab (see Figure 8-17) and you can select from an assortment of included screen savers. Click one to see its preview display on the right side.

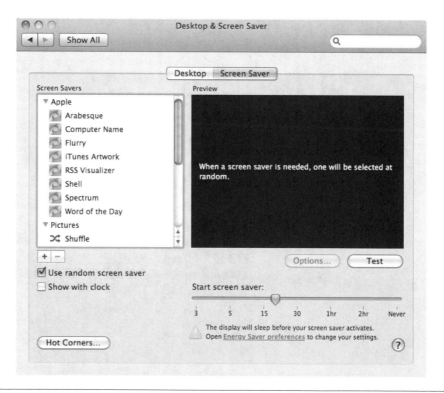

FIGURE 8-17 You can select a screen saver from the list or have your computer choose one at random for you.

The Screen Saver tab offers several options for your screen savers:

- **Use Random Screen Saver**   Check this box to have your MacBook decide which screen saver you will use.
- **Show with Clock**   Check the box to show the time on your screen saver.
- **Start Screen Saver**   Use the slider to tell your Mac when it should activate your screen saver.
- **Test**   Click this button to see a live preview of the screen saver. Move your cursor to exit.
- **Options**   If a specific screen saver has customizable options, you can click this button to access them. For screen savers that don't have additional options, this button will not be active.
- **Hot Corners**   Click this button to select tasks for your Mac to perform when you place the mouse pointer in one of the corners of your screen. Assigning Hot Corners will let you access certain tasks without having to open menus and applications. For example, you can assign your screen saver to one corner. Then, when you want to activate it, just move your cursor to that corner and the screen saver will activate.

Personalize Your Icons

You've been using icons to get around your MacBook, but did you know that you can customize them? While the ones that your computer came with are pretty awesome, if you are so inclined, you can download other icon sets from various websites or even create your own.

An icon, as a general rule, should convey something about the application or task it's assigned to. You can find a lot of themed icon sets online to download and install, such as retro, medical, food, pets, and more! Check out the icons at Smashing Magazine, www.SmashingMagazine.com, and The Iconfactory, http://iconfactory.com/home.

Here's how to customize an icon that's already on your MacBook:

1. Locate an item that uses the icon you want to use for your files or folders. Click it and then go to File | Get Info (or press COMMAND-I). Figure 8-18 shows the Get Info window for an icon.
2. Click the icon in the upper-left corner of the Get Info window. Choose Edit | Copy (or press COMMAND-C). Close the Get Info window.
3. Open the Get Info window for the icon that you would like to replace.
4. Click the icon in the upper-left corner of the window and choose Edit | Paste (or press COMMAND-V).
5. Close the window, and the icon will be replaced.

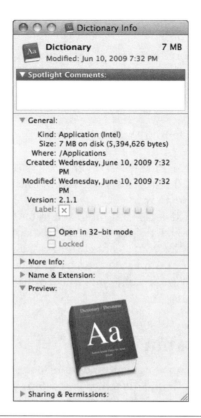

FIGURE 8-18   The Get Info window not only gives you lots of information about an item, but also enables you to change the icon.

Choose Still More Appearance Options

Still not satisfied with how your operating system looks? Well, you can make even more changes to the appearance! Open System Preferences and click Appearance. You can adjust the settings on the Appearance pane to your liking and they will be saved and used whenever you are logged in (see Figure 8-19).

In the first section of the Appearance pane, you can change the look of your buttons and menu as well as what color your MacBook uses when you highlight an item (the default is light blue). The second section allows you to change the options for your scroll bars and scrolling. Use Smooth Scrolling is a setting that you can select to eliminate jumping from one screen to another when using the scroll bar.

Your MacBook has a Recent Items menu that allows you to quickly access your most recent documents, applications, or server connections. You can access this menu by clicking Apple | Recent Items. Use the arrows to adjust how many of each type of file are shown in this menu. You may wish to assign more documents than applications, as you can easily access most applications from the Dock.

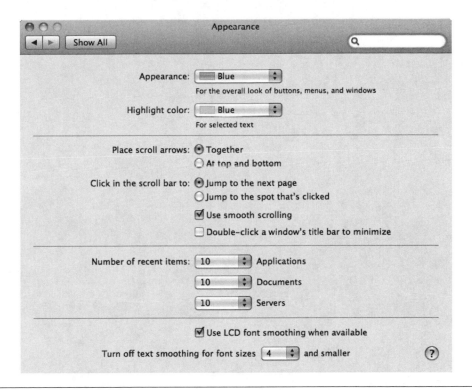

FIGURE 8-19 Change your highlight color and the number of recent items your MacBook displays through the Appearance pane.

Font Smoothing helps to smooth out jagged pixilation, which can occur in some fonts when the size is enlarged. You don't want to use this option if you plan to use small fonts or have a fine screen resolution, as Font Smoothing can make them harder to read, not easier.

Summary

The personalization options on your MacBook allow you to create an environment that is specific to the way you work with your computer. You can make aesthetic changes, such as a desktop picture or custom icons, or make system changes, such as creating the perfect Dock or Finder toolbar for the way you work. There are many ways to make your laptop uniquely yours, and since the settings are easy to change, you can update them as often as you like.

9

Surf's Up: Connecting to the Internet

HOW TO...

- Choose an Internet connection type
- Connect using the Network Setup Assistant
- Create a wireless connection
- Change your network preferences
- Share files with other computers

Your new MacBook is so loaded with great applications that you could probably stay busy for a long time just tinkering with those, but once you connect to the Internet, a whole new world opens up to you. Your MacBook is ready to get online; all it needs from you is a little help.

This chapter covers how to connect your laptop to the Internet through both a wired and a wireless network, as well as how to set up e-mail and surf the World Wide Web. We'll also go over some tips to help keep your computer and your information safe while online, and explore how to network and share files with others.

Get Online

Before you can get online, you need to have an account with an Internet service provider (ISP). ISPs are a dime a dozen, and there are literally hundreds to choose from. Many people find both cost savings and convenience by getting an Internet account as part of a service package from their local phone or cable company. Before you choose an ISP and sign up for an account, you should find out what types of connections are available and decide which best suits your needs.

Types of Internet Connections

Once upon a time, when the Internet was in its infancy, there was only one way to get online: a dial-up modem. The speeds were, by today's standards, unbearably slow, and whenever you were connected to the Internet, your phone line was busy and no one could reach you. You can still get a dial-up account, but there are other, much faster ways to get online, like cable, Digital Subscriber Line (DSL), and satellite.

Dial-Up

Dial-up connections use a regular phone line and a dial-up modem to connect you to the Internet. The available speed has increased a little bit from back in the early days of dial-up, but not much. Dial-up cannot be used for some Internet services, such as making phone calls from your computer with Voice over Internet Protocol (VoIP) or streaming video and music. If you like watching YouTube videos, gaming online, or doing almost anything other than performing web searches and sending e-mail, dial-up is probably not the best choice for you. There are really only a few reasons to consider dial-up at all:

- **Availability**   If you live in a rural area where DSL or cable Internet isn't available, you may only have the option for dial-up Internet. If this is the case, there's not much you can do except call your phone and cable companies to see when they plan to run the proper cables out to your location. Satellite service could be another option if you live out in the sticks, but that depends on availability and your geography. It is also much more expensive. See the "Satellite" section for more details.
- **Cost**   Dial-up is the cheapest way to get online. Some providers offer accounts for free but restrict the amount of time you can spend online and how much you can download. You will also be plagued with advertising. Ad-free accounts sometimes are priced as low as $10/month.
- **Access**   If you travel or spend a lot of time in remote locations, you probably won't always have access to high-speed Internet, but you likely will have access to a telephone line.
- **Usage**   You don't use or plan to use the Internet very often, and when you do, it's mainly for e-mail. Using dial-up for web browsing, watching video, streaming music, playing games, or any other common online activities will be at best frustrating and at worst impossible.

 Your MacBook doesn't have a built-in dial-up modem. If you want to use dial-up, you will need to purchase one separately and install it via USB. Just make sure that you get one that is compatible with your MacBook. Try your local Apple Retail Store or shop online at the Apple Store website (http://store.apple.com).

Digital Subscriber Line (DSL)

DSL and cable are the two most popular ways for people to connect to the Internet. Both offer very high speeds, and you'll probably find that the prices are similar as well. Both cable and DSL are always on, so you never have to worry about missing calls or tying up the phone line when you are connected. They both also use existing wiring—DSL uses your home's telephone lines, while cable Internet uses your existing cable connection, if you have one. There are two factors to consider if you are trying to decide between them:

- **Availability**   Do the telephone cables in your area support DSL? You can usually go to your local telephone provider's website and do a search for your address to see if they offer DSL in your area. To get DSL, you must be within a certain distance of a hub station. Your distance from this station will also affect your speed when you are connected.
- **Cost**   Cable usually costs a bit more, but that really depends on what packages or deals your provider is offering.

Cable

Cable Internet offers the fastest and, depending on your provider, sometimes the more reliable connection. It also usually costs a little more. If you don't already have cable installed in your house, you could incur installation charges and the hassle of waiting for a technician to come out and install everything for you.

The major disadvantage of cable is that your speed is dependent on how many people are logged into and using the network at one time. This shouldn't be a problem if you live in a single-family home in a residential neighborhood, but if you live in an apartment near many other apartment buildings and everyone is using cable Internet, it could really slow down your connection speeds during certain times of the day.

Satellite

In my humble (yet educated) opinion, satellite Internet should be used only when you have no other feasible option. At least at the time of this writing, satellite Internet is unreliable and wildly expensive, requiring multiyear service contracts and costly and intrusive installation.

If you live in a remote area and need high-speed Internet, you may find this to be your only choice. Because satellite Internet works via communication with an actual satellite, your connection can be limited or even unavailable during cloudy or stormy weather. Additionally, physical geographical elements like trees, mountains, and other buildings can interfere with your signal or even prevent you from being able to receive service.

Typically, the satellite company sends the equipment to you and then a service technician comes out to your house to install your satellite dish. The dish is normally mounted on the roof or, if there is interference at that location, on a tall pole.

Whereas when you sign up for broadband, you can usually self-install your connection for free with the instructions included in your modem package, you could end up paying as much as $300 to have satellite installed. Instead of paying month to month as you would with cable or DSL, satellite providers often require two- to three-year contracts with stiff penalties for canceling early.

The speeds available with satellite are better than dial-up but not by much, plus there's a strict limit on how much you can upload and download. You may be surprised at how fast you reach these limits in a month, and once you've exceeded them, your service speed will be hobbled for 30 days. If you really *need* higher speed than dial-up offers and satellite is your only other option, then you have little choice... but don't say I didn't warn you!

Use the Network Setup Assistant

You've already seen in prior chapters how easy your MacBook makes it to set things up, like adding a new printer or other peripheral device. Connecting to the Internet is just as easy! In most circumstances, all you need to do is have your account information from your ISP and run the Network Setup Assistant:

1. Choose Apple | System Preferences and then click Network in the Internet & Wireless area, as shown here.

2. Click Assistant in the resulting dialog box, shown next, to run the Network Setup Assistant. If you already have a network set up on your MacBook, you will see the Network pane. In that case, click the Assist Me button to display the Do You Need Assistance dialog box that's shown here.

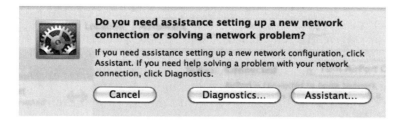

3. Name your location by typing in the text box. Use something descriptive that you can use to tell your network apart from any other available networks in the area. Click Continue.

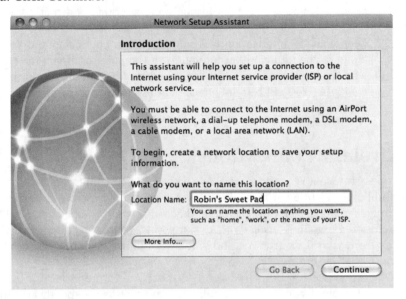

4. Choose the method that you are using to connect to the Internet: dial-up, AirPort (for wireless connections), DSL, cable, or a local area network (LAN).

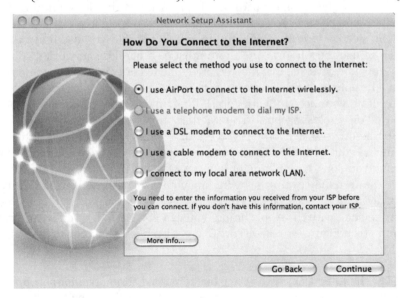

5. Attempt to connect. The Assistant will want to try to connect to the network now. If the connection is successful, you're done! If not, you will need to enter additional information from your ISP that it provided when you signed up for an account. If you still can't connect, contact your ISP directly for support.

Keep your ISP information in a safe place near your computer. You may need it again in the future, either for your own computer or, if you have someone over who wants to use your Internet connection from their own laptop, for your visitor's computer. You will certainly need your username and password to connect for the first time.

Wireless Connections

Wireless Internet is everywhere these days. It's nice being able to get online wirelessly in public places or even throughout your own home. No more Ethernet cables running through the house, tripping people and getting caught on the furniture! Since you purchased a MacBook instead of a desktop Mac, you probably plan to take your computer away from your desk anyway, and you'll want to use your built-in wireless card to connect to the Internet.

When you are at home, you can connect your laptop to the Internet with an Ethernet cable if you want to. You'll generally get faster speeds and maybe a more reliable connection, but if being tethered to a cable is too much of a hassle, connecting wirelessly all the time is fine too.

The wireless adapter card that is preinstalled in your computer is called an AirPort card. If you are connecting to a wired network, you'll use the Ethernet port on the side of your MacBook, but to connect wirelessly, you'll use the AirPort card. In order to use the AirPort card, there must be a wireless network available to connect to.

For now, let's just assume you are going to connect to your home network wirelessly. You'll be able to use the same steps to connect to public wireless hotspots later. When you set up your account with your ISP, you may have been given the option to select a wired or wireless account. The ISP then probably sent you some equipment to set up based on your selection. If you chose wireless, you should have received a wireless router in your setup kit. This allows multiple computers to connect to the same wireless signal. You don't have to rent or buy this wireless router from your ISP, however. You can save more money over time by buying your own. Just make sure that you've read some product reviews and that the company has a decent reputation for tech support. If you want to stick with the Apple brand, you can purchase the Apple AirPort Extreme Base Station (see Figure 9-1) or AirPort Express from an Apple Retail Store or the Apple Store online.

The AirPort Express is the more affordable alternative for networks with fewer than ten connections. It's very portable and also allows you to stream music from iTunes to speakers connected to nearly any stereo in your home.

FIGURE 9-1   You can purchase an Apple AirPort Extreme Base Station for your home wireless network. (Photo by Björn Milcke, Creative Commons)

Did You Know?

Types of Wireless Routers

There are a few different types of wireless networking types, namely G and N. You should select the one that works best with the type of computer user you are. Note that you can use the less expensive and slower routers for things like video and gaming, but the quality may suffer and you could find yourself waiting for the video to load and buffer, which can get irritating! Prices for these products are fairly reasonable, so although the N router is the most expensive, it's still not cost-prohibitive for most people. You should select this type of router if it's within your budget.

- **G**   Routers marked with a G are the most affordable but have the shortest range, are more susceptible to interference from other devices, and are not usually fast enough for streaming video and online gaming. This is a fine basic router.
- **G Plus**   This offers a little bit better speed and range. You could use this for web surfing, e-mail, and streaming music.
- **N**   This is the most expensive of the options but offers the greatest range and the fastest speeds. If you plan on wirelessly streaming video or playing games online, this is the way to go.

Connect to Your Wireless Network

If you've followed the installation instructions that came with your router—whether you purchased your own or received one from your ISP—you may already be connected to the Internet. Open your web browser to find out. If a page loads, you are already connected.

If you aren't connected to the Internet, you should run the Network Setup Assistant again using the same steps as discussed previously in this chapter. To get information about your wireless network, choose Apple | System Preferences | Network to open the Network pane. You'll be able to see if you are connected to a network and what networks are available to connect to (see Figure 9-2). Click Assist Me and then Assistant to relaunch the setup wizard.

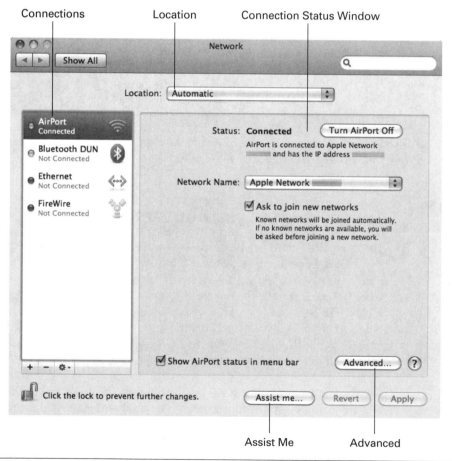

FIGURE 9-2 Find out the status of your network or choose another one to connect to in the Network preferences pane.

When you get to the page where you can choose how to connect to the Internet, select I Use AirPort to Connect to the Internet Wirelessly. You will be provided with a list of available networks to connect to. You may need to enter a network security key in order to connect.

 One of the downsides of wireless connections is that your data may not always be secure. The wireless signals from your router are transmitted over a distance determined by the type of your router and the strength of its signal. If you do not use network security, nefarious hacker types might be able to capture data that you transmit, like bank account information, passwords, and other private records. You'll choose a security protocol when you set up your router. What type you choose will determine what type of security key you need to enter to log onto your wireless network. As a general rule, choose WPA rather than WEP for added security.

Network Preferences

You already visited the Network preferences pane when you ran the Network Setup Assistant. Now we're going to go back to the Network pane and take a look at what we missed the first time. Open the System Preferences window and click Network. The resulting dialog box contains the following elements, which, again, are shown in Figure 9-2.

Location   By clicking the Advanced button, discussed shortly, you can save specific settings that pertain to how you connect to the Internet at various locations. For example, the security key, username, and password that you use to log into your work network are different from those that you use to log in at home. Once you have entered these details for each location and given the locations unique names, you can use this pull-down menu to select the location you want to connect to.

Did You Know?   ## Automatic Network Connections

By default, Mac OS X has a location named Automatic and has set all of your ports to active. This means that your MacBook will search all of your active ports (Ethernet, AirPort, modem, and so on) for a connection to the Internet. So, supposing that you connect your laptop at home wirelessly and at work connect with an Ethernet cable, the Automatic setting will determine which location you are at and automatically connect through the proper port.

Connections   This area on the left side of the Network pane lists the hardware that your MacBook uses to get online. You'll find your wireless, Ethernet, and other connections here. You can add connections, like a dial-up modem or Bluetooth, by clicking the + button, and remove connections by selecting them and clicking the – button.

Connection Status Window   This is the main section of the Network pane. Here you can see if you are connected to a network and, if so, which one you are connected to. You can also find your IP address and other connectivity information.

Assist Me   Click this button if you need to run the Network Setup Assistant again or if you need help troubleshooting your Internet connection.

Advanced   You can access detailed settings for each of your connections by clicking the Advanced button. You may need to access these settings to set up a new network or to connect to some networks. You can do things like specify proxy servers or change from a dynamic to a static IP address. If you don't know what those things are, then you probably won't be accessing the Advanced settings unless directed to by a tech support person.

Share with Other Computers

Your MacBook comes with the capability to share files, printers, and similar items with other computers. These computers don't have to be Macs; they can be PCs running Microsoft Windows or UNIX-based operating systems. All you need to do to set up sharing is open the Sharing preferences pane and change a few settings. Open the Sharing pane now by choosing Apple | System Preferences | Sharing.

The first thing you will see is your computer's name (see Figure 9-3). You should make sure this is something that will easily identify your computer on a network, such as Bob's Computer (assuming your name is Bob). This will help the person who is trying to connect to your computer when you are file sharing.

The sidebar on the left side of the Sharing pane contains a number of services. As you click on each service, options will appear in the main part of the pane that pertain to that sharing service. To activate a service, just check the box next to it. To turn it off, uncheck the box. Pretty easy, right? Let's go through them now so that you can adjust your settings.

DVD or CD Sharing   Turn this service on if you want to allow designated people to access media stored on your optical drive, assuming that you have one in your MacBook model. Likewise, if you have the MacBook Air, which doesn't come with a built-in drive, you could use this service to access the optical drive on someone else's Mac, if they have this setting turned on. This comes in handy if you don't have an optical drive and need to install something from a disc, for example (see Figure 9-3).

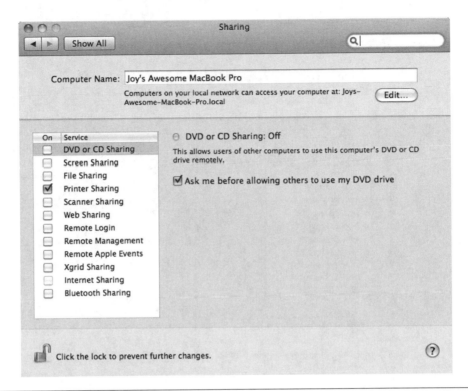

FIGURE 9-3   Tell your MacBook what you want to share and with whom on the Sharing pane.

Screen Sharing   Screen sharing allows someone on another computer to remotely control your MacBook and see what you see on your screen (see Figure 9-4). This is helpful when you are working with a tech support person to troubleshoot a problem with your MacBook. You don't want just anyone creeping around in your MacBook's files, so make sure that you either turn this on only when you need it and then disable it again, or that you only allow very trusted people remote access. Use the + and – buttons to add authorized users.

File Sharing   File sharing allows other people on your network to access specified folders and files on your computer. Turn File Sharing on if you want others to have access, and then specify which folders they can access by using the + and – buttons to add them to the Shared Folders list (see Figure 9-5). You can then select the users who can access these folders.

Tip   You can also select a folder to share by using the Finder. Search for and select the folder, choose Get Info from the File menu, and check the box next to Shared Folder to share it. Uncheck the box to stop sharing the item. If File Sharing isn't turned on already, the Finder will prompt you to do so.

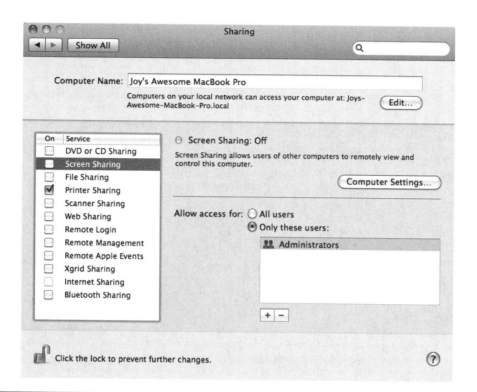

FIGURE 9-4 Do you see what I see? If we have Screen Sharing turned on, you might!

How to... Configure User Permissions

You'll need to configure the user and group accounts so that they have the appropriate privileges to access your shared files. Here's how to do it:

1. In the Sharing pane, select File Sharing in the list of services and select the shared file from the Shared Folders list.
2. Click the + button to add a user.
3. Select an existing user account or group. Click New Person to create a new Sharing Only user account or select a user in your Address Book (also a Sharing Only user account). To create a different type of new user account, use the Apple | System Preference | Accounts pane.
4. Select a privilege option. The default is Read Only, meaning that the user can access the file but not make any changes to it. Read & Write lets them read, copy, and make changes to the files in the folder.

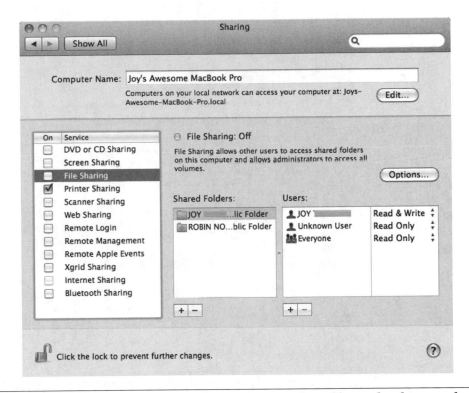

FIGURE 9-5   With File Sharing turned on, you can share files with other people in your network.

Clicking Options lets you select which network protocol will be used when others are accessing your system (see Figure 9-6). There are three options:

- **AFP**   This stands for Apple Filing Protocol. Use this setting to share with other Macs.
- **FTP**   File Transfer Protocol, the setting to use with some UNIX-based systems that don't use SMB. FTP is the least secure of the sharing protocols and should be used only when another isn't available.
- **SMB**   Server Message Block protocol is the best setting for Windows-based PCs and most UNIX-based operating systems.

 You will have to enter the user's password for a user account if you enable it to use SMB.

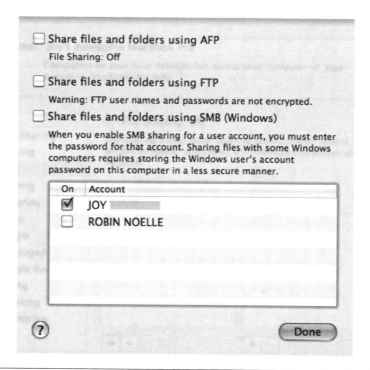

FIGURE 9-6 Select a protocol based on what type of computer the person you want to share with is using: Mac, Windows PC, or UNIX.

Printer Sharing and Scanner Sharing These two services allow others to use printers or scanners that are connected to your computer. To enable printer sharing, simply check the Printer Sharing check box in the Service list on the left of the Sharing pane. Choose which print queue to share by selecting it from the middle pane. By default, all users will be able to print using your shared print queue. To change this, click the + button below the Users list on the right. A drop-down list of users will appear. Select one or more people to add and click Select. Once you do this, only those users will be able to access your shared print queue. The same procedure is used for sharing your scanner after you click Scanner Sharing.

Web Sharing This service allows other users to view web pages on your computer. You might use this if you are hosting a website on your computer.

Remote Login Remote Login lets other people log into your MacBook using Secure Shell (SSH). This is similar to Screen Sharing and should be turned on with caution and only as directed by tech support personnel.

Remote Management This service also allows people to remotely access and control your MacBook, only this time they need to use Apple's Remote Desktop software to do it. Reserve the use of this for troubleshooting, and then only when directed by tech support to do so.

Remote Apple Events   This service allows other people to send Apple Events directly to your computer. Since these events are basically commands for your computer to follow, like running an application, it's best to leave this one turned off, too.

Xgrid Sharing   Xgrid Sharing typically is used in a workplace environment. It allows a group of networked computers to access the processing power of your MacBook when you aren't using it. By combining resources from many computers, complex computational tasks can be performed more quickly. You'll probably never use this.

Internet Sharing   Using this service enables other computers to access the Internet through your computer (see Figure 9-7). Generally, it's a lot easier just to hook up the other computer to the Internet in some fashion, using a wired or wireless connection. Don't bother with this if you have dial-up or satellite Internet, and check with your ISP's Terms of Service before turning this on.

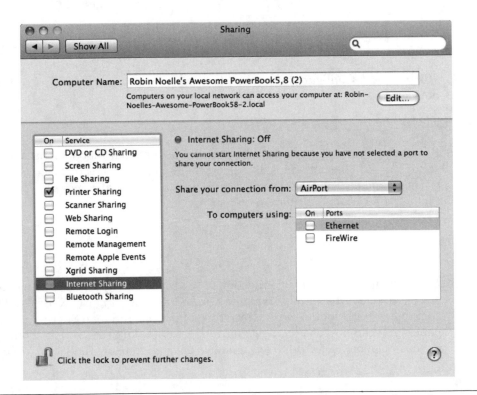

FIGURE 9-7   You can allow other computers to access the Internet through your MacBook, but check with your ISP's Terms of Service first!

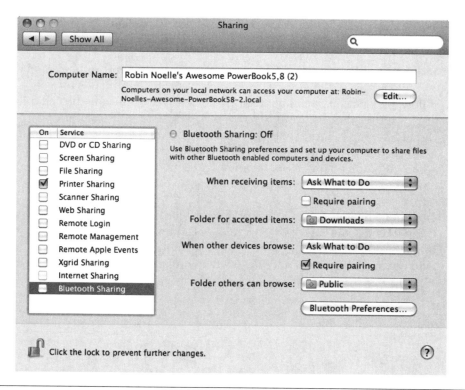

FIGURE 9-8 Configure how your MacBook connects and shares with Bluetooth devices.

Bluetooth Sharing You can alter the settings that your MacBook uses when connecting to Bluetooth devices. Select where you want files received via Bluetooth to be saved and decide whether you require pairing before sharing (see Figure 9-8). See Chapter 2 for more information on pairing.

Summary

By now you should have a connection to the Internet, either wired or wireless. You can share files with friends and family, even those running UNIX- or Windows-based computers. With your new understanding of the Network and Sharing preferences panes, you can now change how you connect to the Internet and how others connect to your MacBook. Read on to learn how to get started using the World Wide Web.

10

Navigating the World Wide Web

HOW TO...

- Use Safari to browse the Internet
- Set Safari's user preferences
- Find information on the Internet
- Create and use bookmarks
- Subscribe to websites with an RSS feed
- Download and use another browser

Once you've established an Internet connection, there's no limit to the things you can do online. Before you can really start accessing it all, you'll need a web browser to display all of that great online content. There are a lot of different browsers out there that you can use, but your MacBook comes with Safari preinstalled. We'll start by exploring how to make the most out of this versatile browser.

Surf the 'Net with Safari

In the previous chapter, you set up your Internet account on your computer. Make sure that you are connected to the Internet and then open Safari by double-clicking the icon in the Applications folder or by clicking the icon in the Dock. This will launch your browser, which should open to the Top Sites page by default during your first use. One of your Top Sites will be the Apple home page. Take some time to explore the website if you haven't visited it before. There's a lot of great information available!

Did You Know?

Top Sites

Safari 4 tracks the sites that you visit and ranks them according to how often you do so. It presents the websites you visit most often in the Top Sites view, with up to 24 thumbnail images of the websites per page. You can pin favorite sites to specific locations on the page—so that you know just where to look next time you open Safari—by clicking the pushpin icon of the site you want to pin. Arrange your Top Sites by dragging the web pages to where you want them to be on the page. Click the X in the corner of a site to remove it from your Top Sites.

Websites with a star icon in the upper-right corner have updated their content since your last visit. To access your Top Sites page, click the Top Sites button in the Bookmarks Bar (described in the "Create and Use Bookmarks" section later in the chapter).

As with other programs, you can use the scroll bar to move the screen's contents up and down, such as when you want to move through lengthy web pages. Occasionally, you will notice that your mouse pointer turns into a hand. This means that the text or image that you are currently centered on contains a link to a website. You can click the active item to go to that site. In the upper-left corner, you will see two arrows. Clicking the left-pointing arrow will move you back to the website that you were on previously, and clicking the other arrow will move you forward to the website that you went back from. Check out Figure 10-1 to view the various buttons and features of Safari.

If you want to make your Safari window larger or smaller, click the resize handle in the lower-right corner of the window. Drag by clicking and holding the icon and moving your mouse until the window is the size you want. After resizing a Safari window, any new windows that you open will be the new size.

FIGURE 10-1   Safari is the web browser that comes with Mac OS X, preinstalled on your MacBook.

Clear Your Browser History

Your web browser keeps a history of all the websites that you visit. Safari uses this information to update your Top Sites (a list of the websites that you visit most often), both to auto-complete web addresses and so that these websites will load more quickly when you visit them again. On the flip side, someone else can come along and see exactly what websites you've visited, which might not be a good idea if you were shopping online for a birthday gift or surprise anniversary vacation. To keep your browsing activities under wraps, click History | Clear History at any time to manually remove your browsing history, or change the preferences in your browser so that your history is erased at regular intervals.

When you want to move to a new site, you can type the address into the address bar at the top of the screen or click a link from a page that you are currently on.

 Safari and other browsers now include "smart" address bars. As you type in a website address, your browser will suggest complete addresses that you can select to jump to that site. It will suggest sites from previously typed entries and from top sites on the Internet if they match what you are typing. Back in the day, you had to type in every character of web address, including the http://, before you could navigate to a site. Now, in some instances, you can just type in a single word and the browser will fill in the rest. Try typing just "apple.com" into your browser's address bar to see how it works!

Change User Preferences in Safari

As with your MacBook and its other programs, you can change your preferences in Safari so that it works the way you want it to when you access the Internet. Click Safari on the menu bar and then Preferences to access your options, as discussed next.

- **General**   On the General preferences tab, shown in Figure 10-2, you can change your default home page, select a new location for saving downloaded files, and delete your browsing history. You can also change how Safari handles links from applications and whether or not it automatically opens downloaded files that it deems "safe." Examples of typical safe files include graphics files, documents, music, and movies; basically, file types that aren't known to be infected with viruses and spyware. If you choose not to open a downloaded file immediately, you can locate it wherever you selected your download location to be.
- **Appearance**   On this tab, you can change the default fonts that Safari uses (see Figure 10-3) and choose whether to display images. If you deselect the Display Images When the Page Opens check box, your pages will load faster but won't include any images. If you have anything faster than dial-up, there's no need to uncheck this box.

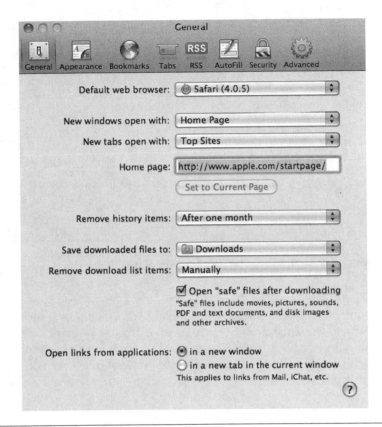

FIGURE 10-2   Set your default home page from the General preferences tab.

How to... Change Your Home Page

If you're like most computer users, you probably want to change your home page to a website that you visit frequently, such as your web-based email, a social networking site, or a news site. You can change your home page using the steps below so that when Safari starts up, it always opens to the page you selected.

1. Navigate to the web page that you want to set as your home page.
2. Click Safari | Preferences. You can also use the COMMAND-, (COMMAND plus the comma key) shortcut.
3. Click the General icon.
4. Click Set to Current Page.
5. Close the preferences window.

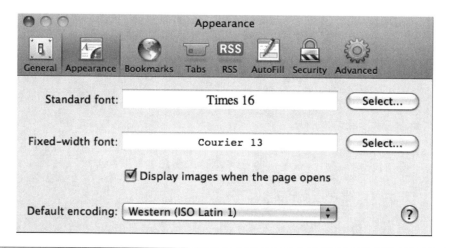

FIGURE 10-3 Choose a default font for Safari from the Appearance tab.

- **Bookmarks** You can set what content you would like displayed in the Bookmarks Bar and Bookmarks Menu here (see Figure 10-4). You can also change the settings so that your bookmarks automatically synch with your MobileMe account (see Chapter 12), which is useful if you want to access your bookmarks from multiple Macs.

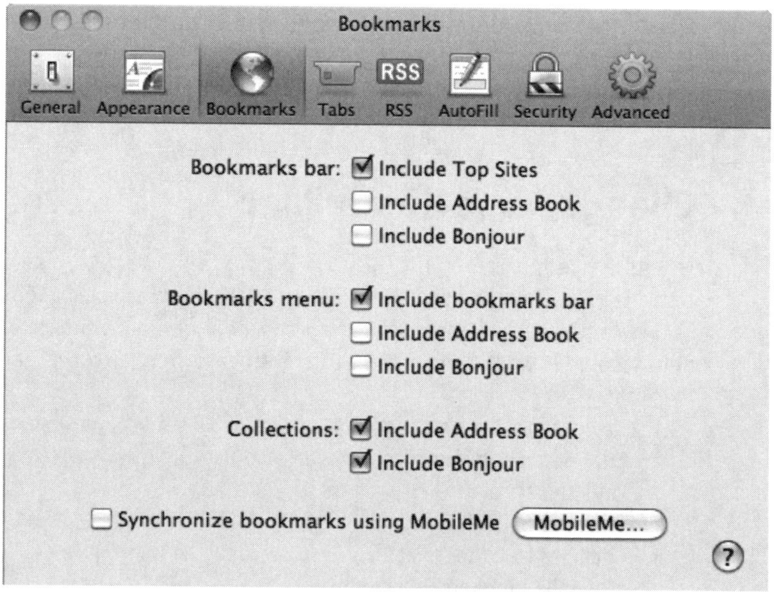

FIGURE 10-4 Use the Bookmarks tab to change how your Bookmarks Bar looks.

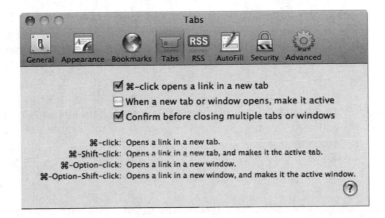

FIGURE 10-5   Tabs are a great way to keep multiple websites open without using separate windows.

- **Tabs**   When you use tabs, you can access different websites from a single browser window instead of opening a new window for each site. You can scroll through the tabs to see the pages, reducing your screen clutter. Very handy! Use the Tabs preferences to change how Safari deals with tabs (see Figure 10-5).
- **RSS**   Use this tab to configure your RSS reader and how often it updates the feeds from your subscriptions (see Figure 10-6). You'll learn more about what RSS is in the "Subscribe to Websites with RSS" section later in this chapter.

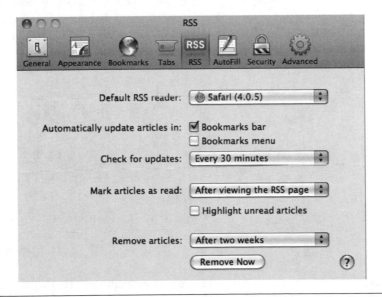

FIGURE 10-6   Keep up with your favorite blogs and websites with a built-in RSS reader.

- **AutoFill**   If you're driven mad by constantly filling out web forms on every site you visit, AutoFill is for you! AutoFill will fill in forms for you by using information that you have previously entered. You can also have it remember usernames and passwords for secure web pages (see Figure 10-7).

Caution   Turning on AutoFill for usernames and passwords will prompt Safari to store this information for all secure sites that you visit. Your stored information is encrypted for your security, but use caution when using this feature. If your laptop is stolen or someone accesses Safari on your computer, they could potentially have access to any secure website that you have visited, including online banking, social networking, and shopping sites.

- **Security**   The Security tab sets how Safari deals with multimedia content, pop-up ads, and cookies (see Figure 10-8). Unless you are having problems with your web browsing experience, it's probably best to leave most of the settings in the Security tab alone. Your browser needs to use plug-ins to display some graphic, audio, and video content. Java and JavaScript are both used by websites for web forms, animation, and other interactive content like games. Under the Accept Cookies area, make sure that the Only from Sites I Visit option is selected. Some websites won't display content if cookies aren't enabled. You should leave the Block Pop-Up Windows check box selected to cut down on annoying and potentially infected pop-up ads.

Note   Cookies are small files that websites use to authenticate users and track your activity while on their website. One example of this is when you do some shopping on a website but don't complete your purchase. When you return to the website, you may find that the items you put in your cart are still there. Generally cookies are harmless, but if you are deeply concerned about privacy, you can either turn off cookies or delete them frequently. If cookies are turned off, some websites will not work for you (including banking and shopping sites).

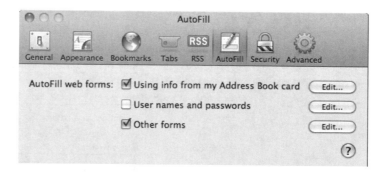

FIGURE 10-7   AutoFill will fill in common web form fields for you with data that you've previously entered.

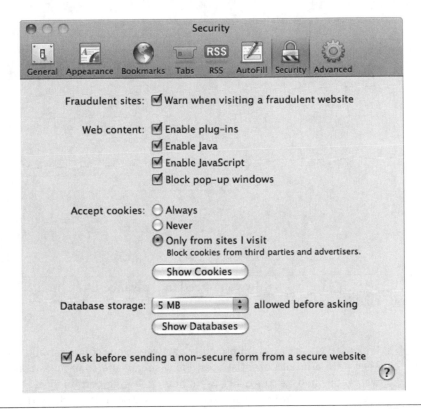

FIGURE 10-8   Your security settings control pop-up ads, animations, and cookies.

- **Advanced**   Set the default size of your font, specify whether you want to use a CSS style sheet to change how websites appear, and change your proxy settings on this tab (see Figure 10-9). Safari is set to allow the user to use the TAB key to move from the address bar to the search field and then to text fields and pop-up menus. If you want to use the TAB key to move through every element on a web page, you can check the box for Press Tab to Highlight Each Item on a Webpage. Most users won't need to change any of the advanced settings.

How to... **Customize the Toolbar**

To change the items on your Safari 4 toolbar:

1. Choose View | Customize Toolbar.
2. In the new dialog box, drag to the toolbar the items that you want to add to the toolbar. You can also drag items off the toolbar to remove them. You can restore the default toolbar by clicking and dragging it from the bottom of the window to the toolbar.
3. Click Done when finished.

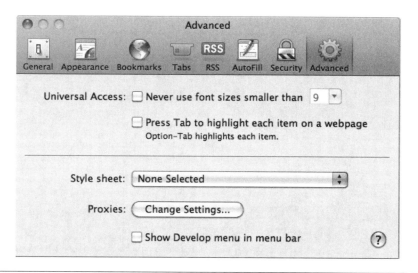

FIGURE 10-9 You probably won't need the Advanced tab, but it's a good idea to know what it contains.

 Proxy servers act as an intermediary between your computer and another server. They have a lot of potential uses. Proxy servers are sometimes used to surf the Web anonymously, to restrict users from accessing certain sites, to track and audit Internet usage, or to circumvent regional restrictions (such as the inability to watch video on Hulu.com if you are outside the United States).

 Click Safari | Private Browsing to start a private browsing session. While in this mode, Safari will not save any information from the websites that you visit, including AutoFill content and cookies. Your search information will not be saved, and anything that you download will be erased from the download history immediately. Pretty handy!

Find Information on the Internet

The Internet's primary function is to help people store, locate, and share information, regardless of their physical location. The Internet is vast and contains literally billions of pages of information, so how do you locate something specific? You use a search engine, of course.

Search engines send out digital scouts called "spiders" that scour the Internet and index the content that is available on every page they visit. This information is stored on the search engine provider's servers and is provided to you when you enter a search term. So, if you are looking for a cheesecake recipe, you would enter "cheesecake recipes" as your search term and the search engine would provide a list of all the pages its spiders have visited that contain those words, with the best matches or paid ads at the top of the page.

There are many search engines to choose from. Google is the most popular—so popular that the term "google" has been entered into the American lexicon as a verb to describe the act of conducting a search—but there are others to choose from as well. Yahoo.com, Bing.com, and Ask.com all offer similar search features, or you can use a site like Dogpile.com that aggregates search results from a number of different search engines.

The key to success when using search engines is to be specific. The more terms that you enter, the more likely it is that the results that are returned will be what you are looking for. For example, searching for "Golden Gate Bridge history" will return more results relating to the history of the bridge than a search for just "Golden Gate Bridge" or "San Francisco." See Figure 10-10 to see Google's results.

When a search engine performs a search for you, it looks for your keywords or search terms throughout all the pages, but doesn't necessarily look for them together. If you want a search engine to look for a specific phrase or word combination, put your terms in quotation marks. A good example is when you are searching for a person's name. Searching for John Smith will bring up pages that contain both of those words, so you might find information on John Peterson and Bob Smith. If you search for "John Smith" using the quotation marks, you will only receive pages that contain the name John Smith.

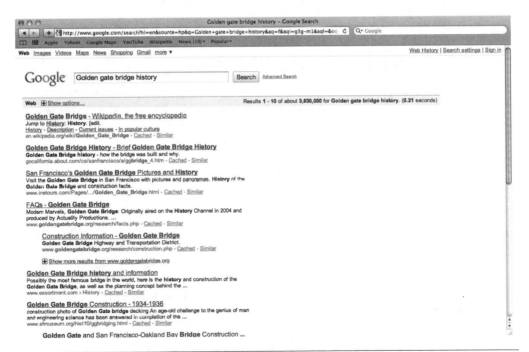

FIGURE 10-10   Be as specific as possible when doing web searches. If your search returns no results, you can try using broader search terms.

How to... **Perform a Full History Search**

As mentioned previously in the "Change User Preferences in Safari" section, Safari saves information about every website that you visit. You can use the Full History Search and Cover Flow options to search through and view any web page that you've visited online (if you haven't cleared your Internet history).

Type a word or phrase in the Search History field in Top Sites and Safari will display a list of results from your browser history in the Cover Flow view. Use the slider or arrow keys to browse through the results and then click the website that you want to view to open it.

Safari comes with a built-in Google search bar right at the top of your screen (refer to Figure 10-1). Just type the search terms you want to find in the box and press ENTER. Your search results will be displayed in the web page below.

Tip You might notice some links at the top of the Google search page, such as Web, Images, Videos, and more. To narrow your search results to just image files, either click Images and use the search box on that page or perform your search and then click the Images link. If you only want shopping results to appear, enter your search terms and click Shopping.

Create and Use Bookmarks

Bookmarks work for the Internet in very much the same way that they do for books; they mark a specific spot so that you can quickly return to it. You can use bookmarks to organize your favorite websites and pages so that you don't have to type in a web address or perform a search to find the page again.

Create Bookmarks

To create a bookmark, first open Safari and head to the web page that you want to add to your bookmarks. Click Bookmarks | Add Bookmark and you will be prompted to name the page that you want to save (see Figure 10-11). Not all web pages have descriptive titles, so make sure that you use a name that will remind you of what is on that specific site or page. After you give the page a name, you can choose where you want to save it in your Bookmarks folders. Access your bookmark by clicking Bookmarks and selecting it from the folder or group that you saved it in.

Keep Your Bookmarks Organized

If you do a lot of web surfing, over time you might accumulate dozens or hundreds of bookmarks. Searching through them all to find the one site that you want doesn't

FIGURE 10-11   Add bookmarks to find favorite websites again quickly.

sound very efficient, does it? Well, you can save yourself a lot of time and trouble if you start organizing your bookmarks from the start. Click the Bookmarks icon in the Bookmarks toolbar to see all of your bookmarks to date (see Figure 10-12).

Just like with your documents or music, you can create folders and subfolders to store your bookmarks in. Apple has provided some preset folders for you, but you can customize them or create new ones as you see fit. You may have a folder for news websites, one for recipes you've found online, one for your favorite shopping websites, and perhaps a folder for websites relating to a favorite hobby or pastime. Use the + button at the bottom of the page to create new collections or subfolders (see Figure 10-13).

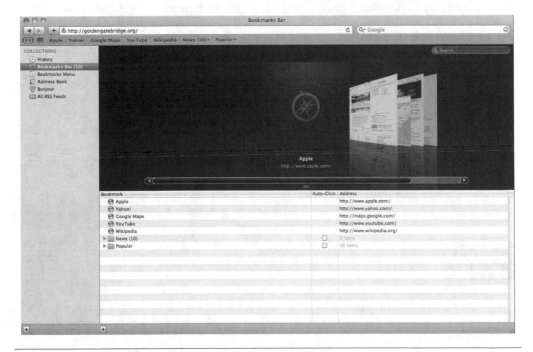

FIGURE 10-12   Clicking the Bookmarks icon will open the Bookmarks Bar, where you can view all of your saved bookmarks.

FIGURE 10-13 Create folders to keep your bookmarks organized.

In the Bookmarks Bar window, your bookmarks are listed by name and the web address appears under the Address section. You can move bookmarks by dragging them to new folders or collections. If you want to keep a copy of the link in the original folder, hold down the OPTION key when you are dragging and dropping it. To delete a bookmark, subfolder, or collection, select it with your mouse and press the DELETE key.

 Quickly add a site to your bookmarks by selecting the address in the address bar and dragging and dropping it onto the Bookmarks toolbar.

Import and Export Bookmarks

As mentioned before, you can easily accumulate dozens or hundreds of bookmarks over the lifespan of your computer. If you lose your bookmarks, it could take a long time to find all the websites again and re-add them to Safari. Luckily, you can back up your bookmarks and then import them to a new computer or browser.

To export your bookmarks, click File | Export Bookmarks and give your file a name. Select a location on your hard drive where you want to save them, and click Save.

 Using a date in the filename, like November_2010, will help you keep track of which bookmark file is the most recent.

To import bookmarks into Safari, click File | Import Bookmarks, browse for your file on your computer, and then click Import. You can use this feature to import bookmarks from friends and family to your new computer or to share your bookmarks with them!

Subscribe to Websites with RSS

RSS is the acronym for Really Simple Syndication, a format used most often by websites that update frequently, like blogs or news sites. There are many different programs you can use to subscribe to and keep track of RSS sites, but Safari comes with an RSS reader built right in, so you don't have to use a separate program if you don't want to.

When you visit a website that uses RSS, Safari will display the RSS symbol in the address bar. If you want to view the RSS feed, just click the icon and the feed will appear in your browser window. You will see the total number of articles in the feed in the upper-right corner of your screen and the number of new articles (assuming you've visited the feed before and not all of the available articles are new to you). Check out Figure 10-14 to see how an RSS feed for the popular news website Fark.com looks in Safari.

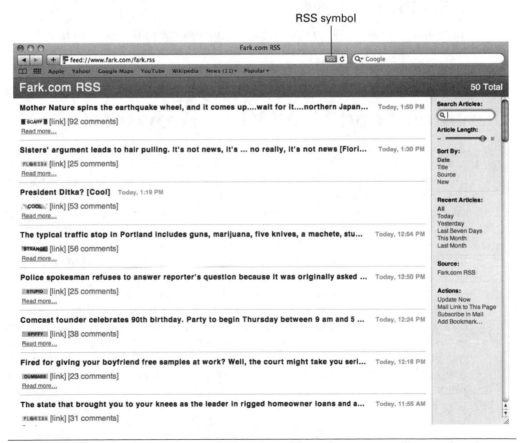

FIGURE 10-14   Click the RSS symbol in the address bar to open the articles in Safari's built-in RSS reader.

In the right sidebar you will see a variety of options pertaining to RSS. First, you can use the slider to select how much of an article appears in your feed. If you just want a small portion to appear, move the slider to the left. For the full article, move it all the way to the right. You can also make a selection under the Sort By heading to sort your articles by title, source, date, or most recent.

Use the Recent Articles options to select articles from a certain date or range of dates. You will find the original source of the article listed under Source. Under the Actions heading you will find options that include updating the RSS feed to see any new articles that have been posted since you opened the feed, sharing the article with someone via e-mail, subscribing to the feed yourself by e-mail, and bookmarking the feed.

 You can bookmark RSS feeds just as you can with regular websites. Save the bookmark to your Bookmarks Bar. The number of unread articles in the feed will appear next to the name of the bookmark.

RSS Preferences

You can access the RSS tab of Safari's user preference to set how often it checks for new articles in your RSS feeds. You can also tell Safari to mark new articles in a different color so that you can easily tell them apart from your previously read articles.

Download and Use Other Browsers

As mentioned before, there are lots of different browsers that you can use on your MacBook; you don't have to stick with Safari if you don't want to. Two other popular browsers are Mozilla's Firefox browser (see Figure 10-15) and Google's Chrome browser (see Figure 10-16).

To download a new browser, you just need to visit the associated website (or use your new search engine skills to find it!) and download the version for Mac OS X. To download Google Chrome, visit www.google.com/chrome. The website should auto-detect your operating system and offer you a download link for Mac OS X. You can download Firefox at www.mozilla.com.

When you click Download at one of these websites, you will be asked to agree to the Terms of Service for the browser. Read them if you like and then accept them if you want to download the browser. You will then start the file transfer. You can choose to save the file and then open it or to open it upon download. Run the file, and the installation application will launch and guide you through the setup process. Once you have installed the new browser, you can launch it from the Applications menu or pin it to the Dock for easy access.

FIGURE 10-15   Visit Mozilla's website to download the Firefox web browser.

Choose Between Browsers

Did You Know?

There really isn't too much difference between browsers. They all operate in more or less the same way, with an address and search bar, bookmarks, and preferences. Some come with slight variations on standard features, and all of them look slightly different. It hasn't been proven conclusively that any one browser is faster than any other, so choose your browser based on any unique features it might offer and its aesthetics.

FIGURE 10-16 Google Chrome is the newest web browser and is available for Windows, Mac OS X, and Linux.

Summary

The Internet is like outer space, a limitless expanse containing more things than one could hope to imagine. Unfortunately, there's a lot of space junk floating around the Internet, too—broken links, outdated web pages, and useless information. Using a search engine helps you weed through the garbage and find the information you are looking for, quickly. You can use bookmarks to organize and share your favorite websites and Safari's built-in RSS reader to keep up with your favorite blogs. When you get tired of searching for information and reading, there's games, videos, music, and so much more to explore online.

11

Staying in Touch: E-Mail, Chatting, Video, and More

HOW TO...

- Configure an e-mail account
- Create a new e-mail message
- Instant message with iChat
- Video chat with friends
- Make phone calls from your computer

While the primary purpose of the Internet revolves around the storing and sharing of information, its secondary purpose is to allow people to connect with other people and interact. If you or people you know enjoy chat rooms, message boards, or online gaming, you most likely have friends all over the world, even if you've never met face to face. That's part of the beauty of the Internet; no matter what you are into, there are hundreds of people who are crazy about the same thing! Your MacBook gives you a lot of ways to connect with people online, including e-mail, instant messaging, video, and even phone calls.

E-Mail Basics

Among the many ways to communicate with people online, e-mail is still the most popular. Billions of e-mails are sent and received every day around the world. Whether the sender is a CEO in a plush corner office or a South American student at a local Internet café, the beauty of e-mail is that it is fast, easy, and free. All you need is an Internet connection, a computer, and some type of e-mail program. Since you have a MacBook, you already have an e-mail program on your computer; it's called...Mail.

Open the Mail application by clicking its icon on the Dock or accessing it from the Applications folder. You will need to set up a new e-mail account before you can start sending out messages.

You will need information provided by your Internet service provider (or e-mail provider, if they are separate) to properly set up your e-mail account. You should locate this information, including your username, password, and e-mail server, before you continue. If you cannot find this information, call your ISP.

Create a New E-Mail Account

Assuming you haven't already set up an e-mail account in Mail for your user account, when you launch Mail, you will receive a Welcome to Mail message, the first step of the setup program. Perform the following steps to get your e-mail account up and running:

1. Enter your name, e-mail address, and password for your e-mail account as provided by your ISP. Click Create or Continue.

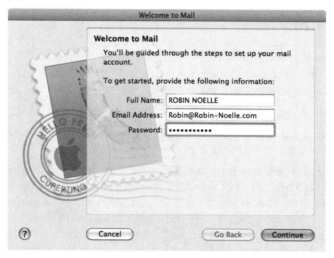

 Mail can automatically configure your e-mail accounts from certain popular ISPs like Gmail, Yahoo, AOL, and more. If you have one of these accounts, just fill in your username, password, and e-mail address and Mail will fill in the rest of the appropriate settings. Click Create to finish creating your account. If Mail doesn't recognize your ISP, you will need to enter additional information for your account and you will receive the Continue prompt.

2. Input your incoming mail server information as provided by your ISP, as shown next. This includes your account type (IMAP, POP, or Exchange), server address, username, and password. You should give this account a descriptive name in the Description field so that you can distinguish between different

e-mail accounts if you have more than one, such as one account for work and another for personal use.

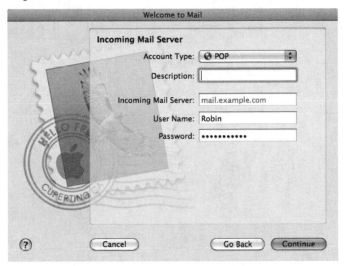

 With an IMAP e-mail account, your e-mail stays on the server, allowing you to access it from different computers or online. With a POP3 account, your e-mail is generally downloaded to the computer that you use to check your e-mail and deleted from the server. Once it's downloaded, you can no longer access it from other computers or the Internet.

3. If you are using a POP account, your ISP will have provided you with information if you are required to use Secure Sockets Layer (SSL) and authentication. If so, check the SSL box, enter the authentication method, and click Continue. If you are using an account type other than POP, or if your ISP doesn't require you to use SSL, click Continue.

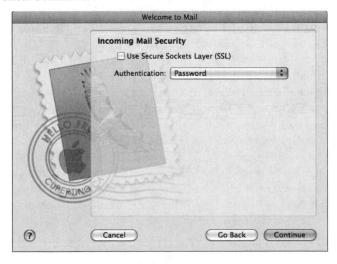

4. Enter your outgoing mail information. If the outgoing mail server requires a username and password, check the Use Authentication box and enter that information in the boxes provided. Click Continue.

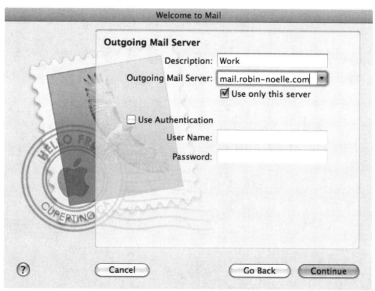

5. Review the Account Summary window for any errors and then click Create to finish your account.

Did You Know?

Choose Your Favorite E-Mail Application

You don't have to use the Mail application that comes with Mac OS X. You can use any of the free web-based e-mail programs available, like Yahoo, MSN, or Gmail, or, if you have Microsoft Office for your MacBook, you can use Entourage or some other e-mail application.

When you use a program like Mail or Outlook, the program downloads your e-mail from a web server into your mail program. Depending on your settings, those e-mails are then deleted from the server or stored indefinitely. When you use web-based mail, your e-mail is always stored online. Of course, some web-based e-mail programs like Gmail have settings that allow you to use them with e-mail programs like Mail. Confused yet?

Generally, if you prefer to access your e-mail from the Internet, go with a web-based program, and if you would rather download your e-mail and be able to view it even when you aren't online, you should choose an e-mail program like Mail or Outlook. Note that you'll still need to be connected to the Internet to send and receive e-mail.

Create a New E-Mail Message

Just as all web browsers share many of the same basic features, so do all e-mail programs. You can send, receive, and organize your e-mail messages in all of them. More advanced features vary by application, and you may find one program to be more aesthetically pleasing than another, so go with whichever one has the features you want and has a look that you enjoy. For the sake of this tutorial, I'm going to assume you are using Mail, but if you use a different program, the steps will be more or less the same.

Once Mail is open, take a moment to review the layout of the toolbars and buttons, as shown in Figure 11-1. Find and click the New Message button, and a new, blank e-mail will open, as shown here.

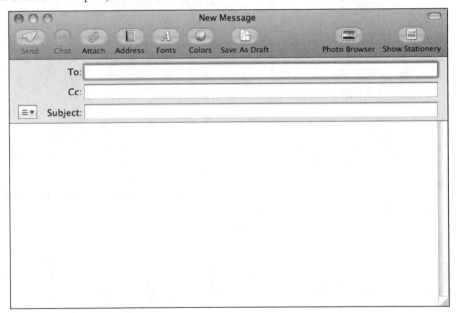

Enter in the To field the e-mail address of the person you want to send your message to, type a subject in the Subject line, type your personal message, and then click Send. That's all there is to it!

Tip Make sure that you enter a person's complete e-mail address correctly or they will not receive your message. There's a big difference between an underscore (_) and a dash (-) in an e-mail address. Always include the @ symbol and domain (@gmail.com, for example). Not all domains are the same. The .com domain is popular, but you may have friends or colleagues who have e-mail addresses that end in .org, .net, or something completely different.

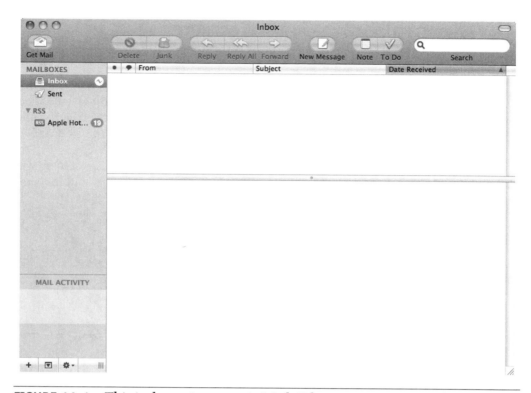

FIGURE 11-1 This is the main screen in Mail. When you receive e-mail messages, they will appear here.

Netiquette

There are certain socially accepted rules to online and e-mail/chat behavior, often referred to as "netiquette." Typing in ALL CAPS IS CONSIDERED THE SAME AS YELLING AT SOMEONE, and could offend someone, or at least irritate them. Likewise, typing in all lowercase with no punctuation just makes your e-mail confusing and hard to read. Using a spell checker is highly recommended, even for personal e-mails. It makes them easier to read and makes you look smarter and more professional. Use exclamation marks sparingly; sentences shouldn't end with multiple exclamation points, or at least not more than one sentence!!! As a general rule, keep smiley faces and other "emoticons" out of professional e-mails altogether and use them sparingly in personal e-mails ☺. Internet abbreviations like LOL (laugh out loud) should be reserved for those rare instances that someone or something really has made you laugh aloud.

Read and Reply to E-Mail

Now that you've sent out an e-mail or two (perhaps announcing your new e-mail address?), it's time to read your replies. Mail will check for new e-mails periodically. You can change how frequently that happens in the General preferences, discussed later in the chapter. When a new e-mail arrives, it appears in your Inbox. If you don't want to wait for the next scheduled mail call, you can click Get Mail to force Mail to look for new e-mail anytime. Click on an e-mail, and its contents will appear in the preview pane below your Inbox, as shown in Figure 11-2. If you want to read the message in a separate window, double-click it.

Once you've received an e-mail from someone, it's easy to add them to your address book. Right-click the name of the person in the From field of the e-mail you received and select Add to Address Book (see Figure 11-3). Later, when you want to send an e-mail to that person, you'll only need to type the first few letters of their name, and the rest of their name and address will be displayed automatically. You can always add a contact manually by opening Address Book and creating a new contact. See Chapter 12 for additional information on Address Book.

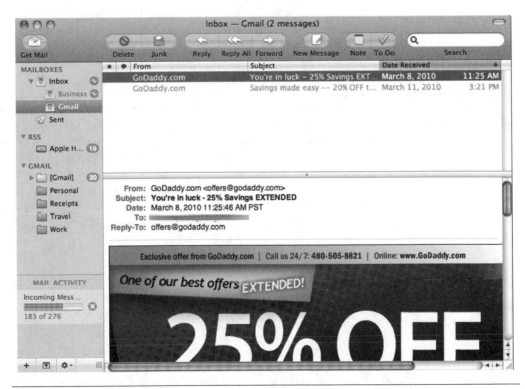

FIGURE 11-2   You can take a quick look at your unread e-mail in the preview pane. Double-click the e-mail to open it in a new window.

FIGURE 11-3 Add to your address book the people with whom you correspond regularly so that Mail can fill in their e-mail address for you quickly later.

Once you've read an e-mail, you might want to respond. Click Reply on the toolbar and a new e-mail window will open. The To address will already be filled in because the reply is going back to the person who sent the e-mail you're replying to. You can change the Subject line if you want, or leave it the same. Mail automatically adds Re: to the beginning of a reply. Enter your response in the body of the e-mail and click Send. Off it goes!

 There are two ways to reply to an e-mail, Reply and Reply All. If the sender of an e-mail sent it to more than one person, the e-mail addresses of all recipients will appear in the original message's To or CC line (that stands for Carbon Copy or Courtesy Copy, depending on who you ask). If you click Reply, your response will only be sent to the original sender. If you click Reply All, it goes to everyone who was included in the original e-mail. Use extreme caution when using Reply All. Make sure that your response is both relevant to everyone on the e-mail list and appropriate to send to a large audience. There have been many cases where someone has accidentally sent an off-color joke or snarky comment to their whole office when it was meant for just one person!

Did You Know?   ## Create a To-Do List

You can create a to-do list item by highlighting text in an e-mail and clicking the To-Do button on the toolbar. You can then set a due date, set an alarm, or assign it a priority rating. Each To-Do item includes a link back to the original e-mail, in case you want to review it, and is added to your iCal calendar.

Delete an E-Mail

It's up to you whether or not to delete your old e-mails. Depending on how much e-mail you send and receive, you may never have to delete a single one. But if you find yourself running out of hard drive space or losing important e-mails amid thousands of old messages, you might want to get rid of the ones you no longer need.

Deleting an e-mail is as easy as selecting it and either CTRL-clicking it and choosing Delete or clicking the Delete button (or pressing the DELETE key on your keyboard).

 If you aren't going to delete your e-mail messages, you will definitely want to keep them well organized. While most e-mail programs have a search feature, it's easier and faster to find what you are looking for if you are searching a folder or two instead of an entire Inbox with 23,000 e-mails in it!

Advanced E-Mail Techniques

By now, you've mastered e-mail basics: sending, receiving, replying, and deleting. But there's a lot more to e-mail than that. You can format your e-mails, send attachments, and create personalized folders to keep your e-mails organized. To truly master e-mail, keep reading!

Organize Your Inbox

Most e-mail programs offer folders to help you keep organized. Mail does too, but it calls these folders *mailboxes*. By creating mailboxes, you can sort your saved e-mails by sender, by topic, or any other way you can think of.

To create a new mailbox, choose Mailbox | New Mailbox. Name your new mailbox something descriptive, as shown in the following illustration. Choose a location for the mailbox and click OK. You might have different mailboxes set up for e-mails from different groups of correspondents, such as family, friends, and work colleagues, for e-mails related to different categories, such as hobbies, newsgroups, and newsletters, or for other types of e-mails you would like to save. You can drag relevant messages into your new mailbox to add them.

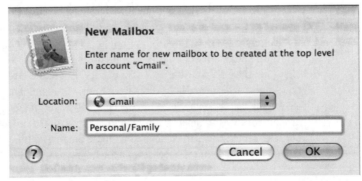

Of course, just as with folders, you can create sub-mailboxes. To do this, follow the steps to create a new mailbox, and in the Name field type the name of the parent folder followed by a forward slash (/) and then the name of the subfolder (Family/ Sister, to create a folder under the Family heading for e-mails from your sister, for example). Remember that the more detailed your mailbox or folder system is, the easier it will be to find what you are looking for later.

Format E-Mail Messages

Until now, your e-mail messages have probably looked pretty boring, but don't worry, you can get more creative with formatting! Start by creating a new, blank e-mail message.

Just like in a word processing application, you can alter the font, font size, and color in your e-mails to add that personal touch. Click the Fonts button in your e-mail message toolbar to see all the fonts that are available on your MacBook (see Figure 11-4). There are many to choose from, so I'm sure you'll find one that appeals to you, but if not, you can always go online and find new, free fonts. Go ahead and use your search engine to look for free Mac OS X fonts!

Smart Mailboxes

Mail also comes with a feature called Smart Mailboxes, which allows you to pull e-mails from various folders and combine them in a new mailbox without actually removing them from their original location.

To create a new Smart Mailbox, choose Mailbox | Smart Mailbox, give the mailbox a name, and then set the criteria you want that mailbox to use in the boxes provided. This is handy if you have e-mails from a specific person scattered throughout different mailboxes and you want to collect them into a single area.

Some examples of Smart Mailboxes that you might want to create follow:

- **Unread Messages** Often our Inboxes become cluttered with e-mails we've read but are leaving in the Inbox to deal with later. If you don't want to lose unread e-mails, you can create a Smart Mailbox with the criteria to move all unread e-mails from a specific date or date range (today, this week) into it. Later, just click this mailbox and browse your unread e-mail.
- **VIPs** Whether it's your boss, your spouse, or someone else important in your life, you can create a Smart Mailbox that contains correspondence from the people you select. This could prevent you from accidentally overlooking an important e-mail.
- **Attachments** Attachments can take up a lot of space on your hard drive or your mail server. Have them sent to a single Smart Mailbox and then just browse through them, deleting unnecessary attachments as you go.

FIGURE 11-4   Pick a font for your e-mail to add a personal touch.

Select the font that you like from the list. You can select the type of typeface that you want and set the size. Keep in mind that people read their e-mails on different types of devices. A tiny font might be fine when viewed on a large monitor, but on a small Blackberry or iPhone, it could be very hard to read.

You can click the Colors button in your e-mail message toolbar to add color to your font or the background of your e-mail. Be wary of using these features in a professional setting; bright colors and wild fonts can be distracting and might look unprofessional. Clicking the Colors button brings up the Colors palette, shown here, where you can select the colors that you want to apply.

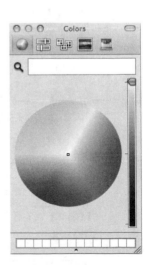

Use Stationery

E-mail stationery is sort of like regular stationery except it's electronic. Stationery templates are included in a number of e-mail programs, and Mail is no different. You can access some of the great templates that Apple has included, shown in Figure 11-5, by clicking the Show Stationery button on the e-mail message toolbar.

Browse through the options until you find the stationery that appeals to you, and then click on the stationery option to apply it. You can then write your e-mail by selecting the dummy text and typing over it. Send it as you would any other e-mail. Assuming that the recipient's e-mail program supports HTML (a language in which most websites are written and that allows the creation of this stationery stuff), they will be able to view your lovely e-mail just as you sent it.

 You can search online for more stationery templates that you can use with Mail. Some are free, whereas you may have to pay for others. Just make sure that you carefully read the system requirements so that you know your version of Mail is compatible, and read the installation instructions for installing the template correctly for use. You can also create your own templates by designing an e-mail and then selecting File | Save As Stationery.

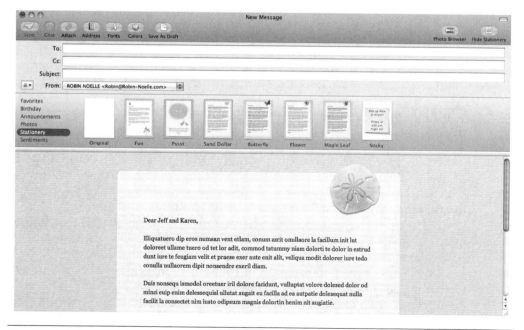

FIGURE 11-5 Stationery templates offer a complete look for your e-mails without having to select each formatting component.

Add Photos and Attachments

You can easily add photos to your e-mail and send them all over the world. Click the Photo Browser button on the e-mail message toolbar to select photos from your iPhoto library or elsewhere on your computer and add them (see Figure 11-6). Once you have added your photos to your e-mail message, you can set their size by using the Image Size pop-up menu at the bottom of your e-mail message.

 You can click the Email button in iPhoto to start an e-mail message in Mail with your selected photo already attached. You can also drag photos from iPhoto into a Mail message to attach it.

You can also add other types of attachments, like Word documents, text files, applications, movie files, and more. To add an attachment, click the Attach button and browse your computer for the file that you want to attach. Click the item to select it, and then click Choose File to add it to your e-mail (see Figure 11-7). You can also drag files into your message, just like you can with iPhoto pictures.

 You can use Quick Look to view some supported attachments (like PDF files or Word documents) in e-mails that you receive. Select the attachment and click the Quick Look button to preview the attachment without actually opening it. This works with photos too.

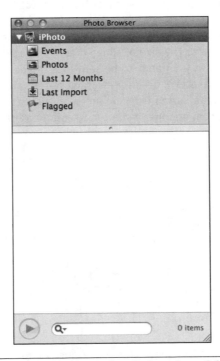

FIGURE 11-6   Share your photos by e-mail with friends and family around the world.

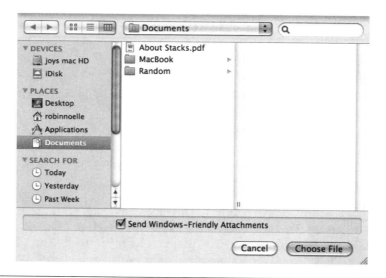

FIGURE 11-7 Send files through e-mail by adding them as attachments. Just make sure the file size isn't too big!

If you aren't sure what type of computer the recipient of your attachment is using, or if you know they are using a Windows PC, make sure to select the Send Windows-Friendly Attachments check box (see Figure 11-7) so that they can read it.

 ISPs set different limits for the types of files that they allow to be sent and received and for the size of those files. Some ISPs will not allow executable files (.exe), such as programs, to be sent or received. If your file is too big for an ISP, you will also receive an error message or returned e-mail message. If you really need to send a large file, there are services that will allow you to do so online, like YouSendIt.com or some instant messaging programs, for example.

Read RSS Feeds

Just as in Safari, you can read RSS feeds in Mail. (See Chapter 10 for more information on RSS.) To add a feed, click File | Add RSS Feeds. This opens a window where you can choose the feeds that you've already subscribed to in Safari, or you can add new ones by entering the RSS feed address. The image here shows an example.

Once added, your RSS feeds will appear in the sidebar along with other mailboxes that you've created. Each feed will have its own mailbox. Select an RSS message just as you would an e-mail message and its contents will appear in the preview window. Double-click the article to read it in a new window.

Use Text to Speech

One really cool feature of Mail is that you can have your MacBook read your e-mail aloud. This is great if you are busy multitasking or just want to relax while Mail does your work for you. It works pretty well for sight-impaired people too.

Open your e-mail in a new window by double-clicking it in your Inbox. Click Edit | Speech | Start Speaking and your MacBook will read your message to you (including the headers). When you get tired of hearing robotic voices, you can click Edit | Speech | Stop Speaking to turn it off again.

 The Edit | Speech | Start Speaking command is available in a variety of applications on your MacBook, not just Mail.

Mail Preferences

You'll want to take a moment to go through the preferences menus of Mail if that's the program you want to use for your e-mail. Like always, you can alter some of the settings to make your experience more personalized to your way of doing things. Choose Mail and then Preferences to access these settings or you can go to the Apple menu | User Preferences | Mail.

Customize General Preferences

Use the General preferences tab to set your default e-mail program, how often it checks for new e-mail, how you are alerted to new e-mail, and other fairly self-explanatory settings (see Figure 11-8).

 If you want invitations that you receive to automatically be added to iCal, you can select that as an option from the pull-down menu.

Customize Accounts Preferences

The Accounts preferences tab has three subtabs: Account Information, Mailbox Behaviors, and Advanced.

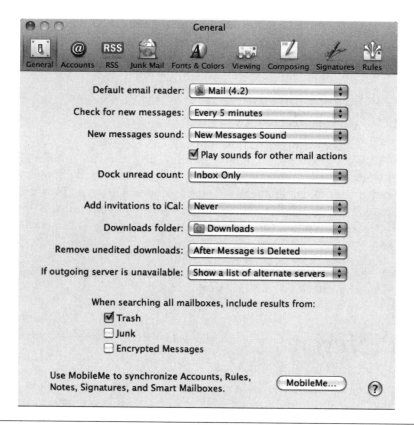

FIGURE 11-8 Change how often Mail checks for new messages from the General preferences tab.

Account Information

Here you can add, delete, and edit your e-mail accounts. You can edit your specific account information, including your username, passwords, e-mail address, and server information. You can also add multiple accounts, such as a home e-mail account and a work e-mail account. Click the + and – buttons below the Accounts list to add and delete accounts. Click an account to see its details (see Figure 11-9).

Once you've added a new e-mail account, its mailbox will appear with your other mailboxes in the Mail sidebar. Click the mailbox to see what e-mail it contains.

 When using multiple e-mail accounts within Mail, all of the e-mail will be dumped into your Inbox. If you want to see which e-mail account it was sent to, you will need to click an account's mailbox.

FIGURE 11-9 You can add, remove, or view the details of multiple e-mail accounts on the Account Information tab.

How to... Select an E-Mail Account to Send From

When you have multiple accounts in Mail, you will need to be careful which account you are sending messages from. Change which account you are sending an e-mail from by selecting the desired account from the pull-down menu under the From field. If you do not see a pull-down menu, here's how you can add it:

1. Create a new blank e-mail.
2. Locate the small list icon to the left of the Address field (refer to Figure 11-4).
3. Click the list and choose Customize.
4. Check the box next to From and then click OK.
5. Select which account you want to send your e-mail from in the pull-down menu.

Mailbox Behaviors

Here you can decide where to save drafts, whether notes should appear in your Inbox, whether sent messages are stored on the server, and how often you want junk e-mails to be deleted (see Figure 11-10). You can also set how often your deleted messages are permanently erased. Remember, once they are permanently deleted, there's no turning back!

Advanced

Turn a Mail account on or off and decide which accounts are checked for new e-mail from the Advanced tab (see Figure 11-11). Checking Enable This Account enables the account to send and receive e-mail. Checking Include when Automatically Checking for New Messages means that this account will be included when Mail checks the servers for new e-mail messages. You can also opt to keep copies of your e-mails on your ISP's server.

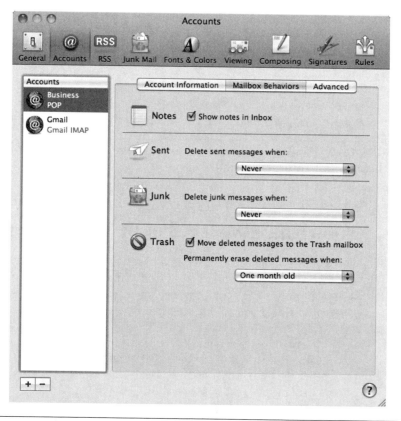

FIGURE 11-10 Change how each mailbox handles e-mail in the Mailbox Behaviors preferences.

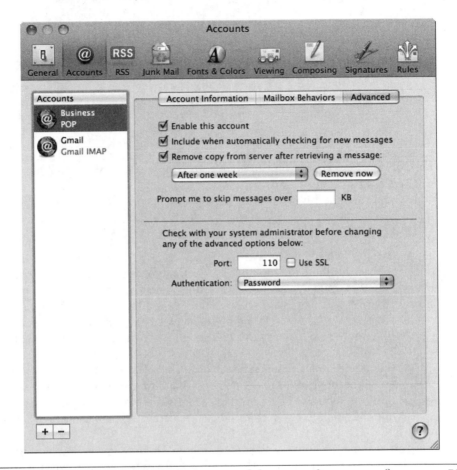

FIGURE 11-11   You can tell Mail to save or delete e-mail messages from your ISP's server on the Advanced tab.

 Once you download your e-mail, if you decide not to keep copies on the server, you will no longer have access to your e-mail from anywhere except the Mail program. That means if your computer crashes or the e-mails get deleted somehow, you will not be able to retrieve them again. If you keep copies on the server, you can download them again any time you want. On the other hand, it takes up space on the server and, depending on the type of account you have, that space may be limited or cost extra if you exceed your storage limit.

Customize RSS Preferences

Use these settings if you want to read your RSS feeds in Mail. You can set how often Mail checks the feed for updates and set Mail or Safari (or another program) as your default RSS reader (see Figure 11-12).

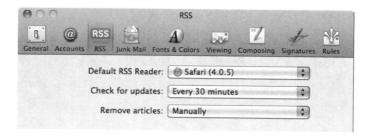

FIGURE 11-12 If you want to view your RSS feeds in Mail, you can change the settings for them here.

Customize Junk Mail Preferences

Ah, junk mail (aka spam), the bane of e-mail users everywhere! Unfortunately, the more time you spend online, the more likely it is that you will receive unsolicited e-mails. Every time that you enter your e-mail address into a website or write it on a form or survey, there's a chance that it will be sold on a mailing list. Since you need to enter your e-mail address to register for shopping websites, news websites, and just about everything else online, there's no real way to avoid spam. You can, however, try to control it.

 One way to dramatically cut back on spam is to use a throwaway or junk mail e-mail account. You can set one up using a free web-based e-mail service like Gmail or Yahoo and then use that address when registering on websites or filling out consumer forms (such as product registration, club cards, and so forth).

You can use the Junk Mail preferences tab to determine how you want Mail to handle your spam (see Figure 11-13). Select which e-mails are exempt and how you want your mail filtered. You can click the Perform Custom Actions radio button and click Advanced to access advanced settings that let you define additional rules for Mail to use when evaluating unsolicited mail.

 No matter how good a junk mail filter is, sometimes e-mail that you want to receive can end up in your spam folder or Trash. It's a good idea to take a quick browse through the e-mails that Mail has marked as spam before you permanently delete them!

 ## You Can Help Mail Block Spam

Mail automatically uses its own junk mail filter and your settings to sift through the e-mail you receive. You can help Mail better learn what e-mail you want to keep and what you want to send to the Trash by sorting e-mails it has missed. If Mail has marked something spam that isn't, click the Not Junk button. If Mail has missed some junk mail and it's in your Inbox, click Junk. Junk mail appears brown in your mail list.

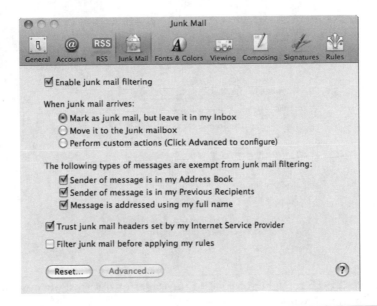

FIGURE 11-13   Use the Junk Mail settings to help Mail sort the spam from the real e-mail.

Customize Fonts & Colors Preferences

You can set the default fonts and colors for your e-mails here (see Figure 11-14).

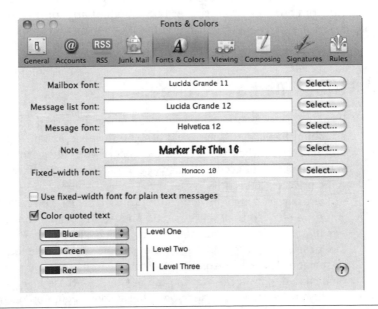

FIGURE 11-14   Pick your favorite font and make it the default for all of your new e-mail messages.

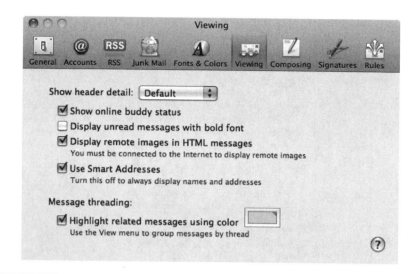

FIGURE 11-15 Highlight related messages or opt to show new messages in bold font in the Viewing preferences tab.

Customize Viewing Preferences

On the Viewing tab (see Figure 11-15) you can decide how you want to view your e-mail in Mail. Headers include the information normally at the top of e-mails, like the From, To, and Subject lines as well as lots of information about how the e-mail was routed and from what ISP. You can set how much, if any, of this information is visible to you. Generally, the default setting will suffice for most users.

Block Remote Images

Remote images are typically used by advertisers. Instead of embedding or attaching the images they would like you to see in e-mail, the images are stored on their server. When you open the e-mail, if you choose to view these images, your computer will access the server and download the images. This could create some privacy and security issues.

For example, simply by connecting to their server, you have revealed that you have received their message and opened it, thereby confirming your e-mail address is valid. You can also be giving them your IP address—that is, the location of your computer on the network. This is valuable information to someone looking to exploit your system. To protect yourself, you can (and should) opt on the Viewing tab not to have these images automatically displayed. A more drastic and somewhat inconvenient approach is to download and then read your e-mail offline.

By checking the boxes, you can select to see the status of your iChat buddies, to display unread messages in bold font, and to display remote images, like those that are usually included in advertisements and newsletters. You can also turn Smart Addresses (AutoFill for the To field) on and off.

Message threading highlights all the messages that are related to the one that you are currently viewing. This is handy if you have sent or received multiple e-mails relating to a single subject and want to find them all.

Customize Composing Preferences

In the first section of the Composing preferences tab (see Figure 11-16), you can decide whether you want to use rich text or plain text. Rich text is what allows you to

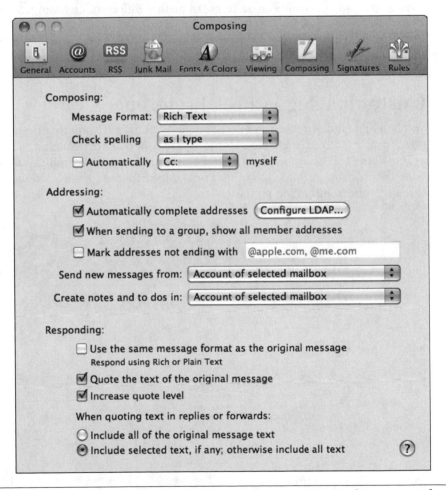

FIGURE 11-16   When you have multiple e-mail accounts in Mail, you can select the default account to reply from in the Composing preferences.

change fonts and add color and graphics, like stationery, to your e-mails. You might want to use plain text, however, if you are sending lengthy e-mails to someone's phone or other mobile device, because the files are smaller and faster to download, plus there's no formatting to be distorted on a small screen. You can also set your spell check options here and opt to copy yourself on all of your e-mails.

In the Addressing section, you can set a default account to send e-mails from, determine how you want them addressed, and specify what the default account is for notes and to-do lists. LDAP is a protocol mostly used by businesses to access company-wide directories. You'll need to talk to your company's IT department to determine whether or not this feature is available and what the settings are.

Mark your options in the Responding section to set what format you will use to reply to e-mails and whether you want to quote e-mails when replying. When quoting, the original message is included in your response. You can increase the quote level to have quotes appear with a colored line to further differentiate them from the reply text.

 If you want to just quote part of a message, you can select what you want to quote and then click Reply.

Customize Signatures Preferences

You can add signatures to the end of outgoing e-mails by creating them on the Signatures preferences tab (see Figure 11-17). You can create as many signature files as you want and assign them to different accounts. Typical signature files include your name, title, website, and other contact information. It's a good idea to keep your signature short and to the point.

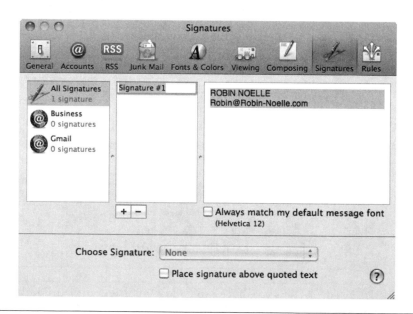

FIGURE 11-17 A signature file should include your name and contact information.

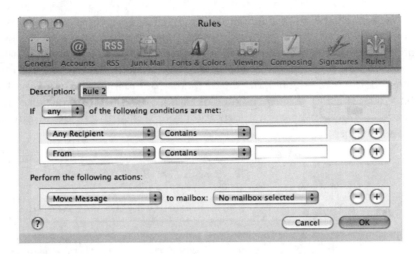

FIGURE 11-18 Rules help Mail sort incoming e-mails by sender, keywords, or other criteria.

Customize Rules Preferences

You can create rules to help Mail automatically sort your incoming mail. You might want to create a rule that says to highlight in blue all the e-mails from your best friend, for example, or to place all e-mails from your boss in a mailbox called Boss.

To create a rule, just click Add Rule and then select the criteria you want to use for it from the boxes (see Figure 11-18). When you have finished defining your rule, click OK to activate it. Just make sure to give it a descriptive name so that you know what that rule does when you want to edit it later!

Text and Video Chat with Instant Messaging and Make Phone Calls

Sending e-mail is a great way to keep in touch but requires time between sending your e-mail and receiving a reply. By using instant messaging, video chat, and Voice over IP (VoIP) phone services, you can instantly see and hear friends, family, and colleagues from around the world while you communicate in real time.

Instant Messaging

Instant messaging (IM) today is used as much in business as it is in personal life. Instead of having to send an e-mail or pick up the phone, you can just quickly instant message someone with a question and get an almost instant response (if they are at their computer!). There are lots of different IM applications that you can use, but since your MacBook comes with iChat, let's start with that one.

Open iChat from the Applications window or by launching it from the Dock. You'll see the Welcome to iChat screen, shown here, that gives you some information about the features included. Click Continue. You will need an IM account to use iChat. You can sign up for a MobileMe or Mac.com account, or if you have an AOL Instant Messenger (AIM), Jabber, or GoogleTalk account (if you have a Gmail account, you have a GoogleTalk account), you can add it as well. Enter your account type and then your account or username information and password. Click Continue and then click Done to finish.

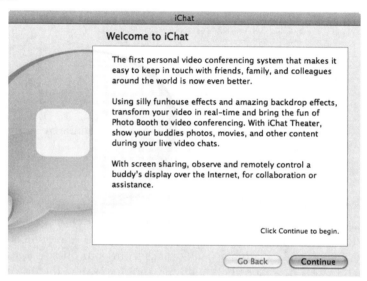

Buddy Lists

You can't chat by yourself, so you'll need to add some friends (or "buddies") to chat with. Add a buddy to your account by clicking the + button at the bottom of the iChat window. You will need to enter account information for your friend, such as their username and the type of account they have. iChat supports accounts from MobileMe, AIM, GoogleTalk, and Jabber; the following illustration shows how to add a friend who uses AIM.

You can organize your contacts in a Buddy List once you have added them all. To see a Buddy List, check out Figure 11-19.

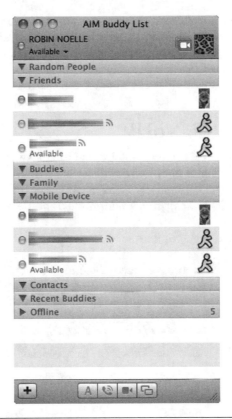

FIGURE 11-19   Once you've added them, your buddies appear in your Buddy List.

Chatting

Double-click a buddy's name to start a conversation with them (assuming they are online). Offline contacts will appear under the heading Offline. A new chat window will open. Type your message and press ENTER or RETURN. When they reply, you will see their text in a different speech bubble next to an icon or photo representing the person you are chatting with, as shown here. You might have noticed that your user photo or icon appears next to your text, too. You can have multiple chat windows open at one time if you are a multitasker.

You can video chat with iChat too. If your contact has video chat capability, there will be a camera icon next to their name. Click the camera to start a video chat. iChat comes with special effects that you can use to liven up your video image, if you're feeling creative (or mysterious).

Tip There are a lot of other chat programs that you can use. Like iChat, most offer multiplatform capabilities (that is, they work with different types of IM accounts). Most are free to use, but some require a small payment to use advanced features like video chatting. Check out Download.com and search for IM programs for the Mac if you want to see what else is out there. Otherwise, you can just stick with iChat!

Voice over IP (VoIP)

Voice over IP (VoIP) is the technology that enables you to make telephone calls from your computer. A lot of people find this to be a great option for keeping in touch with friends and family members overseas because making calls is cheap or free. Some people use VoIP as their primary telephone at home for all their calls. How you use it is up to you.

There are two very popular services for VoIP, although there are a lot more to choose from. Vonage is one you might have heard about (see Figure 11-20). You can sign up for an account and Vonage will send you a special modem that you can use to make calls through your Internet service for a monthly fee.

FIGURE 11-20 Vonage requires a special modem so that you can make telephone calls using the Internet.

FIGURE 11-21   Skype is a popular program to make voice calls, chat, and video chat with people around the world. It doesn't require any special equipment to use.

Skype is another very popular option (see Figure 11-21). It doesn't require any special equipment and can be used for instant messaging with other Skype contacts, video messaging, and video phone calls. Both Vonage and Skype offer paid services that include the option to purchase an 800 number or a virtual local number almost anywhere in the world. This is handy, for example, if you live in San Francisco but have a child attending college in New York. You can purchase a New York virtual number so that whenever your kid wants to call home, the call is free. Likewise, you can purchase international numbers, so a person living in England can purchase a United States number for their U.S. family to call, and vice versa.

Visit Skype.com and Vonage.com for more information on each of these services.

Summary

Congratulations! You have mastered online communication! Now you can e-mail, video chat, and even make overseas phone calls, all from the comfort of your MacBook. With your newfound communication skills, you can start making friends all over the world.

12

Getting Organized with iCal, Address Book, and iSync

HOW TO...

- Organize contacts with Address Book
- Create and share calendars with iCal
- Synchronize handheld devices with your MacBook

In today's age of mobile computing, it's not uncommon for someone to have a laptop computer (like a MacBook), a smart phone (like the iPhone), or another handheld mobile device, like the new iPad. Fortunately, Apple makes it easy for you to share information, such as contacts and calendars, with other people or between devices by allowing you to synchronize data and access it across multiple devices. Once you master these simple tools, you'll be more organized than ever, no matter where you are.

Organize Contacts with Address Book

In the last chapter, you learned how to connect with people via e-mail, and that included adding their contact information to Address Book. Address Book works with several applications on your MacBook, including Mail, iChat, and iCal, so once you have all of your contacts added, you'll always have important addresses and phone numbers on hand regardless of which program you are using.

Address Book creates a virtual card (vCard) for each contact. Like a paper address book, these cards have dedicated space for phone numbers, e-mail addresses, and home/work addresses too. You can import cards from other people's address books and send them yours as well, allowing you to easily share information with other Mac users. By using iSync, you can synchronize your contacts between your phone or PDA and MacBook, so you always have the most updated information regardless of which device you are using. Launch Address Book by clicking its icon in the Dock or by clicking the icon in the Applications folder. Figure 12-1 shows the Address Book layout.

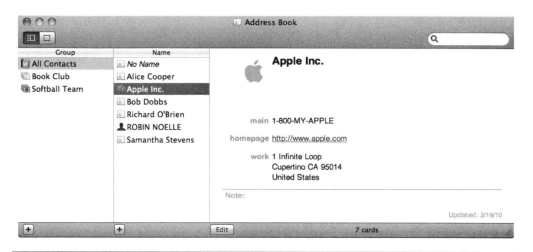

FIGURE 12-1   The default layout of Address Book

Add Contacts

There are several ways that you can add contacts to Address Book:

- Choose File | New Card.
- Click the + symbol under the Name column.
- Use the COMMAND-N shortcut.

Once a new card is created, all you need to do is fill in the missing information (see Figure 12-2). You'll notice that in some fields, a pop-up menu will appear so that you can select an appropriate label for the entry. For example, when you enter a phone number, you can choose a label such as Work or Mobile, as shown here. You can add as much or as little information as you want to each card. You can even add a photo to your contacts by double-clicking the square next to the contact's name and browsing for a photo or dragging one and dropping it into the square. Choose Card | Save to save your contact.

You can add your contacts to Safari too. Open Safari and go to Safari | Preferences. Click the Bookmarks tab and check the box Include Address Book in the Bookmarks Bar. If you have contacts in Address Book that include website URLs, they will be added in a new folder for you to access.

FIGURE 12-2   Fill in as many details as you want for your contacts. You can even add a photo.

 Edit an existing card by clicking on the contact and clicking Edit at the bottom of the screen. To add additional fields, such as a birthday or website, choose Card | Add Field. More fields appear in a submenu that you can select from, as shown here.

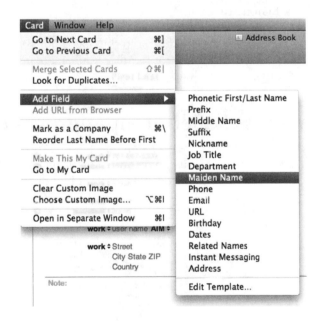

Create Contact Groups

Creating a group of contacts is useful when you regularly e-mail several people, such as family members or coworkers. It saves you the time of having to select each contact or type in multiple e-mail addresses. Once you've created a group, you can click on the group's name to see what contacts are associated with it.

You'll notice in the Group column of Address Book that Apple has created your first group for you; it's called All Contacts. Everyone in your address book is listed in this group. To create new groups, just click the + button at the bottom of the Group column, or choose Card | File | New Group. Enter a descriptive group name in the available text field.

To add contacts to your new group, you can click the group to select it and then create new contacts to associate with it or drag and drop your existing contacts into your new group. Don't worry, they will still appear in your All Contacts group too.

Create a Smart Group

Smart Groups automatically update themselves when a new contact is added that meets the criteria that you've defined when you created the group. For example, you could create a Smart Group for your company. Whenever a new contact is added and associated with that company, Address Book will automatically place them in the company Smart Group that you created.

To create a new Smart Group, select File | New | Smart Group. Name your new Smart Group and set the search criteria in the dialog box that appears, as shown in Figure 12-3. Create Smart Groups for family members, team members, online friends, coworkers, or any group you like.

Print Address Labels from Address Book

If you've ever printed address labels before, perhaps by using spreadsheet and/or word processing software, you know it can be quite a hassle! Now you can quickly print out your contacts in Address Book onto labels for your big (or small) mailing projects.

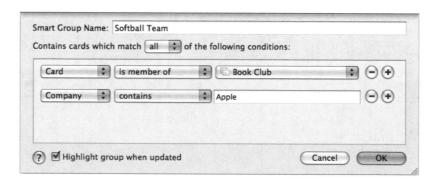

FIGURE 12-3 Smart Groups automatically update based on the criteria you select.

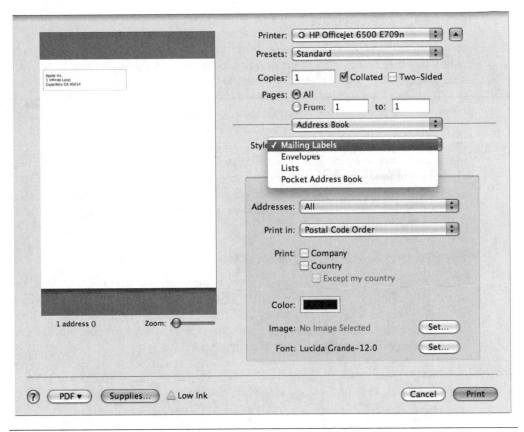

FIGURE 12-4   Choose the format that you want to print your contacts to.

To print your contacts, simply select File | Print. In the Print dialog box (see Figure 12-4), you will see formatting options that include Mailing Labels, Envelopes, Lists, and even a Pocket Address Book format. In the attributes section, you can select which elements of your contact card that you'd like to print. If you are printing a Pocket Address Book, you might want to include the address and phone numbers but not the photo, job title, or other ancillary information. It's all up to you!

Manage Your Time with iCal

Apple has provided a very effective but easy-to-use program called iCal to help you track important dates, schedule appointments, and even share your calendar entries with friends and family.

Of course, there's more to iCal than just entering appointments and remembering someone's birthday; you can set alarms for important events or dates and create your own events that you can invite your contacts to.

Create Calendars

How you set up your calendars is completely up to you. You can have a single master calendar with all of your events and schedules on it, or you can create multiple calendars for different aspects of your life.

To create a new calendar, first open iCal by clicking the icon in the dock. You will be presented with two premade calendars—Home and Work (see Figure 12-5). To add a third, either select File | New Calendar or click in the calendar window and then click the + button in the corner of the iCal window (see Figure 12-6). Enter a descriptive name for your new calendar. iCal organizes multiple calendars by color, so you can also click the small box to the right of the name and turn calendars on and off. To change a calendar's default color, click the name of the calendar you want and then click Edit | Get Info. Select a new color from the pull-down menu (refer to Figure 12-6).

Create a Calendar Entry

To get started with creating entries in your calendar, you first need to click the name of the calendar you want to work with. Once you've chosen the correct calendar, you can drag your mouse across the day and time that your event takes place and then click it to access more options. Your selection doesn't have to be perfect, because you can correct any errors in the forthcoming dialog box.

FIGURE 12-5   The main iCal display

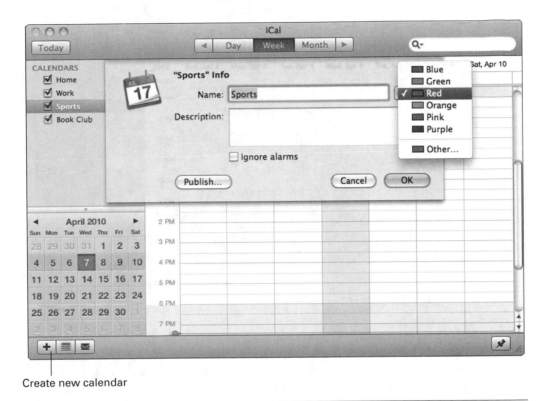

Create new calendar

FIGURE 12-6 View different calendar entries in different colors.

>
>
> **Tip** How you add an event depends on what view you are in. If you are in Month view instead of Week view, double-click the day to add something to your calendar instead of dragging your mouse across the preferred day and time.

Enter a name for your event (see Figure 12-7), correct start and end times, if necessary, and a location or any other additional information, and then save your entry to add it to the calendar. Some of the options that you have for each entry include setting a reminder alarm, repeating events (such as birthdays and anniversaries), and adding a guest list. You can always edit your entry by double-clicking it on your calendar or by selecting the event name and then selecting Edit | Get Info.

> **Tip** You can create line breaks in your calendar entries by pressing OPTION-RETURN. Use this feature to create lists within an event, such as to assign dishes to people for a potluck or to accomplish anything else you can think of.

Share Your Calendar Online

There are a lot of reasons to share your calendar. Perhaps you and your spouse need to coordinate taking the kids to soccer or picking them up from school. You could share a family calendar that each of you could access from your own MacBook

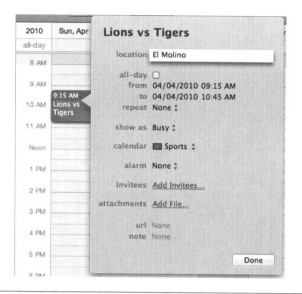

FIGURE 12-7 Name your event and add pertinent details before adding it to your calendar.

computer, with alarms to remind both of you whose turn it is to do carpool duty. You could create a work calendar to share with your coworkers to coordinate vacation plans or to plan meetings, brainstorming sessions, or presentations.

By publishing your calendar online, you can invite people to check out your schedule or subscribe to receive updates whenever you make changes. They can view it online and see instantly whether you are busy at a certain time or on a certain day. You will need a MobileMe account to publish your calendar unless you use another server, like one from a hosting company for a personal website or a corporate server.

 If you are publishing to another server, you will need server and login information for that server account. If you aren't sure what this information is, you will need to check with your hosting provider.

CTRL-click on the name of the calendar that you want to publish and select Publish to see more options (see Figure 12-8). You can choose which elements you want to make available to viewers and subscribers, such as your notes, alarms, and to-do lists. Select where you want to publish your calendar to, either a MobileMe (.Mac account) or another server. If you want to stop publishing your calendar, you can CTRL-click and select Unpublish.

 You can share your address book too. Open up Address Book and go to Address Book | Preferences. Click on the Sharing tab and check the box next to Share Your Address Book. You can allow someone with a .Mac account to view your address book by clicking the + button. If you select Allow Editing, they will be able to make changes to the entries.

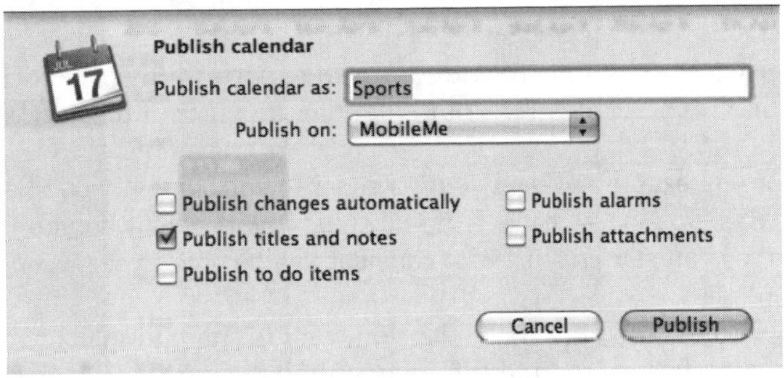

FIGURE 12-8 Publish your calendar online to share it with coworkers, friends, or family.

Subscribe to a Calendar

You can also subscribe to other people's calendars just as they can subscribe to yours. Choose Calendar | Subscribe. Enter the web address (URL) of the calendar that you want to subscribe to and then click Subscribe. You can opt whether to remove things like attachments and alarms and set how often you want iCal to check for updates to the schedule (see Figure 12-9).

Check out the iCal library at www.apple.com/downloads/macosx/calendars/ to see many calendars that you can subscribe to, including sports schedules, TV schedules, movie release schedules, and more. Apple isn't the only place to find these calendars; use your favorite web browser to find even more.

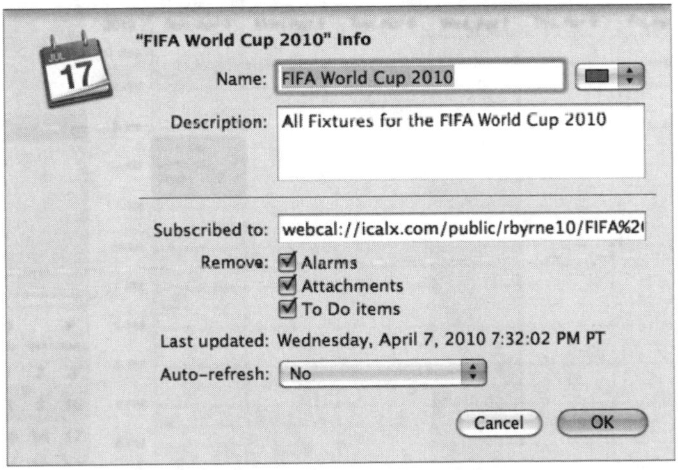

FIGURE 12-9 Subscribe to the calendars of your friends or your favorite sports team.

Import and Export Calendars

Another way to share your calendar is to export it into a file format and e-mail it. Once the recipient receives your calendar, they can import it to their iCal program.

If you export and send your calendar to someone, it won't be automatically updated when you make changes. If you share it with them through the Publish feature, they can subscribe to your calendar and be able to see when changes are made.

Click the name of the calendar you want to share to select it. Choose File | Export | Export. Attach the exported file to an e-mail to share it. If someone sends you their calendar in return, you can download the file and then select File | Import | Import instead. Browse to the location where the file has been saved and click Import to add their calendar to your list.

Print Your Calendar

There's another way to share your calendar: the old-fashioned way, on paper! You can print out your calendar to share it or just to have a copy in your day planner, on your fridge, or in your car. Choose File | Print and you will be presented with a dialog box of options.

You can customize your calendar print options. Use the check boxes to choose the calendars that you want to print. Select the view (Day, Week, Month, or List), the paper size, the time range, and other options (see Figure 12-10). Click Continue when you are ready to move to the Print dialog box.

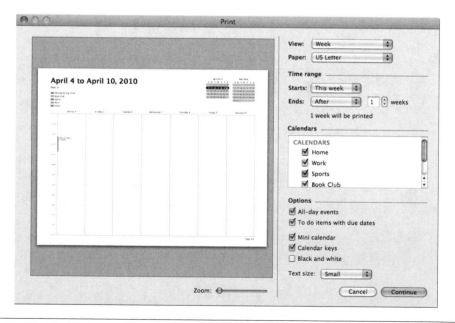

FIGURE 12-10 Print a calendar to share or keep with you. You can even print a mini calendar.

Synchronize Data with Your Handheld Devices

As much as you love your MacBook, it's probably not feasible to take it with you everywhere you go. But if you are like most people, you probably have a handheld device or two that you take everywhere you go, such as an iPhone for example.

You can synch up your calendar entries, Address Book contacts, and more by using iSync. Synchronizing ensures that your most recent updates made on one device are shared with your other devices, so you never have out-of-date information. If you run into a friend at the grocery who just moved, you can input their new address into your Palm PDA and the date of their housewarming party. Later when you run iSync, the new address will be added to your contacts and the housewarming party information will be sent to iCal. Easy!

In order to use iSync, your device must be compatible with the application and able to connect to your MacBook via USB cable or wireless Bluetooth connection. Visit this website to see if your device is listed: http://support.apple.com/kb/HT2824. If your device is compatible, connect it to your MacBook using one of the methods previously listed.

 iPods and iPhones use iTunes to sync information. For more information, see the iSync support information on the Apple.com website.

Add a Device to iSync

Before you can use iSync, you need to add a device for it to sync with. Open iSync and select Devices | Add Device. If you have connected your handheld device to your MacBook already, iSync will scan the computer looking for compatible devices and list them for you. If you haven't previously connected your device to your MacBook, the Bluetooth Assistant will appear and prompt you to add a Bluetooth device (see Figure 12-11).

 Make sure that your handheld device is in discovery mode and ready for pairing.

Once iSync has found your device, it will list it in the Add Device window. Double-click the name of the device to add it to iSync and then exit the Add Device dialog box. If your device has been added correctly, it will appear in the iSync window. If not, try adding it again.

Sync Your Devices

Once your device is added, you can start syncing. Click the icon for your handheld device to see your sync options. On your first synch between your MacBook and a device, you will have two options. You can merge the data onto both devices, or you can erase the data from your phone or PDA and replace it with the more up-to-date information contained, presumably, on your laptop.

iSync window

Add Device window

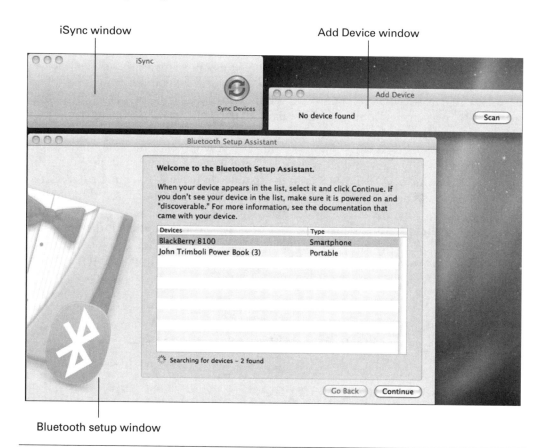

Bluetooth setup window

FIGURE 12-11 iSync automatically scans your system to look for compatible devices and starts the Bluetooth assistant if it can't find one.

Make sure that the Turn on Synchronization box is checked prior to attempting to sync. Next you can select what items you would like to sync, such as contacts or calendars. Click More Options to see more options related to syncing. When you are ready to synch, click the Sync Devices button in the upper-right corner of the screen. A progress bar will help you keep track of the process. If you haven't synced with a device before, you will be warned that iSync is changing more than 5 percent of the information on your device. Go ahead and click Allow. In just a few moments, everything will be synced up and ready to go on both devices. That's all there is it!

Summary

With the help of iCal, Address Book, and iSync, you will be more organized and connected than ever before. But remember, they only work if you use them!

13

Anything Windows Can Do, Mac Can Do Better: Running Windows Programs

HOW TO...

- Install Windows on your MacBook
- Switch between Mac OS X and Windows

While Apple and Microsoft have had some rivalry in the past, there was a time when they worked together. After all, once upon a time there was even Internet Explorer for the Mac! Thanks to the inclusion of a utility called Boot Camp in Mac OS X, Apple and Microsoft can play nicely together again.

Boot Camp allows Mac users to install Windows on their computer. Why would you want to do a crazy thing like that? Well, because there are some programs that are only available for Windows, for one reason. You might also have recently switched from a Windows PC to your new MacBook and thus already have a lot of software for Windows. Whatever your reason, you can easily install Windows right alongside Mac OS X and decide which one you want to load each time you start your computer.

Microsoft recently released Windows 7, which, while still new, is the best version to date in terms of reliability and functionality. You might notice how similar Windows 7 is to Mac OS X in a lot of ways. This chapter is going to focus on Windows 7, but you can also install Windows XP and Windows Vista using Boot Camp. You can refer to the Apple Support website for specific information on system and software requirements if you plan on installing either of these previous versions of Windows.

 Always back up your entire system before performing a major change, such as creating a partition and installing Windows. Refer to Chapter 19 for information on backing up your data.

Install Windows 7 with Boot Camp

Your MacBook doesn't come with Windows, so if you want to install it, you need to purchase your own copy if you haven't already. You will need your original installation discs, so if you already have a copy of Windows, make sure you locate these before you start. You can only install Windows on internal hard drives, not external drives.

Installing Windows 7 requires Mac OS X v10.6 Snow Leopard and the Boot Camp 3.1 Update. Before you run the Boot Camp Assistant, run the Software Update by clicking Apple | Software Update and selecting all of the available updates. You will need to enter your administrator password to complete the update. Your MacBook will check for updates to hardware drivers and software, including your operating system. You may need to restart your computer after the update process is complete.

 If you are using a wireless mouse and/or keyboard, switch to wired prior to the installation or use the built-in keyboard and trackpad. Your wireless devices will not work until the device drivers have been installed at the end of the installation process.

Here's how to install Windows 7 using Boot Camp:

1. Open Boot Camp from the Applications | Utilities folder by clicking the Boot Camp icon. Do yourself a favor and print out the Installation & Setup Guide before you continue (see Figure 13-1).
2. Click Continue.
3. Determine how much space you want to give Windows. You can divide your hard drive space equally between the two operating systems (which is optimal if you use Windows a lot) or drag the small dot between the partitions to the left or right to manually set a partition size (see Figure 13-2).

 Check the Windows system requirements to make sure that you set aside at least the minimum Windows needs to install and operate properly. You will need at least 20GB of space for a 64-bit installation of Windows 7, but be sure to increase this figure to 32GB (or more) if you are going to be running resource-intensive applications like Adobe Photoshop (or similar programs) or playing graphics-heavy games.

4. Click Partition to create the space for Windows.

 Make sure that you select to install Windows to the Boot Camp partition. If you install it to the Mac OS X side, you will wipe out your whole operating system!

5. Insert your Windows installation disc and click Start Installation (see Figure 13-3). Your computer will boot up to the installation program. Refer to the Installation & Setup Guide as you follow the installation procedure.

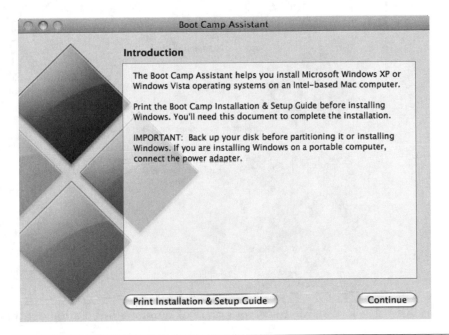

FIGURE 13-1   The Boot Camp Assistant walks you through the installation. It's a good idea to print the Installation & Setup Guide before proceeding.

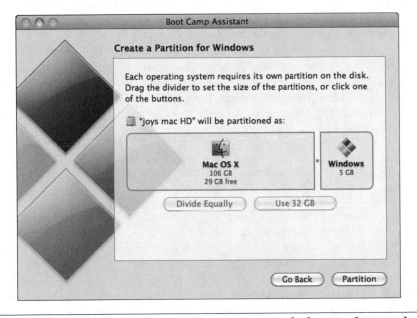

FIGURE 13-2   You can decide how much space to provide for Windows and any Windows software that you want to run.

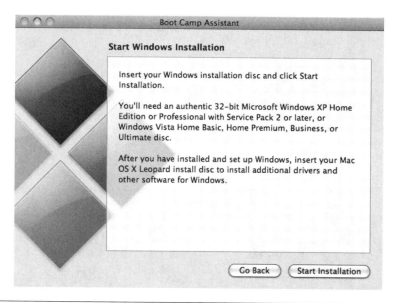

FIGURE 13-3   You will need your original Windows installation disc to continue
with Boot Camp.

If you insert the wrong Windows disc during installation, it can become stuck
in the drive. To remove the disc, restart your computer and hold down the Eject
button on the keyboard. The disc will eject.

6. Pick a format for your Windows partition, either NTFS or FAT. FAT has the
   advantage of allowing Mac OS X to read and write from the partition even when
   you didn't boot to Windows, but you can't have a partition larger than 32GB.
   With NTFS, you can have a partition larger than 32GB but you will need to load
   Windows to write to it.

Windows 7 and Windows Vista both require NTFS.

7. When your MacBook boots into Windows, insert your Mac OS X installation disc
   so that necessary drivers can be installed. Click Next.
8. Install the Apple Software Update for Windows. Wait until you see the Finish
   button, click it, and reboot your MacBook.

When you first run Windows, you should install antivirus software for Windows and
then run Windows Update to make sure you have important security updates installed.

Remove Windows from Your MacBook

If you've decided that running Windows on your Mac just isn't for you, you can easily uninstall it. Just make sure that you've backed up your system and important data first because all Windows files and software will be erased forever.

1. Log out all users (except your Administrator account) and close all open applications.
2. Choose Applications | Utilities | Boot Camp to open the Boot Camp Assistant.
3. Select Restore the Startup Disk to a Single Volume, and then click Continue.

Refer to the Boot Camp Support website at www.apple.com/support/ bootcamp/ for additional support.

Choose an OS to Boot Up

You can easily switch between Windows and Mac OS X by using the Boot Camp Control Panel.

- From Windows, go to Start | Control Panel | Boot Camp Control Panel. In the Startup Disk tab, you can select Mac OS X and click Restart to load it.
- From Mac OS X, go to Apple | System Preferences | Startup Disk and select Windows. Click Restart to boot into Windows.

Tip   If you want to select which operating system to boot to when you first turn on your MacBook, hold down the OPTION key when you hear the startup tone. Keep holding the key down until you see the Windows and Mac OS X icons appear. Select the one that you want to load.

Summary

Boot Camp makes it easy for people to use both Windows and Mac OS X on their MacBooks. This is a great option for people who have recently switched from a Windows PC to a Mac, or for people who have a need to use software that is only available on Windows.

14

But Wait! There's More: MacBook Application Basics

HOW TO...

- Discover what applications are included with your MacBook
- Perform shared application tasks

You can purchase a lot of different software products for use with your MacBook, but before you do, it's probably a good idea to familiarize yourself with what software it already contains. This chapter will give you an overview of all the programs and utilities that your MacBook comes preloaded with, as well as some of the basic commands that many programs share.

Additional information about some of the programs is included in other chapters (like iChat and Mail in Chapter 11), while other applications have whole chapters dedicated to them (like Safari in Chapter 10 and iLife in Chapter 16). You can refer to the index to find out where more detailed application information is included in this book. If you still can't find the specific application information you are looking for, you can always refer to the Apple website at www.Apple.com/Support.

Discover What Applications Are Included with Your MacBook

One of the great things about Apple is that it includes a ton of software in its products, and your MacBook is no different. There are a lot of useful programs for you to explore, and you should do so before going out and buying expensive software. You might already have an application that does just what you are looking for. You will find each of the programs discussed in this section in the Applications folder.

Explore Applications

If you've ever wondered what all those icons are in your Applications folder, wonder no more! Below you'll find brief descriptions of every application included on your MacBook.

 Address Book The Address Book is where all of your contacts are stored. Other programs can access your contacts through Address Book, like Mail and iCal. Check out Chapter 12 for more details.

 Automator The Automator is a handy little application that is actually quite powerful. It automates repetitive tasks for you, such as resizing a group of photos for uploading onto the Web, renaming a batch of files, or burning DVDs and CDs for you.

 Calculator You can use the calculator in basic, scientific, or programmer mode. You can also perform conversions with it.

 Chess You can play chess against another player or against your computer at a variety of difficulty levels.

 Dashboard The Dashboard provides access to small applications called Widgets that perform a variety of tasks. You can check sports scores, flight information, or weather using Widgets, and that's just the start! If you run out of Widgets that you want to use, you can create your own.

 Dictionary You have a built-in dictionary and thesaurus right on your MacBook to help you with your writing projects or just to build your vocabulary.

 DVD Player What would a laptop computer be without a DVD player? Watch your favorite movies while you're on the go.

 Font Book You can manage the fonts on your MacBook, including adding new ones, through the Font Book.

 Front Row Front Row is your MacBook's media management program. You can view iPhoto slideshows, watch movies, or listen to iTunes with it. It's easiest to use if you have the Apple Remote, but you can use keyboard shortcuts as well.

 iCal iCal keeps all of your appointments and important dates organized. You can set alarms and reminders, synch with your iPhone or iPad, and even share calendars with friends and family online. See Chapter 12 for more information.

 iChat Text or video chat with your iChat contacts using this multiplatform instant messaging application. See Chapter 11 for more information on using iChat.

 iDVD You can create DVDs of your home movies or other video, including creating menus and adding music using iDVD. This application is part of the iLife suite. See Chapter 16 for more information.

 Image Capture Grab images from a digital camera or scanner with this handy application.

 iMovie You can create your own cinematic masterpieces with this easy-to-use video-editing application. iMovie is part of the iLife suite and is covered in more detail in Chapter 16.

 iPhoto Edit, organize, and share your photos using this application. iPhoto is also part of iLife and covered in Chapter 16.

iSync Synch your MacBook contacts and other information with your iPhone, iPad, or another Mac using iSync. See Chapter 12 for more information.

 iTunes Manage your music collection with iTunes. You can purchase music or audiobooks online, burn music CDs, and watch music videos with this popular application. Chapter 17 has more details.

 iWeb If you have a MobileMe account, you can quickly and easily create and publish web pages using iWeb.

 Mail Covered in Chapter 11, Mail is a program for sending and receiving e-mail and reading RSS feeds.

 Photo Booth Use your MacBook's built-in camera to take photos of yourself and get creative with fun effects using Photo Booth.

 Preview View PDF or image files (like JPG or GIF files, among others) using this helpful application.

 QuickTime You can watch TV shows and movies or listen to music using this audio-video player. See Chapter 17 for more information.

 Safari Use Safari to surf the Internet, find information, or read RSS feeds. See Chapter 10 for more details.

 Stickies Jot down your notes and memos on these virtual Post-it notes.

 System Preferences Change how your MacBook works with these settings.

 TextEdit Perform basic word processing tasks with this simple text-editing program.

 Time Machine You can use Time Machine to back up and then restore your system files and folders. See Chapter 19 for more information.

Identify Utilities

Utilities are used to perform system tasks and operations such as taking screenshots (pictures of your computer screen, like many of the images in this book) and repairing your hard drive. Your MacBook comes with a lot of utilities already installed. You may find that you rarely, if ever, use most of them, but here's an explanation of what they are, just in case.

 Activity Monitor If your MacBook is running slow, you can use Activity Monitor to see what processes are running and how your computer resources are being used.

 AirPort Utility Set up and manage wireless devices like the AirPort Extreme Base Station or AirPort Express using this utility.

 AppleScript Editor Create and edit scripts to automate tasks using this script-editing application.

 Audio MIDI Setup Configure your audio devices in the Audio MIDI Setup application. You can add external microphones, speakers, and musical instruments to your MacBook with this utility.

Bluetooth File Exchange Use Bluetooth to communicate with other Bluetooth-enabled devices like cell phones, printers, and smart phones.

Boot Camp Assistant Install Microsoft Windows on your MacBook with Boot Camp. See Chapter 13 for information on how to install Windows and switch between operating systems.

 ColorSync Utility If you work with graphics, you can use ColorSync to manage color profiles and any devices that use them, like printers and scanners.

 Console If you need to troubleshoot your MacBook, Console will allow you to access the detailed logs your computer keeps of all of its activities.

 Digital Color Meter You can use the Digital Color Meter to measure colors on your MacBook screen and match them in a graphics program.

 Disk Utility Use the Disk Utility to perform tasks on your internal and external drives. You can create a disk image, repair a damaged file, or burn files using your optical drive.

 Exposé Organize all of your open windows using this handy utility. See Chapter 6 for additional information on using Exposé.

 Grab Grab can be used to take pictures of your screen (called screenshots, like those contained in this book). You can take a picture of the whole screen or just a part of it.

 Grapher Make detailed graphs with this program.

Java Preferences Java is a programming language that any operating system can use. It is often used on websites and for animation. You can change your computer's Java settings here.

 Keychain Access Keychain Access can store all of your passwords and other private information.

 Migration Assistant Easily transfer all of your important information from one MacBook to another using this utility. When you are ready for a new MacBook, you can use this to copy your user accounts, files, and more.

 Network Utility If watching network activity excites you, you can use this utility to view a graphical representation of it. You can also use this to view your network traffic if you experience a slow connection.

 Podcast Capture Podcasts are audio or video recordings that people post to the Web for download by iPod users. You can use Podcast Capture to record one.

 Remote Install Mac OS X You can use the optical drive on another Mac to install Mac OS X if, for example, your MacBook doesn't come with an optical drive (like the MacBook Air).

 Spaces Multitask with Spaces and organize your workspace into separate areas. See Chapter 6 for more information.

 System Profiler Anything and everything you wanted to know about your MacBook's system is contained here. You can see what hardware is installed and find information on your software here.

 Terminal Terminal will be familiar to DOS and UNIX users. Terminal is a command-line program that enables you to type in commands for tasks you aren't normally able to perform from the Mac OS X GUI. It is a great way to access hidden features... as well as to completely break your system if you don't know what you are doing. I recommend leaving this alone unless you are absolutely confident that you won't do some serious damage.

VoiceOver Utility   VoiceOver helps sight-impaired people navigate the Mac OS X system by speaking to them directly. It describes what is onscreen and can read text.

 X11   Run X Window System applications using X11. If you don't know what those are, you aren't a developer or UNIX user and thus won't need this utility.

Find Shared Tasks in MacBook Applications

Many of the applications included on your MacBook have tasks in common, such as finding application information, launching an application, or creating a new document. Once you familiarize yourself with these commands, you can perform them in a wide variety of programs.

Open an Application

You can launch any of the applications on your MacBook by double-clicking the program icon in the Applications or Utilities folder. If the application is also located on the Dock, you can click the icon from there instead. If you aren't sure where an application is located, open a new Finder window and type what you are looking for in the search box (or use Spotlight). The results will appear in the Results window (see Figure 14-1).

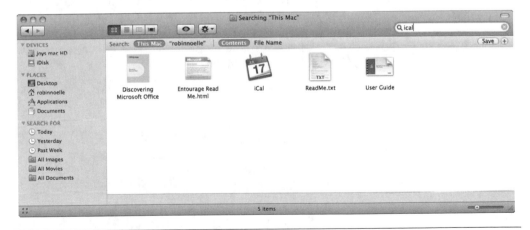

FIGURE 14-1   Can't find what you are looking for? Use the Finder to search your MacBook for applications.

Red × button

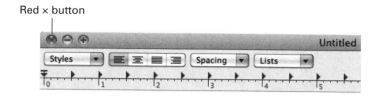

FIGURE 14-2 Click the small red × button to close a window or use the File |
Close command.

Create a New Document

There are a lot of programs in which you'll need to create a new document to
get started. These include word processing programs (TextEdit, Microsoft Word,
OpenOffice.org Writer), graphics programs (Adobe Photoshop, GIMP), page layout
programs (QuarkXPress, Adobe InDesign), and many others. You can create a new
document by selecting File | New. You can also use the keyboard shortcut COMMAND-N.

Open, Close, and Save Documents

Also available from the File menu are the commands to Open, Close, and Save
documents. Select Open and a new dialog box will appear so that you can browse to
the document you want to open (the type of document depends on the program). You
can close a document by selecting File | Close or by clicking the red × button in the
upper-left corner of the window (see Figure 14-2). To save your document, select File |
Save (or try COMMAND-S). Name your document and choose a location to save it to
(see Figure 14-3). Click Save and you're done!

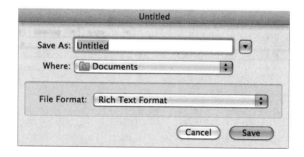

FIGURE 14-3 COMMAND-S opens the Save dialog box.

When browsing in a folder, you can open a document with its associated program by double-clicking it. This will launch the appropriate application as determined by the file type (image files will be opened by a graphics program, text files by a word processing program, and so on). To find out what the associated program is for a file, CTRL-click (or right-click) and use the shortcut menu. Select Open With to choose another application instead of the default.

If you want to save a copy of a document and not overwrite the original, you can use the Save As command. This allows you to rename the document and save it as a copy or, in some cases, as a different format. For example, you could open a .gif image file in Photoshop and use Save As to save it as a .jpg file. Or, you could open a Word document and save it as Plain Text (.txt extension). You will find the Save As command in the File menu below Save.

Print Documents

While having digital documents has saved a lot of trees, occasionally it is necessary to print them out. You can easily print documents by opening the document that you want to print and clicking File | Print. This opens the Print dialog box. In the first box, you can select which printer you want to send your document to, in case you have more than one available on your network. Click the up-facing arrow next to the printer selection box to expand the dialog box and see more Print options (see Figure 14-4).

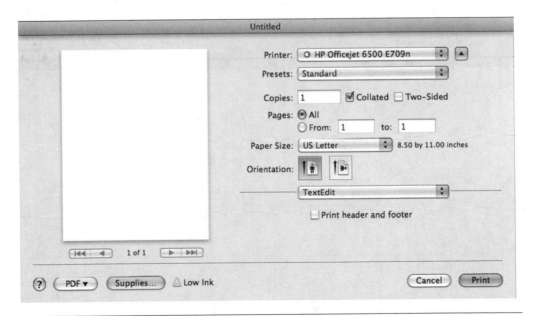

FIGURE 14-4   You can change your printer settings and page layout in the Print dialog box.

With the expanded options, you can change the paper size and the page layout and set how many copies you would like to print. You can also opt to print the header and footer, collate your copies, or to print your file to PDF format (when applicable).

 The Print dialog box will also tell you if your printer is running low on ink. You might want to check this before printing a ten-page document!

Resize Windows

You can resize any of the windows on your MacBook by clicking and dragging the small arrow in the lower-right corner of the window (see Figure 14-5). If you want to fully open the window, click the green + sign in the upper-left corner. Your MacBook

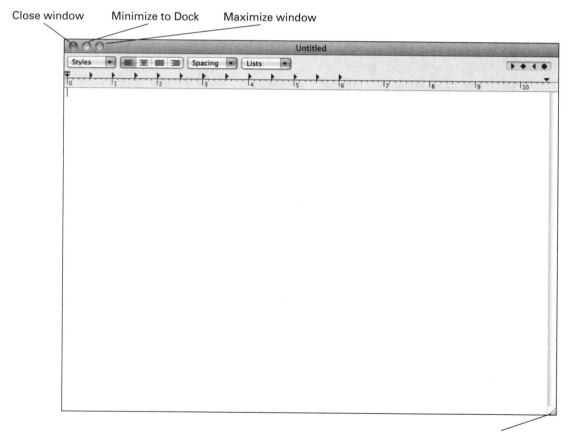

FIGURE 14-5 Change your window size by dragging the resize icon until the window is the size you desire.

will determine the best size of the window based on its contents. You can manually resize it from there if you want it bigger. You can click the yellow – symbol to minimize the window to the Dock.

Find Application Information

Occasionally, it might be necessary to find out what version of an application you are using, like when calling tech support or deciding when to upgrade, for example. You can access this information when the application is open by clicking the application menu located next to the Apple menu in the upper-left corner of your screen. From this menu, choose About *Application Name*. A new window will appear with the name of the program (in this case, TextEdit) and its version number (see Figure 14-6).

Change Preferences in an Application

Nearly all applications come with some type of options or user preferences (see Figure 14-7). You can quickly access them by clicking the application menu and choosing Preferences or by using the COMMAND-, (comma) keyboard shortcut. While the default settings are usually the most popular, each application will allow you to alter at least some of these settings. Every application offers different options, so check them out!

Exit an Application

While clicking the red dot with the × in it will close a window, it doesn't actually exit whatever program you were using. Instead, the application is still running in the Dock. You don't have to exit every program to use another, but some programs (such as Photoshop) require a lot of memory and having them open could slow your other programs down.

TextEdit

Version 1.6 (264)

Copyright © 1995–2009 Apple Inc.
All rights reserved.

FIGURE 14-6 Use an application's information window to find out what version of a program you are running.

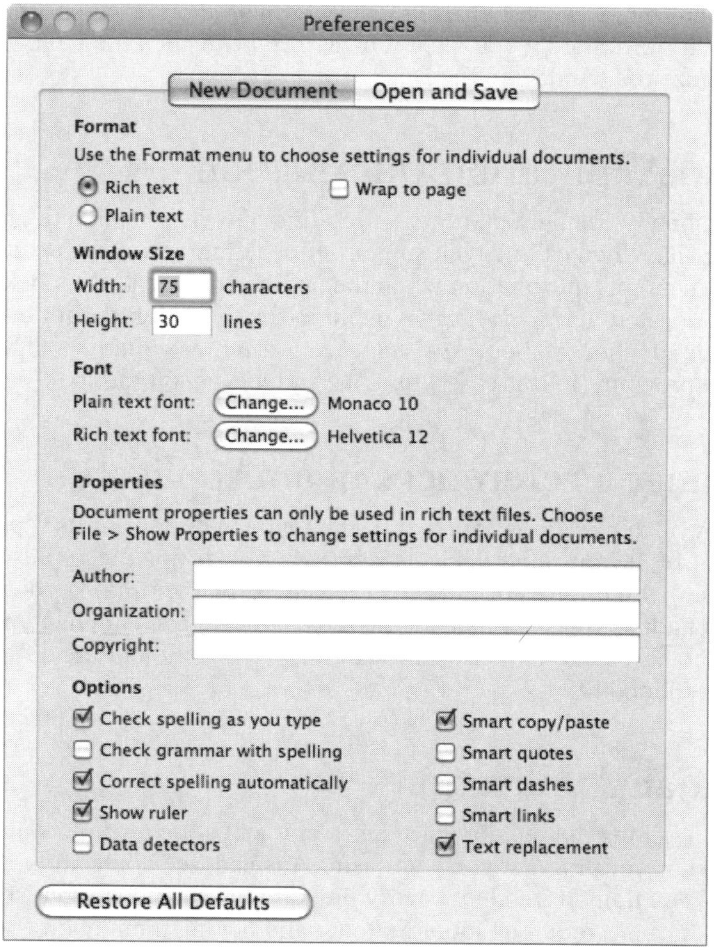

FIGURE 14-7 Set your user preferences using the Preferences window, like this one from TextEdit.

If you want to quit an application properly, you need to go to the File menu. Select Quit and wait for the application to exit. If you have open and unsaved documents, you will be prompted to save them before the program closes.

Tip You can also exit an application by clicking the icon on the Dock and holding your click until a menu appears. Select Quit to exit.

Summary

Now you have a nice overview of all the applications and utilities contained within your MacBook. By using the basic commands found in this chapter, you will be able to easily navigate the most commonly used applications.

15

Your Virtual Office: iWork for Productivity

HOW TO...

- Perform common tasks across iWork applications
- Create word processing documents in Pages
- Design presentations in Keynote
- Build spreadsheets and graphs in Numbers

While your MacBook is great for surfing the Web and chatting online with friends, you can also, not surprisingly, use it for work! iWork is the productivity software suite that is available for your MacBook, and it's composed of three programs:

- **Pages**   Word processing software *a la* Microsoft Word
- **Numbers**   Spreadsheet software *a la* Microsoft Excel
- **Keynote**   Presentation building software *a la* Microsoft PowerPoint

 iWork may be included already on your MacBook as a trial version. You must purchase the license to continue using it after the trial period has ended. You can purchase iWork with your MacBook for only $49, or purchase it for $79 on its own. If your MacBook doesn't have iWork already installed, you can download the trial version from the Apple website and use it free for 30 days to see if you like it. If you have more than one Mac in your household, you can purchase the Family Pack of iWork for $99, allowing you to install it on up to five computers.

This chapter is meant to give you an overview of the types of tasks you can use iWork for, not a complete tutorial, since the program is not part of your MacBook's software bundle. You will find much more information on how to work with the various iWork programs on Apple's website at www.apple.com/findouthow/iwork/, or you can search online for a variety of video tutorials. iWork also comes with a user manual in PDF format on the installation disc.

To get started, you can open your Applications folder and then locate the iWork folder. Inside you will find icons for each of the applications.

Get to Know iWork

The iWork productivity suite is designed to handle common business tasks such as correspondence, budgets, and presentations. Some of the programs do double duty, however, such as Pages, which you can use as a word processing program and for page design. In addition to the installed iWork applications, you can use the new iWork.com website (currently in beta testing) to upload and share documents.

 Beta testing is when a company releases an early version of a software program for people to try, before the company is ready to release the program to retail outlets. Public betas, like iWork.com, are usually fairly stable but may offer limited features and contain some flaws (called bugs). During this beta period, the company requests feedback from users and tries to incorporate suggestions into the program and/or fix any bugs before it is released for retail purchase by the general public.

Did You Know?

Microsoft Office and iWork

Depending on what your needs are, iWork might be a fine substitute for Microsoft Office. iWork is compatible with Office document formats, but there are a few things to keep in mind when considering whether to purchase iWork, Office, or both.

iWork doesn't open Office files; it imports them. This means that not all of the features from an Office document may work or look the same in the corresponding iWork program. In many cases, especially if you are a casual Microsoft Office user, this will be fine and any formatting issues will be easy to fix. However, if you rely on some of the more complex features of Office, you might find that iWork just won't cut it. You should also note that iWork '09 will only handle Office 97 and newer file formats, so if you have any Word Perfect or earlier Office version documents, you're out of luck.

Is iWork a substitute for Office? It really depends on what you want to do. For day-to-day correspondence, creating a spreadsheet budget, or preparing a business presentation, it's probably a good substitute, but if you routinely create long documents or use templates in Word or need to use functions and databases in Excel, then it certainly is not. You'll be better off with Office for Mac.

Identify Common Tasks Across iWork Applications

As you've probably noticed, Mac OS X shares commands throughout the operating system to make it easier to transition during tasks. Actions like opening a document, launching an application, and accessing help remain consistent, regardless of where you are and what you are doing. iWork is no different. The toolbars look the same in all of the programs, and there are four tasks that are performed the same throughout the suite:

- **Inspector** While you will notice that there is a formatting bar along the top of the screen in Pages, Numbers, and Keynote, the real tools are stashed away in the Inspector. Click the Inspector button (a circle with an *i* in it) to access all of the available formatting tools (see Figure 15-1). The top row of the Inspector window contains buttons to access different pages of tools (text, photos, charts, and so forth). You can open multiple Inspector windows by holding down the OPTION key when clicking the Inspector icon.

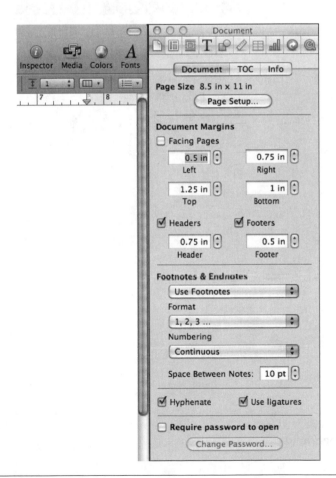

FIGURE 15-1   Access all of your formatting tools through the Inspector window.

- **Media** If you want to add elements to your documents such as audio or a photo, you can use the Media icon to access the Media Browser. This allows you to search your computer for the file that you want and insert it into your document (see Figure 15-2). Once you've located the item you want to insert, just drag and drop it into place. You can also drag and drop items from your desktop or Finder windows without having to use the Media Browser.
- **Colors** Click the Colors icon to access the palettes and color wheel you need to add exciting color elements to your projects, like to borders, lines, and text (see Figure 15-3).
- **Fonts** Using the same font for everything isn't very stylish or exciting. Click the Fonts icon to change your fonts and font size and to add effects like bold and strikethrough (see Figure 15-4).

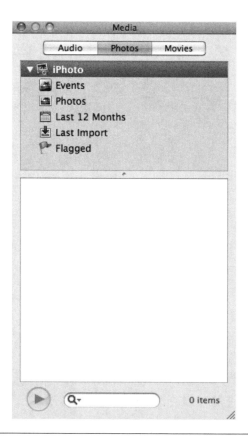

FIGURE 15-2 Use the Media Browser to add audio, video, and pictures of your documents.

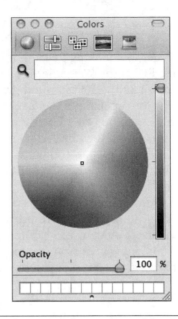

FIGURE 15-3   The Colors window allows you to add color to your text, borders, lines, and other design elements.

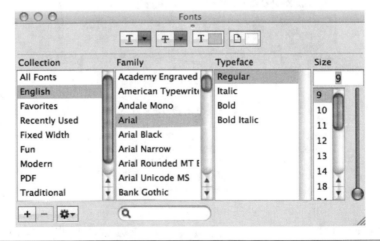

FIGURE 15-4   Create appealing documents with an array of fonts and font styles.

Pages

When you first open Pages, by clicking its icon or launching it from the Applications folder, you are presented with the Welcome screen (see Figure 15-5), which directs you to valuable resources like the iWork training tutorial videos. You can watch the intro video or videos that are specific to the tasks you want to learn about. You can also choose to keep this Welcome screen active every time you launch the program or choose not to see it again, via the check box in the lower-left corner. Click Close to continue.

On the next screen, you will find the Template Chooser (see Figure 15-6). Because Pages has two capabilities, word processing and page layout, the pane on the left side of the screen is divided into these two sections (top and bottom). In the top section of the left pane, you will find common word processing activities like resumes and letters. In the lower section, you can select from more design-orientated projects like brochures, flyers, and business cards. You can pick a template to start from or you can select Blank in either section to start a document from scratch.

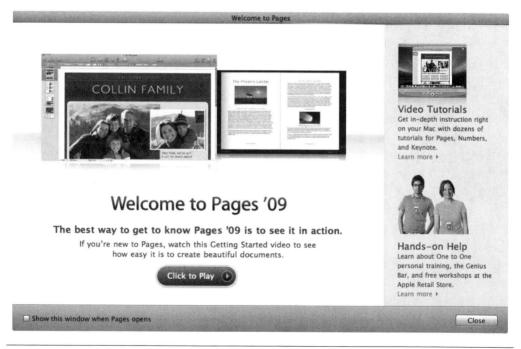

FIGURE 15-5 The Welcome screen offers an intro video and access to more detailed iWork video tutorials.

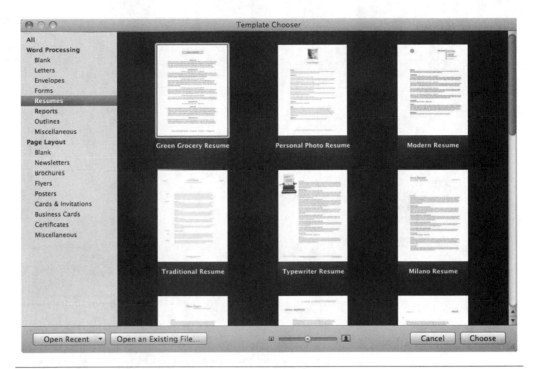

FIGURE 15-6   Select a template from the Template Chooser to get started on a project fast.

Use Templates

If you're just typing up a grocery list or some casual correspondence, you probably don't need to use a template, but if you're working on something a little more complex, take a look at what templates are available before you decide. Apple has provided some lovely templates to help you create clean, professional documents.

 Use the slider at the bottom of the Template Chooser window to increase or decrease the size of the template icons. Increasing them will show less in the preview window but you will be able to see more details.

   To see how templates work, click on one to select it and then click Choose to get started. Your template will open and you'll see some placeholder text plus any images associated with the document. Click on a section of text to select it and then start typing to replace it (see Figure 15-7). When you want to replace a photo, click it to make it your active selection and then use the Media Browser to find a new photo and drag it over the existing one. The photo will be resized to fit the existing space. If you want to resize the image further, select the photo with your pointer and then drag the size adjuster in the lower-right corner until you reach the dimensions that you need.

FIGURE 15-7 Templates come with placeholder text and images that you can replace with your own.

 To start a new document from a template, select File | New from Template Chooser.

Create Blank Documents

If you want to get started without the help of placeholder text and photos, you can select a blank word processing or page layout document in the Template Chooser window. If Pages is open and is the active application, you can start a new document by choosing File | New or pressing COMMAND-N. The Template Chooser will open and you can select a new blank document.

FIGURE 15-8 Explore each tab of the Inspector window to see all of your document formatting options.

There are many formatting tools that you can use within your documents, located in the Inspector window. Just click the Inspector icon to open the window and click the graphics along the toolbar to switch between Inspector views (see Figure 15-8). You can also perform the standard document management functions through the File menu, such as saving, opening existing documents, and printing. Common word processing shortcuts also apply, such as using COMMAND-C to copy and COMMAND-V to paste.

Change the color of selected text by clicking the Color icon and using the palettes to choose a new color.

Numbers

Numbers is the spreadsheet application included in the iWork suite. Spreadsheets are used to store and manipulate data. They are used frequently in business for accounting and for performing complex math functions with large data sets, but they have practical uses at home too. You can create budgets, calculate interest on loans or credit cards, design task checklists, or track your daily spending. As with Pages, when you launch Numbers, you will see the Welcome screen and can view various video tutorials to get started (see Figure 15-9).

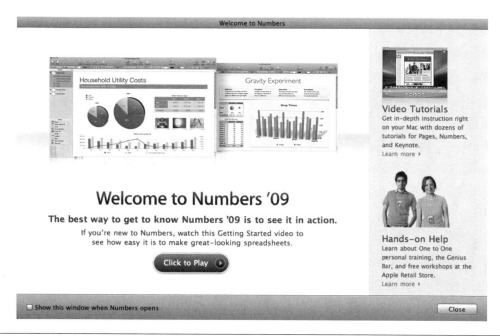

FIGURE 15-9 If you haven't worked with a spreadsheet program before, you should take the time to view some of the basic tutorials.

Create a Spreadsheet

Just like with Pages, the Template Chooser pops up when you launch Numbers (see Figure 15-10). You can click the categories on the left to select Personal, Business, Personal Finance, or Education template sets.

Click on a template that you want to work with and click Choose. Templates work the same in Numbers as they do in Pages. Just select the placeholder data and type in your own information (see Figure 15-11). Since the graphics in Numbers, like graphs and charts, are data driven, they will change as you enter your figures. Use the tools in the Inspector window to modify the template however you wish.

You can also create blank spreadsheets and design them to meet your needs. If you really want to learn to use a spreadsheet program like Numbers or Excel, it's worth it to purchase a book that focuses on that program or to watch tutorials online. Spreadsheets are very powerful tools, and there's a lot to learn that we can't cover here.

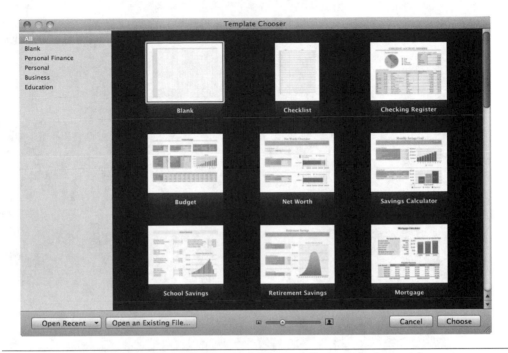

FIGURE 15-10   Browse through the available templates and choose the one closest to your needs.

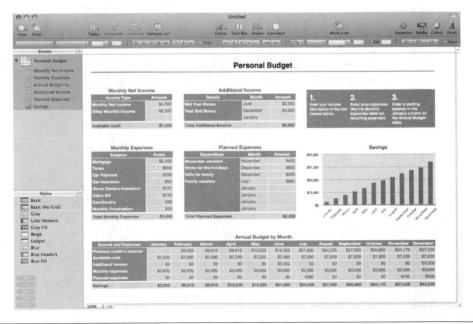

FIGURE 15-11   Open a template and enter your data or use the Inspector window to modify the template.

FIGURE 15-12 Choose a theme for your presentation and set the size of the slides.

Keynote

A beautiful presentation can be used in many situations, from the classroom and office to organization meetings and wedding receptions! Keynote will help you design the best-looking presentations around. It has an easy-to-use interface, so even novice users can create dynamic slideshows.

Create a Presentation

When you first open Keynote, the Welcome screen appears and you can choose to watch some or all of the tutorial videos. Click Close and the Theme Chooser will open (see Figure 15-12). Here you can select a theme that works for the type of presentation that you're designing. Use the Slide Size pop-up menu on the right side of the screen to select what size you want your slides to be.

Tip If you are going to be projecting your slides onto a screen, you should stick with a smaller slide size, like 800×600, so that everyone in the room can read the text.

Each theme comes with a set of master slides, accessible from the Masters button in the main toolbar (see Figure 15-13). Each master slide uses the theme you selected, providing style elements that tie them all together. The formatting and design options that are available are ones that have been selected to complement the theme and will remain consistent throughout the presentation. All the hard work of choosing the right colors, fonts, and styles that work well together has been done for you!

Once you've selected your theme and you have access to the master slides, all you need to do is select the slide that has the elements you want and then replace the placeholder images and text with your own. You can pick and choose from the

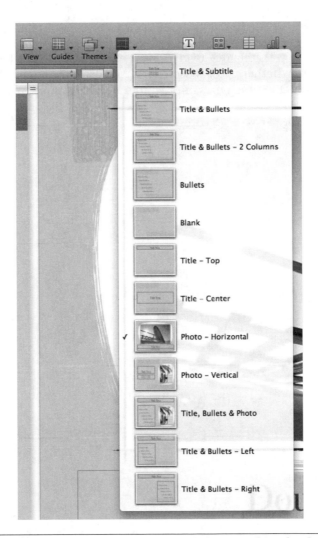

FIGURE 15-13   When you need a new master slide to work with, click the Masters button and select the one you want.

different master slides as you create your presentation based on the content of each slide. There are slides with bullets, graphics, columns, and combinations of elements. To add a new slide to your presentation, click the + button in the upper-left corner. That will add a new slide based on whichever master slide you have selected at the time. When you're done, you'll have a gorgeous and congruent slideshow. To view it, click the Play button.

 You can change your theme at any time by clicking the Themes button at the top of the screen. Select a new theme and it will be applied to all of your current slides.

Summary

This chapter was intended to give you a brief overview of what productivity suites can be used for. Whether you choose iWork, Microsoft Office for Mac, or even OpenOffice .org for Mac OS X, the types of programs and their functions will be similar.

16

Creative Spaces: iLife for Music, Movies, and Websites

HOW TO...

- Organize and edit photos with iPhoto
- Create and edit movie clips in iMovie
- Record music in GarageBand
- Design websites with iWeb

Apple brands the iLife applications as a "lifestyle suite." Regardless of how you refer to it, iLife is a pretty cool set of applications that will allow you to tap into your creative side. If you've ever wanted to record music, design websites, or create and edit your own movies, this is the suite for you. These programs are

- **iPhoto**   Manage your photos by organizing, editing, or adding fun photo effects.
- **iMovie**   Create movies from video clips. Edit and add effects to them.
- **iDVD**   Create DVDs from your own movies and photos.
- **iWeb**   Design your own website with iWeb.
- **GarageBand**   Record musical masterpieces in your own virtual recording studio.

 iLife is included in all new MacBook models so, unlike iWork, you don't need to initially purchase it to use it. Apple releases a new version every year, which you will have to purchase if you want to upgrade the software.

This chapter gives you an overview of each of the iLife applications and what it can be used for. You'll learn how to perform some of the basic tasks, such as creating new projects or documents. You will find much more information on how to work with the various iLife programs by visiting Apple's website at www.apple.com/ilife/ or searching online for a variety of video tutorials. iLife also comes with a user manual in PDF format on the installation disc.

Explore iPhoto

iPhoto is more than just a photo management program. You can do all kinds of neat things, like create photo books, calendars, slideshows, and cards and add special effects to your photos. iPhoto even helps you share your photos online.

iPhoto imports photos from your digital camera and from other places, like your e-mail, jump drives, hard drive, or scanner. Once they've been imported, you can organize them, edit them, and share them (among other things).

Import Photos to iPhoto

Before you can get started, you need some photos on your computer. The easiest way to do this (assuming they are on your camera) is to import them.

1. Launch iPhoto by clicking the icon on the Dock or from the Applications folder.
2. Turn off your camera.
3. Connect your camera to your MacBook using the mini-USB cable that came with your camera.
4. Turn the camera on.

 If you have a MacBook Pro with an SD card slot, you can remove the SD card from your camera and insert it into the slot to transfer your pictures.

Once you've completed these steps, your camera should appear in the Devices section of iPhoto and your photos should appear in the viewing pane. You will be asked to label them with an event name, like Steve's Birthday, for example. This will help you distinguish one downloaded batch of photos from another.

 Don't forget to drag your camera's icon located on the desktop to the Trash or click the Eject button next to the camera listing in the Source list to safely eject it. You can then turn off the camera and remove the USB cable from your MacBook.

Organize and View Photos

Once you have your photos loaded into iPhoto, you can begin working with them. It will be easiest to find the photos you are looking for later if you keep them organized now. By giving each downloaded or imported group of photos an event name, you will be able to access these events from the Source list. Under the Library heading, click Events to see photos grouped by event name.

Sort Photos

One way to organize your photos is through the Sort views. Click Photos and then select View | Sort By. You will be presented with a submenu that gives you four options for sorting your pictures:

- **By Date**   Sort your photos by the date they were taken.
- **By Keyword**   You can assign keywords to your photos to help you find them quickly. Read on to find out how to do this.
- **By Title**   Arrange your pictures alphabetically by title.
- **By Rating**   You can rate your photos and then use this option to sort them by your rating.

You can also perform sorting functions in the Events view.

How to...   ## Add Keywords to Your Photos

Keywords, aka tags, are words assigned to an item to help group it with similar items when using a search function. For example, you can tag a picture of your sister's birthday party with the keywords (or tags) birthday, family, celebration, sister, and perhaps the name of the city where your sister lives. Later, when you are searching or sorting by keyword, you can type Sister and all the photos that have tags for your sister will appear in your results. Here's how to do it:

1. Select the photo that you want to add keywords to by clicking on it in the Events or Photos window.
2. Click Window | Show Keywords to bring up the Keywords window.

3. Click the words that you want to associate with your photo. To deselect a word, click it again.

You can add as many or as few keywords as you want to each photo. You can also add your own keywords to the list Apple provides. In the Keywords window, click the Edit Keywords button and then the Add button. Type your word and press ENTER.

Later, when you want to find your photos, click the Search icon on the bottom task bar and then enter the keyword to search for. All photos tagged with that keyword will appear in your results.

How to... **Rate Your Photos in iPhoto**

You won't be able to sort your photos by rating until you've rated some photos.

1. Choose View | Rating.
2. Place your cursor over a photo and five dots will appear below it.
3. Click the dots to set your rating; for example, clicking the fourth dot will rate your photo with four stars.

Create Albums

Just like physical photo albums, Albums in iPhoto help you organize your photos. You can name your Albums anything you want, organizing your photos by person, date, event name...the possibilities are endless.

Create a new Album by clicking File | New Album. Enter a name into the text box and then click Create (see Figure 16-1). Drag the photos that you want to place inside the Album over from the Library pane. If you prefer, you can also select all the photos that you want to place in an Album and then, while the photos are still selected, create your Album and make sure to check the Use Selected Items in New Album check box; all the photos will automatically be placed inside the new Album.

Remember the Smart Mailbox from Mail and Smart Groups from Chapter 11? Well, you can create Smart Albums too. Start by selecting File | New Smart Album and then select the criteria you want iPhoto to use when adding pictures to it (see Figure 16-2).

Build a Slideshow

You can make really cool custom slideshows with your favorite photos to share with friends or just to show them off. You can even add background music and transition effects. To get started:

1. Select the albums or individual photos from the Library that you want to include.
2. Select File | New Album and then click the Slideshow button in the New dialog box.

FIGURE 16-1 Keep your photos organized by creating Albums.

FIGURE 16-2   iPhoto will add photos to your Smart Albums based on the criteria you select.

3. Name your slideshow and click Create.

4. Reorder your pictures in the photo browser at the top of the iPhoto window. Drag them into the order you want. You can add a theme and music to your slideshow using the appropriate buttons, if you wish.
5. Click Play to start your show!

 To select multiple photos, click the first photo and then press and hold the COMMAND key as you select more. If you accidentally select a photo that you don't want to add, click it again (while still holding down the COMMAND key) to deselect it.

Once you have your slideshow arranged in the way that you want it, you can use the options to add music or cool transitions between slides.

 You don't need to create a new slideshow if you just want to view a series onscreen. Just select the photos or album you want to view and click the Play button in the bottom left-corner.

Edit Photos

What good would a photo management program be if you couldn't edit your photos? Not much, which is why iPhoto gives you the tools to crop, rotate, retouch, and add effects to your pictures. You can even remove the dreaded red-eye effect!

Select a photo and then click Edit to start Edit mode (see Figure 16-3). This will give you access to the following tools:

- **Rotate**   Click this button to rotate your picture by 90 degrees counter-clockwise. Keep clicking until it's rotated to the position you want. Use OPTION-click to rotate your photo in the opposite direction.

FIGURE 16-3   Crop, rotate, or remove red eye with iPhoto's editing features.
(Photo by Stewards of the Redwoods)

- **Crop**   Clicking the Crop button allows you to position your cursor in a photo and drag to select just the part of your picture that you want to keep. Make sure the Constrain box is checked if you want your cropped photo to conform to a certain ratio.
- **Straighten**   Gently nudge your crooked photos in the right direction with Straighten. You can rotate photos in up to 10-degree increments in either direction with this tool.
- **Enhance**   Enhance allows iPhoto to determine what the best contrast and brightness settings are for your photo. COMMAND-Z or Edit | Undo Enhance Photo will reverse the changes.
- **Red-Eye**   Do your friends, family members, or pets look like they are possessed in your photos? You can use the Red-Eye tool to remove sinister glowing eyes. Click the Red-Eye button and drag the size slider to set the size of your crosshairs. Place the crosshairs over an eye and click the button again. Exorcism complete!
- **Retouch**   Smooth or blend areas of your photos.
- **Effects**   Choose one of eight effects to add to your photos, including changing them to black and white, to sepia, or creating a vignette effect (see Figure 16-4).
- **Adjust**   Manually adjust the contrast, brightness, color, and other elements of your photo here.
- **Done**   Exit Edit mode.

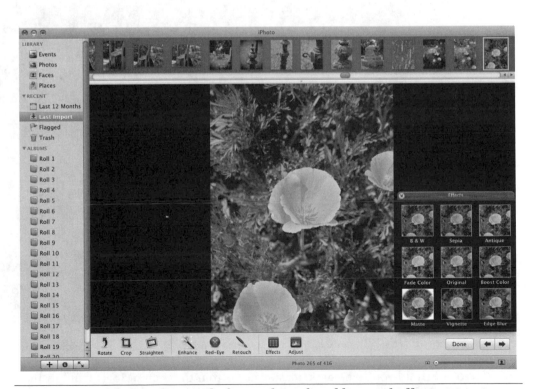

FIGURE 16-4   Change the mood of your photos by adding cool effects. (Photo by Stewards of the Redwoods)

Tip Although iPhoto protects your original image, it's still a good idea to make a duplicate before editing your photos. Do this by pressing the COMMAND-D keys or by clicking File | Duplicate when a picture is selected. If you do not make a duplicate, you can undo any changes by choosing Photos and then Revert to Original.

Explore iMovie

You can use iMovie to sort and organize your movie clips from a variety of sources. You can also combine them, edit them, and create your own movie clips. Once you've imported your video into iMovie, all of your clips will be readily available for viewing with just the click of a few buttons. Figure 16-5 shows the main iMovie window.

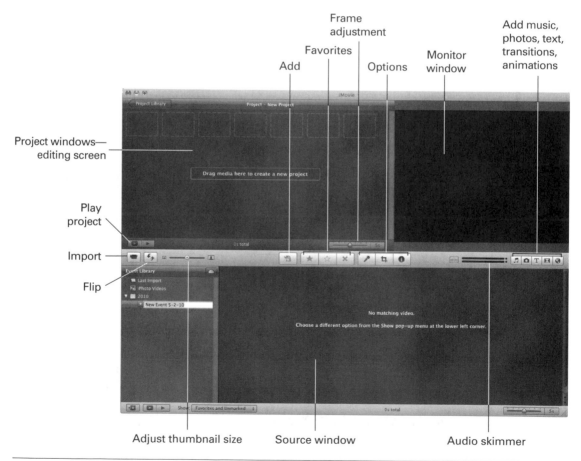

FIGURE 16-5 Build your cinematic masterpiece from the main iMovie window by dragging your video clips into the strip.

Import Video to iMovie

If you have a digital video camera or digital camera, you can easily import your video clips by connecting it to your MacBook, with a mini-USB or an appropriate FireWire cable.

 Some video cameras also support FireWire, which is a data transfer protocol that is particularly great for video transfer. Currently, only the MacBook Pro comes with a FireWire port. If you are working with a MacBook or MacBook Air, you'll have to stick with USB 2.0 and a random access device (RAD) that stores video on flash memory or an internal drive. Your MacBook comes with a FireWire 800 port, so if your video camera uses FireWire 400, you will need to purchase a 400-to-800 adapter.

1. Open iMovie by clicking its icon in the Dock or launching it from the Applications folder.
2. Connect your device to your MacBook with the USB or FireWire cable (when applicable).
3. Turn on your device and wait for it to connect to the computer.
4. Select the clips that you want to import in the Import window. Click Select All to import all video.
5. In the Save To dialog box, choose a location on your hard drive where you want to save the imported items to.
6. Create a new Event to help you organize your video clips, or add them to an existing Event by selecting one of these choices from the pop-up menu.

The time it takes to import your video depends on the length and size of the video. Time can range from minutes to hours. iMovie displays a progress bar to enable you to track the time remaining; just make sure that you do not shut down your computer or disconnect your device until this process is complete.

Import Movie Files from Your MacBook

In addition to downloading videos from a camera or video camera, you can import them from a CD, DVD, jump drive, or your hard drive. Just click File | Import Movies and then use the browser to select a location to search for video clips.

Did You Know?

Importing High-Definition Video

If you are importing high-definition video (1080i), the 1080i HD Import dialog box will appear so that you can select the size that you want it imported as. Full size for 1080i video is 1920×1080 pixels and can take up a lot of disk space (40GB for an hour of HD video), but it is your best bet if you are cropping your video. You can choose to import it in the large format, which is 960×540. This will save you a lot of space yet still look good on a TV or computer screen, but it is not sufficient if you plan to use a serious video editing program like Final Cut Pro.

You follow the same steps as previously described except you will be asked if you want to transfer the files to the new location or just make a copy of the movie. Any video that you downloaded into iPhoto from your digital camera will automatically appear in iMovie without having to be imported.

Create an iMovie Project

Now that you've gathered all of your video into the iMovie library, you are ready to create your first cinematic masterpiece. Once you've created an iMovie project, you can share it, upload it to the Internet, or transfer it to your iPod or iPhone.

Create a New Project

Before you can begin, you will need to create a new iMovie project:

1. Select File | New Project.
2. Name your project.
3. Choose an appropriate aspect ratio. Your choices include Standard (for televisions and computer screens), iPhone (for viewing on mobile devices like the iPhone and iPod), and Widescreen (for widescreen monitors or televisions).
4. Click a thumbnail to add a theme to your project (see Figure 16-6). Once you've selected a theme, iMovie will add transitions and titles for you. If you prefer to add them yourself, you can deselect that box when you choose your theme.

 You can use video and still images in your projects that differ in aspect ratio. Just select the most appropriate format for the majority of the video and then later you can crop or otherwise edit the varied media if you don't like how it appears in the end project.

How to... **Record to iMovie from Your MacBook**

You don't have to have a digital video or still camera to create video for iMovie. Your MacBook comes with a built-in iSight camera that you can use to directly record video. Here's how:

1. Click the Import button.
2. Select your camera from the device pop-up window.
3. Click Capture.
4. Select a Save To location and name your Event.
5. Click OK to start recording.
6. Click Stop to pause recording. You can start and stop as often as you want.
7. Click Done to finish your recording and exit Capture mode.

FIGURE 16-6   When you add a theme to your project, like Comic Book, the transitions, titles, and overall tone are determined for you.

Add Video to a Project

You can add video from a single event or from multiple events to your project. Video clips are combined within your project in the order that you add them, but you can always edit the video later to rearrange the clips and add more elements like music and effects.

1. Click a video clip to select a frame range to add to your project. iMovie automatically selects 4 seconds, but you can alter this to add all or part of the clip.
2. Click the Add Selection to Project button (in the middle of the iMovie toolbar) to add the selection to your project, or drag a video clip into the Project window. Add as many clips as you want.
3. Drag the clips into the order you prefer.

How to...   **Preview Your Project**

Once you have your clips arranged how you want them, you can preview how your project looks.

- **Start from the beginning**   Click the Play Project from Beginning button below the Project window or press the backslash (\) key.
- **Start from any point**   Double-click the frame where you want to begin playing or press the SPACEBAR.
- **Stop playing video**   Press the SPACEBAR or click anywhere in the iMovie window.
- **Play a selected frame range**   Press the forward slash (/) key.

Add Music to Your Project

What better way to add ambience and mood to your movie than through the use of a great soundtrack? With iMovie's help, you can score your film with your favorite songs from iTunes or use iMovie and iLife sound effects to liven things up.

While your project is open, select Window | Music and Sound Effects or press COMMAND-1. Browse through the sources and select the songs or sound effects that you want to add. Drag them to the background of your project. Avoid dragging the songs onto clips; aim for the space around the video.

After you've added music, a green background appears behind the video clips. The background indicates how long the music is relative to the video clips. If the video ends before the music, a music indicator appears at the last clip. To trim the music to better fit your video, click the green background and then choose Edit.

If you want to learn more about adding music and sound effects, open iMovie Help and search for Enhancing Audio.

Share Your Movie

Once you've completed your epic cinematic masterpiece, you'll want to share it! You can use iMovie to export your movie to YouTube or to a MobileMe account, or you can export it to a file and then upload it or e-mail it whenever you want. Here's how to export your project to a file.

1. Choose Share | Export Movie to export your project to an MPEG-4 file.
2. Use the chart in the Export dialog box to determine what size of file you want and then name your project and select an export location. Click Export.
3. Locate the file on your hard drive to attach it to an e-mail or upload it online.

 If you want to export your project as a QuickTime movie, use the Share | Export Using QuickTime option.

Explore iDVD

Now that you've created your exciting slideshows and dramatic movies, all you need to do is use iDVD to burn them to a DVD that anyone can play.

Create a Magic iDVD

A Magic iDVD helps you create a cohesive DVD of your video and/or photos, using Apple-provided themes for your menus. Launch iDVD (see Figure 16-7) and select Magic iDVD to get started. Name your DVD in the Title box and select a theme for

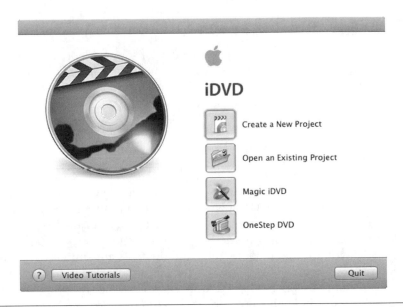

FIGURE 16-7   iDVD offers several options for creating your own DVDs that work in any modern DVD player.

your menus from the Theme chooser provided at the top of the screen. Don't worry— you aren't married to your choice. You can always go back and change it later.

Use the Media Browser on the right side of the iDVD window to select movies and photos for your DVD. You can drag single clips and photos or whole events over to where it says, "drop photos/movies here." Arrange your clips or photos in the order that you want them to play in.

Use the Media Browser again to select music. Drag a song over to an Event or to individual movie clips to add background music. A speaker icon will appear in your selection to indicate that music has been added.

Once you've completed adding your content and enhancing your slideshow with music, you can click the Preview button to see exactly how your finished project will look. The main menu will list Movies and Photos. Click one of them to see the contents. The titles of your media and Events will be listed. Play them if you wish. If something doesn't look right, now is the time to correct it. This is your last chance to change your theme, too, because next you're going to burn it to disc. Click Exit on the iDVD remote control icon to return back to your project screen.

When you are satisfied with how your project looks and sounds, click the Burn button. You will be prompted to place a blank, writable DVD disc into your optical drive. A dialog box will appear so that you can track the burn process. When you are all done, your new DVD will work in any DVD player or computer with a DVD drive.

Create a OneStep DVD

If you simply want to make a playable disc of some video, you can use the OneStep DVD feature. Connect your video camera or digital camera to your MacBook and turn it on. Open iDVD, click OneStep DVD, and insert a blank DVD into your optical drive. iDVD will do the rest! You can also use video clips already located on your drive.

Create a Custom Project

You put together a custom project very similarly to how you created the Magic iDVD, except that you have much more creative control over the details. To start a new custom project, click the Create a New Project button on the iDVD opening screen. You will still choose a theme for your project, but you can customize the buttons and add more features than with the Magic iDVD option.

The layout of the project screen and the tools are similar to the Magic iDVD process (see Figure 16-8). If you want to learn more about creating a custom project, there are some excellent video tutorials on the Apple website, located at www.apple .com/ilife/tutorials/#idvd, or click the link in the Project Chooser dialog box.

FIGURE 16-8 Drag and drop your video files, music, and photos into place to create your perfect DVD.

Explore iWeb

iWeb is an application for creating web pages. It works very much the same as the other iLife applications. You can begin from scratch or from a template (see Figure 16-9). You replace placeholder images and text, add themes, and, in this case, eventually upload your project to a MobileMe account or to an Internet host provider via FTP. You can add photo albums, multimedia, widgets, and even interactive maps to your projects (see Figure 16-10).

To learn more about using iWeb, check out the tutorials at www.apple.com/ilife/tutorials/#iweb.

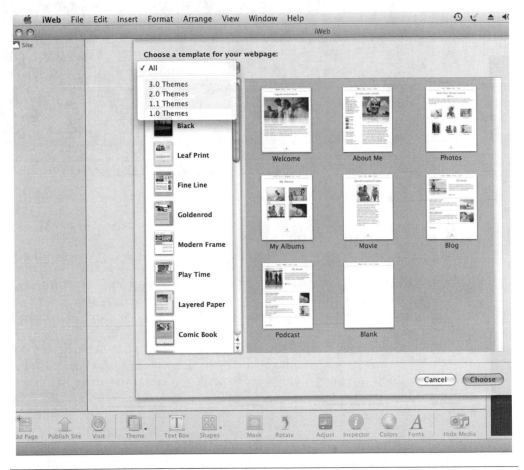

FIGURE 16-9 Build a professional-looking website through the use of templates.

FIGURE 16-10 Add dynamic content to your site with Widgets, movies, and audio.

Explore GarageBand

GarageBand is a complete recording studio right on your MacBook. You can create, arrange, and record your own music or even learn to play an instrument. You can add your own instruments, like a USB keyboard (musical, not computer!) or an electric guitar, or you can choose from the included instruments and sounds to create a musical showstopper.

Because recording studios can get pretty complex, in this book we are just going to cover how to start a new GarageBand project and how to use GarageBand to learn to play music. You can learn more about recording, mixing, and creating music from the online video tutorials or from the GarageBand help file.

Start a New GarageBand Project

Launch the GarageBand application by clicking its icon in the Dock. You will be presented with a project window. Here you can select what type of project you want to start, such as one for voice, guitar, or keyboards or one to create a podcast or iPhone ringtone. Just like with the Magic iDVD, you can use the Magic GarageBand project to determine a theme for your music, like rock, reggae, or blues (among others). Here's how to start a new project:

1. Click File | New or, if you've just opened GarageBand, select one of the templates to get you started, and then click Choose.

2. Name your project in the New Project dialog box and browse to the location where you want to save your project. Click Create.

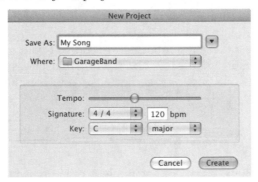

Each GarageBand project includes settings for tempo, key, and time signature. When you add in beats or additional tracks (such as Loops), GarageBand matches them to the project tempo and key that you've selected so that they work together and sound good. You can choose the project tempo, key, and time signature in the New Project dialog box when you create a new project.

3. Create your music in the main project screen. You can do so in the following ways: record music through your built-in microphone or an external microphone, through a connected electric guitar, or through a connected USB (or MIDI) keyboard.

Learn to Play Piano or Guitar

GarageBand can also help you learn to play an instrument. It comes with a basic lesson for both the piano and the guitar. You can download additional lessons or purchase more-advanced lessons online.

To get started, just select Learn to Play in the GarageBand dialog box (see Figure 16-11). You can then select the instrument lesson that you want. A video window opens in which the lesson plays, and an animated representation of your instrument appears below it (frets for guitar, keyboard for the piano). You also have access to a control panel where you can stop, pause, play, or slow down your lesson. You can even record your own instrument as you play along.

Each lesson contains two sections, a learning lesson and a play-along lesson. In the learning lesson, the instructor explains to you how to play the song; in the play-along session, you can play through the piece or choose sections of it to practice. Downloaded lessons and lessons from the Artist series may include more chapters or parts. Just move your cursor over to the left side of the video screen and select which lesson or chapter you want to play.

Connect an Instrument to Play Along

You won't get much out of the lessons if you can't play along, so you can use these steps to connect an instrument to GarageBand. Open a lesson and then use the following steps to add your instrument. A guitar is used in the example steps, but you can connect a keyboard in a similar fashion.

1. Click Setup in the upper-right corner of the screen.
2. Choose the input source for your guitar from the My Input Device pop-up menu. If you used the audio input port to connect your guitar, select Guitar. If you are playing using your MacBook's microphone, choose Internal Mic. If you are using an external microphone connected to your computer, choose External Mic.

How to... **Use Apple Loops**

GarageBand comes with prerecorded riffs that you can add to your projects, such as drums, bass, and other instruments. You can browse which ones are available in GarageBand by clicking the Loop button that looks like an open eye on the lower-right corner of the screen. You can search using Button view or Column view. For the sake of example, we will use Button view.

1. Open the Loop Browser by clicking the Loop button.
2. Select Button view from the view option in the upper-left corner of the Loop Browser.
3. Click the keywords to find the type of loop you want to add. The results will appear below.
4. To preview a loop, click it in the Results list. Click it again to stop the preview.
5. Drag a loop to the timeline to add it to your project.

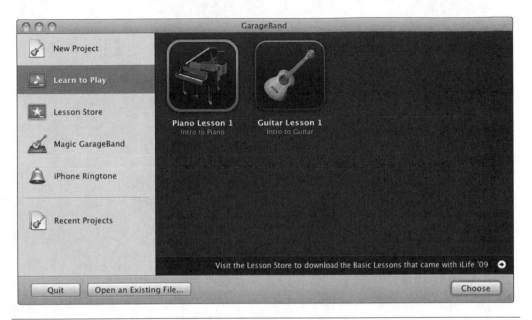

FIGURE 16-11   GarageBand will help you learn to play either the guitar or piano. Download more lessons online.

 If you're playing your guitar using a microphone, choose Monitor Off to avoid feedback.

3. Click Setup again to return to your lesson.

Summary

Now you have a brief overview of the types of projects you can create with the iLife application suite. You can develop any number of creative projects with your personal style. Create a movie and photo slideshow, write the musical score, and then burn it all using iDVD to create a playable DVD of your masterpiece. Talk about cool!

17

Leisure Time: Games, Music, and Movies

HOW TO...

- Find games for your MacBook
- View movies in QuickTime
- Catalog and listen to music in iTunes

Most of the applications covered in the previous chapters are useful for getting things done, both at home and at work, but what about when you just want to relax? Well, your MacBook can help you unwind and forget your daily cares with a host of entertainment options. You can play computer games from your MacBook or online, watch movies from the Internet or a DVD, and listen to and burn CDs of your favorite music.

Play Games on Your MacBook

While PCs have long held the position of best computers for serious gamers, the MacBook still comes with some great hardware and accessories for gaming. You shouldn't have any trouble playing today's hottest and most graphics-intensive games, especially if you have the more robust MacBook Pro model.

The only real game that is included on your MacBook is Chess. You can play against the computer or against another player. You can change the difficulty and even use voice commands to play. Launch Chess from the Applications folder or by clicking its icon on the Dock.

Another way to get some simple gaming time in on your MacBook is through Widgets. There's even a little tile-swapping "game" included in your preinstalled Widgets (called Tile Game). You can download new games by visiting the Dashboard Widgets download center on the Apple website: www.apple.com/downloads/dashboard/games/. There are many types of games available, from action games to word games, many of which are available for free (see Figure 17-1).

If you are serious about gaming, you will want to purchase and install your own games. Before purchasing a game for your MacBook, you should check the system requirements and make sure that you meet or, better yet, exceed the recommended resources. Apple has a gaming page on its website, located here: www.apple.com/games/ (see Figure 17-2).

You can see the hardware specifications for each MacBook model and the recommended games for your system by clicking the Game Hardware tab. Click the Getting Started tab on the site to find a list of available guides that covers topics like online gaming, multiplayer gaming, and even game modifications (mods) (see Figure 17-3).

Apple also provides some solid gaming accessories to help make the most of your system. These accessories include things like trackballs, joysticks, gaming

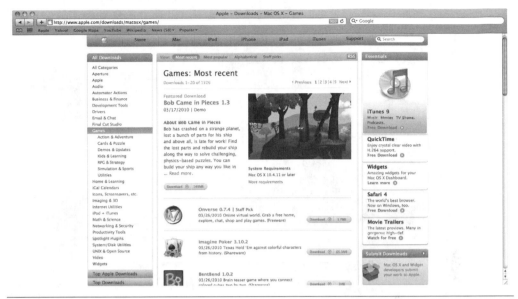

FIGURE 17-1   Download new Widget games from the Apple website.

FIGURE 17-2   Check out the latest information on gaming on your MacBook on Apple's Games page.

FIGURE 17-3 Your window to the world of MacBook gaming—Apple's Getting Started game page.

headsets, and surround-sound speaker sets. You can purchase these from the Apple.com online store or from mass retailers like Amazon.com or Best Buy. Just make sure that whatever you purchase is compatible with Mac OS X by checking the system requirements on the side or back of the packaging.

 If you are dying to play a game that is Windows-only, check out Chapter 13 for how to install and run Windows using Boot Camp.

Watch Movies on Your MacBook

There are a couple of ways to get a great cinematic experience on your MacBook. It already has everything you need to play movies in most of today's popular formats. You can download movies, stream them online, or play them from a DVD.

Get to Know QuickTime Player

QuickTime is one of the best multimedia players on the market today and, best of all, it's free. It's already loaded onto your MacBook with Mac OS X and is located in the Applications folder. With the QuickTime program, you can view video files, record audio and video, and watch movies on the Web.

Watch Video Files in QuickTime

If you want to view a video clip or movie file in QuickTime, all you really need to do is double-click the file and, assuming it's in a format that QuickTime recognizes, it will open and begin to play. If you prefer, you can open QuickTime and then go to File | Open and browse your computer for the file.

Use the controls at the bottom of the screen to stop, pause, fast forward, or rewind the video. You can also adjust the volume with the slider on the left side of the screen. The tracking bar at the bottom shows how long the clip is and how much time remains (see Figure 17-4). You can choose a screen size from the View menu or resize the window with the sizing handle.

Tip For a true cinematic experience, watch your movies in full-screen view. Press COMMAND-F or click the Full Screen button (two arrows pointing in opposite directions). To exit full-screen mode, just press the ESCAPE key on your keyboard. Note that low-resolution videos will look better in the normal view than in full-screen view.

Record Movies with QuickTime

You can also make short movies with QuickTime. Open the QuickTime application and choose File | New Movie Recording. QuickTime will use your MacBook's internal microphone and iSight camera to record your clip unless you have external devices installed. Click the Stop button to stop recording.

Record Your Screen

If you've spent much time online, you've probably come across some video tutorials, maybe even on the Apple website. You can use QuickTime to record your movements

FIGURE 17-4 Control your video playback from the onscreen controls.

around your computer screen and then share the files. Say, for example, that you want to show someone how you performed a task in iPhoto. You can open QuickTime and go to File | New Screen Recording.

A new dialog box appears, asking if you are sure that you want to record and instructing you how to stop recording (COMMAND-CONTROL-ESC, or the Stop Recording button on the menu bar). Click Start Recording and the window will close so that you have an unobstructed view of your screen.

Are you sure you want to start recording the screen?

This window will be hidden during recording so that the rest of the screen is not obstructed.

After recording starts, you can stop by:

• Clicking ■ Stop Recording in the menu bar. (Show Me)

• Pressing Command-Control-Esc

(Cancel) (Start Recording)

View Video Online

You don't have to do anything special to view movies online with QuickTime, but there are some places you should know about to find great content to watch:

- Visit the QuickTime Guide on the Apple website to find the latest movie trailers, music videos, and even video game trailers. Check it out at www.apple.com/quicktime/guide/.
- For just trailers, check out this page on the Apple website: http://trailers.apple.com/ (see Figure 17-5).

Playing Different Video Formats

QuickTime supports many of today's popular video file formats, but not all of them. You can download a small open-source component that will allow QuickTime to play some of these formats, including AVI, DIVX, and MKV. Visit http://perian.org/ and download the file.

Double-click the downloaded file and it will be installed on your MacBook, and that's it! Note that Perian only works with Mac OS X 10.4.7 and later, so check your OS version (Apple | About This Mac) before installing it.

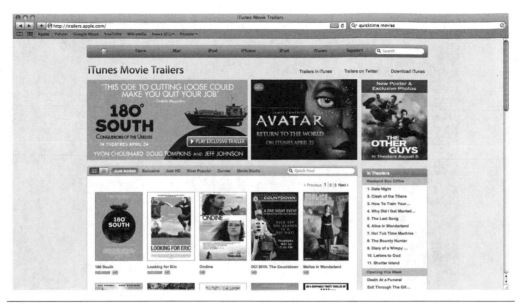

FIGURE 17-5   Watch today's latest movie trailers with QuickTime online.

Watch a DVD on Your MacBook

Of course, you don't have to download video files or watch them online; your MacBook is a full-fledged DVD player too (unless you have a MacBook Air, in which case you need to add an external DVD drive). You don't have to do anything special to watch a DVD on your computer; just insert the DVD into your DVD drive slot. Once inserted, the DVD player will open and your DVD will begin.

Use your mouse to make selections from the DVD menu or to use the DVD Player Controller (see Figure 17-6). You can also purchase the Apple Remote Control ($19) and use that to control the DVD player. Change the size of the window from the View menu.

If you are watching a movie in full-screen mode, you won't see the menu bar. Access it by moving your cursor to the top of the screen.

When you're done watching, you can drag the DVD icon on your desktop to the Trash (which will turn into an eject symbol) or you can click the Eject button on the controller. If your keyboard has an EJECT key (an upward-facing arrow with a line underneath), you can press that to eject a disc as well.

FIGURE 17-6 Use the DVD player remote control to perform standard DVD playback commands.

Master Your Music with iTunes

Many people were introduced to iTunes when they purchased their first iPod. iTunes is Apple's music management application for the iPod and iPhone, and it's available for both Windows and Mac. If you have somehow managed to avoid iTunes until now, we're going to cover how to import your music, organize it, burn CDs, and make purchases from the iTunes store.

Discover iTunes

When you first open iTunes, the iTunes Setup Assistant starts. The Assistant will search your computer for music files to import to your library. Depending on how many music files you have, this could take a while. Let it finish the search and populate the main screen. See Figure 17-7 to view the main parts of the iTunes window.

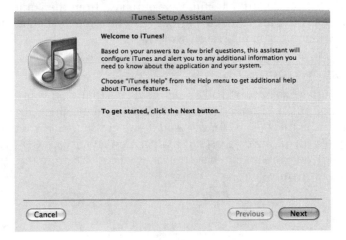

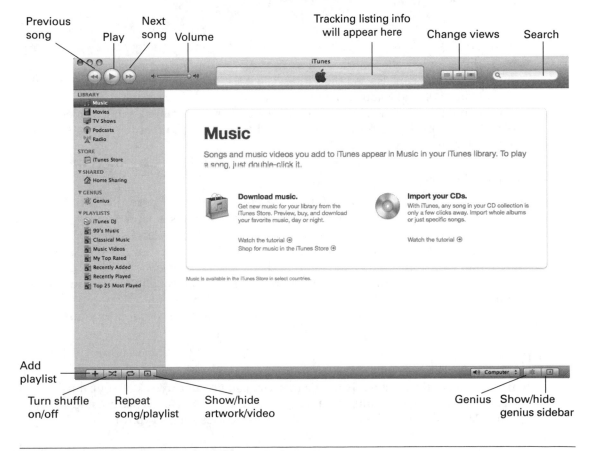

FIGURE 17-7   This is the main iTunes window.

As you can see, iTunes has already helpfully organized your media by type: music, movies, TV shows, applications, books, podcasts, and radio. These are all types of files you can import into iTunes or purchase from the iTunes store. If you want to see what titles are contained under each heading, just click the heading and the results will appear in the results window.

Import Music

While iTunes has imported all of the media currently on your hard drive, you can always add more. If you place a music CD into your optical drive, you will be prompted to import the tracks into iTunes. (And if you are connected to the Internet, iTunes will search an online database for information about your CD while you import it.) Likewise, you can also purchase tracks or whole CDs from the iTunes store and add them to your collection.

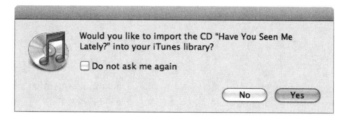

If you've downloaded music to your hard drive from the Internet or perhaps from a jump drive, you can also add those files. Click the File menu and select either Add File to Library or Add Folder to Library. In the dialog box, browse to the location on your computer where the file or folder is located that you want to import. Select it and then click Choose Folder (or File), and after the importation process is complete, the tracks will appear in your Music library.

Switch Views

You can view your music in one of three views: List, Grid, or Cover Flow. List view is the most practical because you can view more tracks per screen without scrolling, but Grid view is a nice choice if you want to view your CDs as icons. The text is also larger, making it easier to read if you have eyesight issues. Cover Flow, as you may remember from other chapters in this book, offers large icons (of cover art if available) with track listings below. It can be fun to scroll through your album covers! Figure 17-8 shows Cover Flow view.

To change your view, you only need to click one of the three view buttons at the top of the screen to the left of the search field.

Create Playlists

One of the cool things about iTunes is that you can create playlists of your music by genre or for special events like a party or workout mix. iTunes has created a few Smart Playlists for you already, organized in categories such as your top-rated songs

FIGURE 17-8   Cover Flow makes it fun to scroll through your CD artwork.

or most recently added songs. You can click these playlists to see their contents. If you want to listen to one, just select it and click Play.

Tip   Do you see the stars under the Rating column (in List or Cover Flow view)? You can rate all of your songs with 1 to 5 stars. Anything that you rate 4 or 5 stars will appear in your Top Rated playlist automatically. Rating is also helpful when you sync with your iPod using the AutoFill feature (more on this later). You can tell iTunes to select your highest-rated music first.

How to... Create a Smart Playlist

Remember the other Mac OS X "smart" features, like your Smart Mailbox and Smart Groups? Well, in iTunes, you have Smart Playlists. Some are already created for you, including Top Rated, Recently Played, and Recently Added. You can create your own Smart Playlist by choosing File | New Smart Playlist. Select the criteria that you want iTunes to use when adding tracks to your new playlist. Then, whenever you add a track that meets that criteria, it will automatically be added to your playlist.

Smart Playlist
☑ Match the following rule:
Artist ⬍ contains ⬍ Robert Burns, Traditional ⊖ ⊕ ⋯
☐ Limit to 25 items ⬍ selected by random ⬍
☐ Match only checked items
☑ Live updating
? Cancel OK

Create your own playlist by clicking the + button in the lower-left corner of your screen or by choosing File | New Playlist. A new list will be added and you can type in a descriptive name, like Road Trip, Birthday Mix, or whatever you want.

Once you've created your playlist, click Music under Library to access all of your music titles. You can drag the songs that you want to include over to your playlist. Hold down the SHIFT or CTRL key to make multiple selections.

Tip Once you've rated your favorite songs, click your Top Rated playlist and use the Shuffle feature to listen to hours of only your favorite music!

Purchase Music, Movies, and More from the iTunes Store

One of the easiest places to find new content for iTunes is, conveniently, the iTunes store. While you can find some free content to download, for most files, you'll need to create an iTunes store account and pay for them. Just like the categories in iTunes, you can select from music, movies, podcasts, books, and even games for your iPod.

To access the iTunes store, just click the Store menu while iTunes is open and choose Home (or click the iTunes Store listing in the left sidebar). Assuming you are connected to the Internet, the bounty that is the iTunes inventory will appear in your iTunes window (see Figure 17-9). Use the tabs at the top of the screen to sort the content and use the scroll bar to scroll through the available titles. To get more information on a title, just click its icon and you will be taken to its product page. There you will have the option, in the case of CDs, to purchase tracks separately or to buy the whole album.

Tip   Double-click or COMMAND-click the iTunes store in the left sidebar to choose to open it in a new window. This way you can shop and still listen to your playlists at the same time.

FIGURE 17-9   You can find movies, TV shows, applications, and music in the iTunes store.

Once you click the Buy button, you will be prompted to create an iTunes account. You'll have to enter a credit card number to complete your purchase. Once you have created an iTunes account, you will be logged in whenever you use iTunes.

 Once you create an iTunes account, you can utilize the new Genius feature. Genius searches your music library and creates music mixes of songs it considers "complementary." Once you've activated Genius, it sends the data of your entire library to Apple. Click the Show/Hide Genius Sidebar button to activate Genius (see Figure 17-7).

Burn CDs

It only makes sense that if all of your music is in one place and you've created all of these wonderful playlists, you should be able to burn them to disc to take them with you or to share. The easiest way to do this is to select a playlist that you would like to burn (or create a new one and add tracks to it), and then click the Burn button in the lower-right corner. You will be prompted to insert your blank CD, and iTunes will handle the rest. You can also CTRL-click the playlist and select Burn Playlist to CD from the menu.

You can opt to burn an audio CD, playable in most of today's modern CD players, or you can burn an MP3 disc. MP3 discs are only playable in CD players with MP3 capabilities, but they use better compression, so you can fit more music on them. You may be able to put as many as 19 or 20 tracks on a music CD (depending on the length of the tracks) or more than 150 on the same CD using the MP3 format. If the playlist that you've selected will not fit on one CD, iTunes will warn you before it starts to burn your list to disc. You can then either remove tracks so that they all fit onto a single CD or use multiple CDs to burn your playlist to.

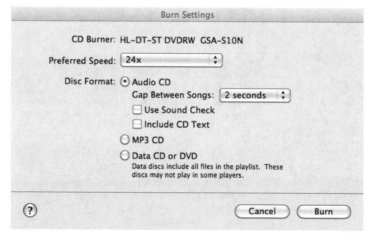

 You can also burn files to CDs and DVDs using the Data option. Use this option to back up important files. To access the data, you will need to open the disc using a computer with a CD/DVD drive (depending on which type of disc you burned).

iTunes Preferences

You can access the iTunes preferences by choosing iTunes | Preferences from the menu bar.

General

On the General preferences tab (see Figure 17-10), you can change the name of your iTunes library and choose what categories/types of files iTunes lists in the sidebar. You can also set your preferences for importing CDs and set your text size.

Playback

On this tab, you can select from options that affect how iTunes plays your music and videos (see Figure 17-11). You can check the Crossfade Songs box to have songs that are ending fade out and new songs fade in. You can also tell iTunes to play videos in a new window or to play them in full screen by default (once they are playing, you can always change your view). This is where you can also select to use closed captioning when available as well as subtitles.

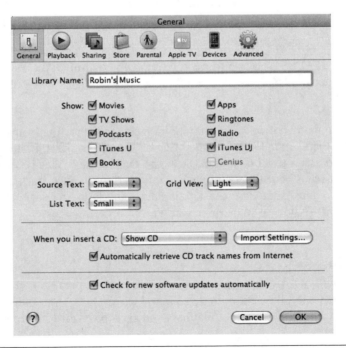

FIGURE 17-10   Change the name of your iTunes library in the General preferences window.

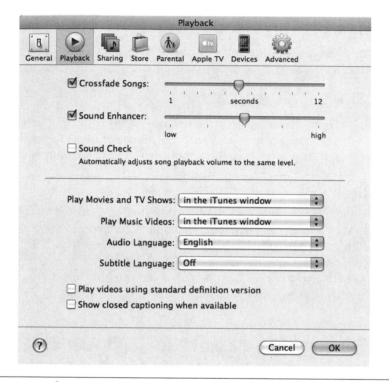

FIGURE 17-11 Select options to enhance your music playback in the Playback preferences.

 You may notice when listening to music in iTunes that some songs are louder than others. Sound Check is an option on the Playback tab that supposedly allows you to listen to all of your music at the same volume. When Sound Check is turned on, it scans your library for volume information for each track and then stores it in the music database or ID3 tag. Sound Check doesn't seem to be very effective, so there's no real value in activating it.

Sharing

If you want to give someone access to your library, you can change your Sharing preferences to allow them to do so (see Figure 17-12). You can share your entire iTunes library or just select playlists and set a password for remote users to access

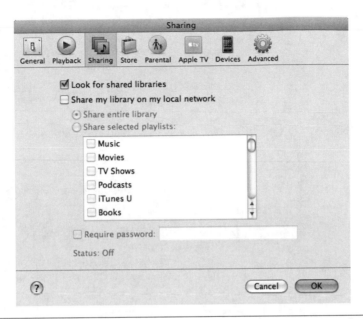

FIGURE 17-12 You can share your iTunes library with remote users if you activate file sharing.

them with. You can also search for other shared libraries on computers connected to your network. You can only share with five computers per day.

Store

The Store preferences relate to what the iTunes store can and can't do automatically, like whether it can automatically download prepurchased files or missing album artwork.

Parental

With these settings, you can restrict the type of content your children have access to (see Figure 17-13). You can also use content ratings to restrict access to certain materials. If you don't want your children running up your credit card in the iTunes store, check the iTunes Store check box to disable it and then click the lock in the lower corner to prevent further changes without a password.

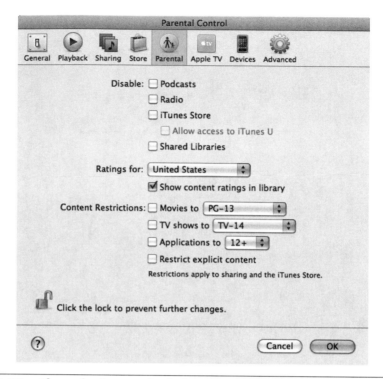

FIGURE 17-13 If you don't want the kids running up your iTunes store tab, you can restrict their access to that and more.

Apple TV

Sync your iTunes content with your Apple TV using this tab.

Devices

This is where you can change options relating to the syncing of devices like your iPod, iPhone, and iPad (see Figure 17-14). If you like to manually select your music, make sure to select the Prevent iPods, iPhones, and iPads from Syncing Automatically check box.

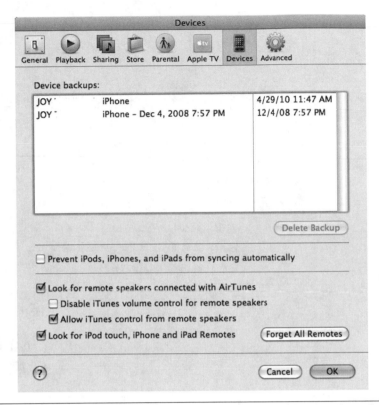

FIGURE 17-14   Set your syncing preferences for your iPhone, iPad, and iPod.

Advanced

On the Advanced tab, you can change your default iTunes library location, tell iTunes to keep your files organized, and tell iTunes whether or not to make copies of files that you add to your library (see Figure 17-15). You can also make changes to how iTunes windows work.

Note If you choose to have iTunes make a copy of your files as you add them, you will end up with duplicate audio files on your hard drive. Once iTunes has copied them to the iTunes folder, you can delete the file from its original location to save disk space.

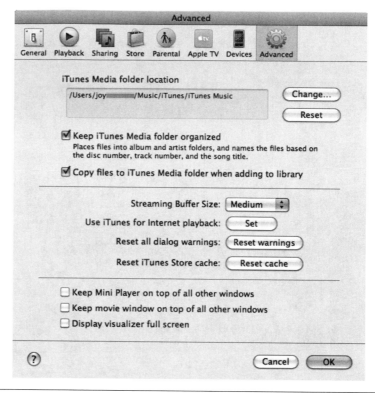

FIGURE 17-15 iTunes will keep your music files organized if you select that as an option on the Advanced preferences tab.

Summary

Your MacBook is a complete multimedia entertainment system, ready to take with you anywhere. You can watch movie files and DVDs, play games, and listen to music. By using the powerful iTunes software, you can create CD mixes for your friends or burn CDs to take with you in the car.

18

Staying in Sync with MobileMe

HOW TO...

- Establish a MobileMe account
- Access MobileMe web applications
- Keep your devices in sync
- Find a lost iPhone or iPod touch

MobileMe is a web-based service that Apple introduced in 2008 that helps you to keep all of your devices in sync. It also includes a set of Internet applications, including mail, contacts, and a calendar that you can access online from anywhere, very similar to the applications on your Mac computer. Through the MobileMe service, you can share information and post media such as photos and movies online. The main advantages of this service are that you can keep your devices all in sync with each other without having to connect them directly via USB cable or Bluetooth and you can share extra-large files.

MobileMe is a paid subscription service and is available as a single-user account for $99/year, which includes 20GB of online storage, or as a Family Pack for $149/year, which includes one master account with 20GB of storage and four family accounts, each with 5GB of storage space. You can sign up for a 60-day free trial from the Apple.com website to get started.

 You can purchase discounted MobileMe subscriptions from Amazon.com, Buy.com, and other online retailers, often saving up to $40!

Get Started with MobileMe

To get started with MobileMe, you first need to create an account.

1. Run the software update application on your MacBook by choosing Apple | Software Updates.
2. Install updates as necessary.
3. Open System Preferences by choosing Apple | System Preferences and then click MobileMe in the Internet & Wireless category.
4. Click Learn More to open Safari and visit the MobileMe website.

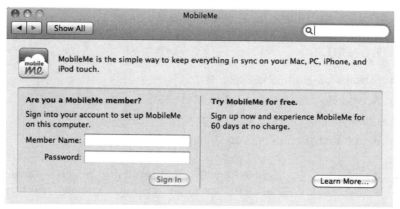

5. Click Free Trial to get started.
6. Create your user account by filling in the web forms and click Continue.
7. Enter your credit card information (you will not be charged until after the 60-day trial period is complete) and complete the signup process. Once you complete your signup process, you will have your new MobileMe username and account information. Don't lose it!

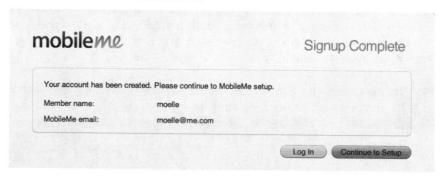

8. Click Continue to Setup.
9. Enter your new username and password and click Sign In.

Once you've signed in, you will be presented with your MobileMe account information screen (see Figure 18-1). It will tell you what type of account you have, how long you've been a member of MobileMe, your online storage capacity, and when

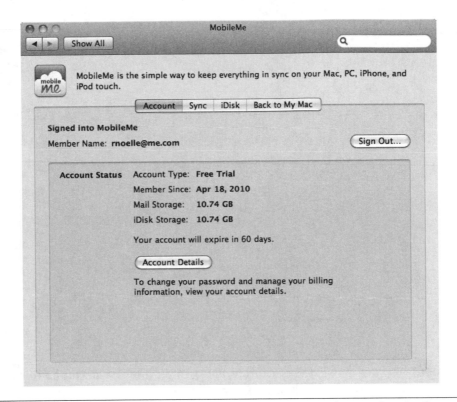

FIGURE 18-1   The account information screen gives you relevant details about your MobileMe account, including when it is set to expire.

your account will expire. You can click the Account Details button to change your billing information and other account settings.

Set Your Sync Preferences

You can use MobileMe to keep all of your devices synced up, including your iPhone, iPod, iPad, MacBook, and even your PC.

1. Click the Sync tab in the MobileMe preferences window (see Figure 18-2).
2. Click the check box next to Synchronize with MobileMe.
3. Use the pull-down menu to select a synchronization frequency.
4. Check the boxes next to the items that you'd like to sync, using the scroll bar to see all of your options.
5. Click the Advanced button to see which devices will be synced.
6. Click Sync Now to send your information to MobileMe for storage and syncing with other devices.

The sync status date and time will be updated to reflect your latest syncing.

FIGURE 18-2 Use the Sync preferences to set how often MobileMe syncs with your devices and what items it syncs.

Set Your iDisk Preferences

iDisk is your online storage system that you can access through MobileMe. You will have 20GB of storage space with a single-user account. You can click the iDisk tab in the MobileMe preferences window to see how much space you have used (see Figure 18-3). You can also set up your public folder, with options to allow others to write files to your space and to set passwords for those who do.

Did You Know?

Managing Your Passwords

Keychain is a password management utility available in Mac OS X. You can use it to store and automatically enter passwords to your favorite websites and to your e-mail account, among other things. You can also enter your MobileMe password information into your Keychain and then sync it with your devices. This allows applications like Mail, Address Book, iWeb, and iPhoto to automatically connect to your MobileMe account with each use, rather than requiring you to input your password each time. If you want to sync your Keychain, make sure to select its check box during the sync process. If you want to see what information is stored in your Keychain, open the Keychain Access utility from Applications | Utilities.

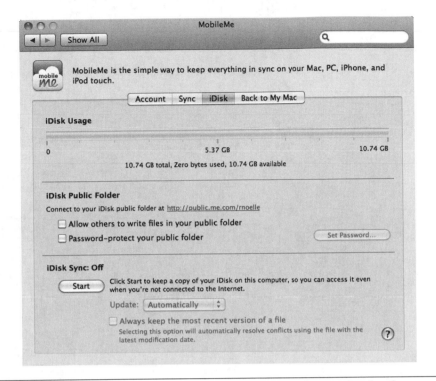

FIGURE 18-3   Keep track of your iDisk space usage on the iDisk tab of your MobileMe preferences.

You can also choose to sync your iDisk with your MacBook so that you can access anything saved online from your computer even when you aren't connected to the Internet.

Enable Back to My Mac

Back to My Mac is a service that allows you to access your MacBook computer from other computers if this feature is enabled on both machines. You can share files or turn on screen sharing from this tab (see Figure 18-4).

In order for Back to My Mac to work, your router needs to have NAT Port Mapping Protocol (NAT-PMP) or Universal Plug and Play (UPnP) enabled. If you receive the error shown in Figure 18-4, you will need to refer to your router documentation to find out how to enable NAT-PMP or UPnP.

Use the other buttons on the tab to enable file sharing and to turn on Wake for Network Access, which allows you to "wake" your sleeping MacBook when you want to access it remotely from another computer. For more information on Back to My Mac, click the ? button in the lower-right corner to access Mac Help.

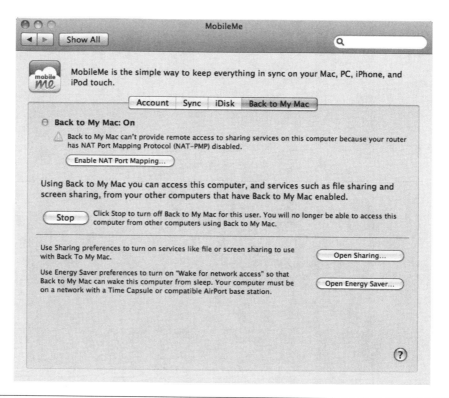

FIGURE 18-4 If you want to be able to access your MacBook from another computer, both computers must have Back to My Mac enabled and meet the router specifications.

Use MobileMe Online

Once you've synced your information with MobileMe, you can access applications like Mail and Calendar through Me.com. Open Safari (or the browser of your choice) and go there now.

You'll be presented with a login screen (see Figure 18-5). Enter your MobileMe username and password to log in and you'll be directed to the www.me.com/mail screen (see Figure 18-6). From there, assuming you've synced your contacts, you can send e-mail using your MacBook Address Book and access other applications like your calendars and MobileMe Gallery.

Send E-Mail with MobileMe Mail

If you use Mail as your primary e-mail program, MobileMe Mail won't look that much different. You can do all of the same things as you can in Mail: create folders, compose e-mails, save drafts, and integrate with other programs.

FIGURE 18-5   Sign in at Me.com to access MobileMe Mail, Calendar, Contacts, and Gallery online from any computer.

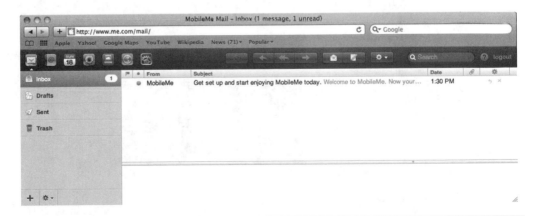

FIGURE 18-6   When you first sign in to MobileMe online, you will be directed to the Mail program.

Click the Compose New Message button (the pad of paper and pencil icon). In the composition window, click the Address Book icon to access your synced contacts. You can select which recipients to add to your message. You can also just start typing the first few letters of the person's name and, if they are in your Contacts, their name will appear in the address box for you to select them. Type up your e-mail and click Send. MobileMe will automatically sync this sent e-mail with your Mail program.

If you're checking your e-mail online through MobileMe and just want to quickly reply to an e-mail you've received, you can use the Quick Reply feature. Click the Quick Reply arrow next to the e-mail and the Quick Reply box will open. Type in your reply and click Send. There's no need to open the e-mail!

Allow Others to Upload/Download in Your MobileMe Gallery

If you recall from previous chapters, you can publish your photos and movies to your MobileMe gallery, but that's not all you can do. You can also allow your friends and family to upload their own photos to your albums and to download their favorites of your photos.

1. Click the Gallery icon in the MobileMe toolbar to open the My Gallery window, shown in Figure 18-7.

FIGURE 18-7   Click the Gallery icon to view the main My Gallery window.

2. Create a new album in your MobileMe Gallery by clicking the + button.
3. In the Album Settings dialog box, name your album.
4. Select the settings that you wish to apply to your album.

5. To allow people to upload photos to your gallery, select Allow: Uploading of Photos via Web Browser.
6. To allow people to download your photos, select Allow: Downloading of Photos or Entire Album.
7. Click Create.

Tip   You can also allow people to publish photos to your gallery via e-mail or from their iPhone. Select the check box next to this option to enable this feature.

Now when people visit your gallery online, Upload and Download buttons will be active if you've enabled these options; otherwise, the buttons appear but are grayed out (inactive) (see Figure 18-8). Visitors can select a photo and click Download to transfer the file to their own computer, or they can click the Upload button and add their own photos to your album.

Note   If you want to change the permissions of an existing album, click the album to select it and then choose Adjust Settings from the toolbar.

Share Large Files with MobileMe

If you've ever tried to send a large computer file via e-mail, you probably already know what a hassle it can be. Slow upload times and limits on file sizes and types can make it a Herculean task even when using compression software. To avoid these issues, you can use MobileMe iDisk to share your large files.

1. Click the iDisk icon (the cloud icon) in MobileMe online.
2. Click the directory that contains the file you want to send. If the file you want isn't already synced with MobileMe, click the Upload button to upload a file from your computer (see Figure 18-9).

FIGURE 18-8 If upload/download permissions aren't set in your albums' preferences, the corresponding buttons will be inactive when your gallery is viewed online.

3. Click the file, and in the next column, click Share File (see Figure 18-10).
4. Enter the recipient's address in the new window. Type a personal message if you want and then click Share.

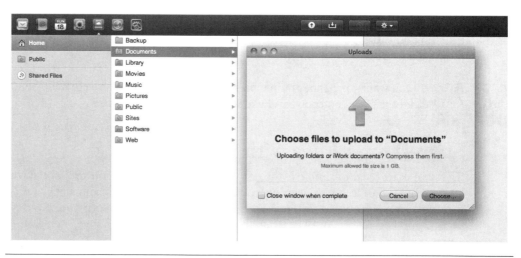

FIGURE 18-9 Upload large files to iDisk to share them without having to worry about e-mail file size and type limits.

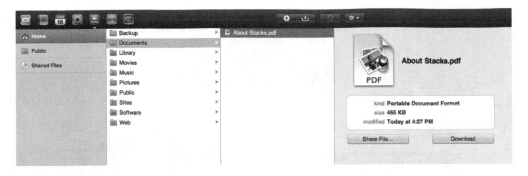

FIGURE 18-10   Send a link to your file with the Share File feature. You can even add a password to keep your file private.

  If you don't want to make your file completely public, you can choose to password protect the file and set an expiration date using the other options in the Share dialog box.

Once you've clicked Share, an e-mail will be sent to the people you've selected with a link so that they can download the file.

Find a Lost iPhone, iPad, or iPod Touch

One really cool thing that you can use MobileMe for is to find a lost iPod touch, iPad, or iPhone. Click the Find My iPhone button in the MobileMe toolbar and you'll be taken to the location page. You must register your device and make sure that it is running the appropriate software before this service will work.

Once you've registered your device, as long as your iPhone (or iPad/iPod touch) is on, you will be able to track its location on the map (see Figure 18-11). You also have the ability to send a message to your iPhone that will appear on the main screen or to play a tone, even if the iPhone is in silent mode.

If you've simply misplaced your iPhone or left it somewhere where it can be retrieved, you can remotely place a lock on the iPhone so that no one will be able to use it until you return for it. Perhaps most importantly, if you believe you will not be able to recover your iPhone (if you know it's been stolen, for example), MobileMe gives you the means to perform a remote wipe of the system. This wipe will remove all of your data, personal settings, and personal information from your iPhone or iPad and restore it to factory settings. It will not, however, affect your wireless service.

  If you perform a remote wipe on your iPhone or iPad, you will no longer be able to locate it using this service. This function should be used as a last resort!

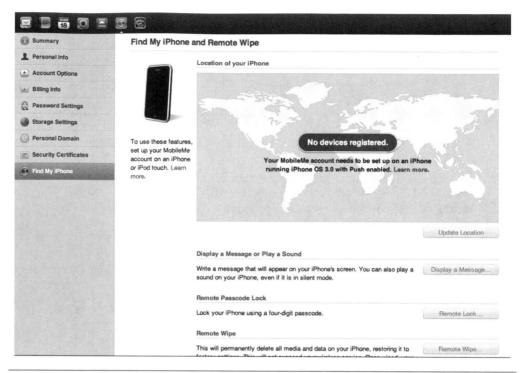

FIGURE 18-11 Track, lock, or completely wipe your iPod touch or iPhone through MobileMe.

Summary

We've covered just a few of the functions that are available to you through the MobileMe subscription service. By using MobileMe, you will be able to publish photos and movies to the Web, use e-mail, contact, and calendar functions online from any computer, allow people to upload and download from your personal MobileMe gallery, and even track and disable your iPhone, iPad, or iPod touch.

19

Under the Hood: Tune-Ups and Basic Maintenance for Your MacBook

HOW TO...

- Update your system and applications
- Check your hard drive health
- Back up your data
- Clean your MacBook

The chances are good that you could own your MacBook for a long time and never have to perform any maintenance, but periodically doing so will reduce the risk of system or hardware failure. Note that I said "reduce the risk," not "eliminate the risk," which is why routinely backing up your data is critical. In this chapter we are going to cover some simple maintenance tasks (including backing up your system) as well as how to keep your computer spick-and-span.

Perform Software and Application Updates

The best way to keep your system running smoothly and prevent system problems is to perform regular updates to both your system and your third-party applications. Your MacBook computer comes with a handy update utility so that you can easily update your operating system files, and many third-party programs come with an update utility, too.

Update Your MacBook

Apple regularly releases updates to its operating system. These updates sometimes contain security updates or fixes to previously unknown problems (those pesky bugs again), or even add new features to your computer.

The update utility on your MacBook, Software Update, will help you keep your operating system and your Apple software products up to date. You can access this utility by choosing Apple | Software Update.

 Make sure you are connected to the Internet before you run this program.

Once you start Software Update, your MacBook will connect with Apple's servers and check which updates are available that you do not already have installed (see Figure 19-1). When it finds a more recent version of your software, it will provide a list of available updates to download. Check the boxes next to the items you want to update and click Install.

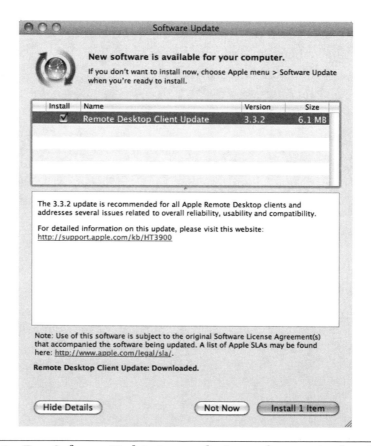

FIGURE 19-1 Run Software Update to see what's new for your Apple software and firmware.

Once you've installed your updates, the program will run again to see if there are additional files that you need to download. This happens because some updates must be installed first, before installing a more recent update. When you reach the point where Software Update says that no more updates are available, you're done!

 Sometimes you will be required to restart your computer to apply an update. This happens, typically, because some of the files that require updating can't be changed when they are in use, so they are updated as they are loaded into your system during a reboot.

Schedule Automatic Software Updates

While you can run Software Update manually, it's a lot easier to just schedule your system to check for updates so that you can forget about it. Open the Software Update preferences window by choosing Apple | System Preference | Software Update.

On the Scheduled Check tab (see Figure 19-2), you can schedule how often your MacBook checks for software updates. Weekly is a good setting to make sure that you don't miss something important for too long, but you can change it to daily from weekly, if you prefer. If you want your computer to go ahead and download the updates automatically, check this box. You will still need to give an okay before these updates are installed.

The Installed Software tab provides a list of updates that your MacBook has downloaded and installed, including the version number and the date of installation (see Figure 19-3).

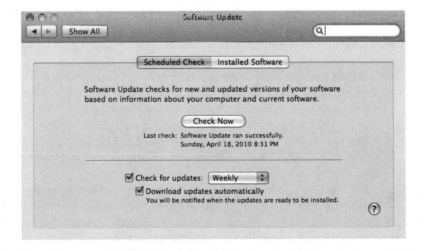

FIGURE 19-2   Set your Software Update schedule from System Preferences and then forget about it!

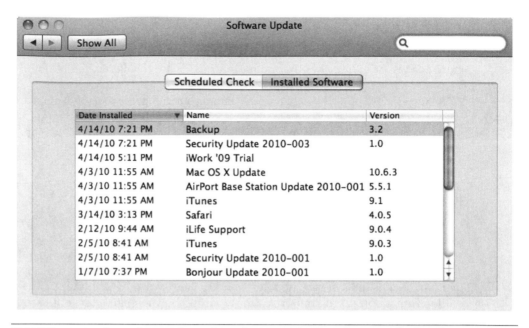

FIGURE 19-3 See what updates have been applied on the Installed Software tab.

Update Third-Party Applications

You can use the Software Update utility to check for and install updates to your Apple software products, but Software Update won't update the third-party applications that you've installed or plan to install. Adobe products like Reader, Acrobat, and Photoshop are used by many people, as is the ubiquitous productivity suite Microsoft Office.

These bigger programs or suites usually have an update utility included in them. You can usually find these utilities under the File menu, Help menu, or About menu. They work in very much the same way as Software Update, querying a server to see what the latest version is and comparing it to what you have installed.

If your software application doesn't have an automatic update utility, you should check the developer's website from time to time for updates. You can find these updates on pages within the main website, usually under Support or Downloads. Instructions on how to update the program will be included, and it's important to follow them carefully to avoid potentially corrupting the program or your system.

Don't feel like checking third-party vendors for updates to your software products? You can opt to sign up on a site like VersionTracker.com or MacUpdate.com, each of which maintains a free list of current software updates. For more features, such as e-mail alerts about updates and update-tracking software, you can purchase a membership to either site ($40–50 annually).

Why It's Important to Update

You probably won't even notice the majority of upgrades and security patches to your system that come from updates, but that doesn't mean they aren't important. The most critical reason to update your software is to apply security fixes, particularly to programs that access the Internet, like Mail, Entourage, Safari, Firefox, and so forth. These updates fix flaws in the program that could allow viruses or hackers to access your system, so make sure you check for updates to these types of programs frequently.

Maintain Your Hard Drive

You've probably figured out already that your hard drive is where all of your data is stored, so you can imagine what a potential crisis it would be if your hard drive were to suddenly fail, taking your photos, movies, documents, tax returns, and banking information with it. While regular maintenance can't prevent damage to your hard drive from a catastrophe such as a house fire or accidentally dropping your MacBook in the hot tub, it can help prolong the life of your hard drive over time and, hopefully, alert you to potential problems before they manifest.

Work with Disk Utility

The Mac OS X Disk Utility can help you maintain and repair your hard drive (and other disks). It also offers other features like tools for formatting disks, tools for creating partitions, and even tools for making images of your disks for archival and storage.

Launch Disk Utility from the desktop by choosing Go | Utilities, and then double-clicking Disk Utility. Figure 19-4 shows the main Disk Utility window. After you select a disk in the left pane, you can click the following buttons in the toolbar at the top of the window to perform the actions described:

- **Verify**   Prompt Disk Utility to check the drive for errors.
- **Info**   View detailed technical information about your disks.
- **Burn**   Burn disk images to an optical disc.
- **Mount/Unmount**   Click Mount to "mount" the disk (including virtual disks), which means to register it on your computer and make it available for use. After you have mounted a disk, you can click Unmount to remove the disk.
- **Eject**   Eject (or unmount) a selected disk or other mountable media (flash drive, DVD).
- **Enable Journaling**   Journaling keeps a record of changes made to your disk.
- **New Image**   Create a copy of the selected disk. These copies, called *disk images*, can be burned to disc or used in virtual drives.
- **Convert**   Convert disk images from one type to another.

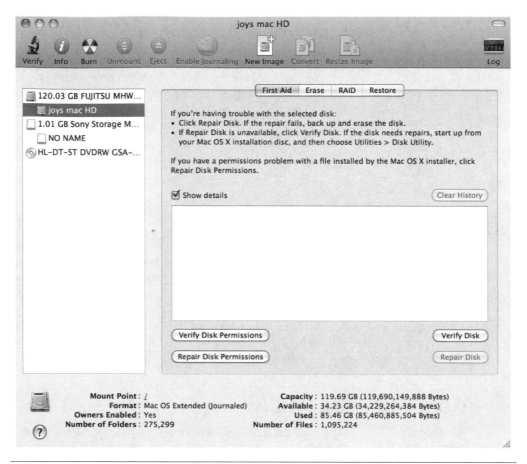

FIGURE 19-4 Use Disk Utility to scan and repair hard drive problems.

- **Resize Image** Alter the sizes of your disk images.
- **Log** Access the log of all of Disk Utility's activities.

 Disk images are exact copies of a disk, including all files and the file structure. You can also make a blank disk image, which you can use to store data on a physical disk.

Explore the Disk Utility Tabs

You can choose a disk from the pane on the left and then use the functions available on the Disk Utility tabs to work with the disk.

 Always back up your system before working with utilities!

- **First Aid**   You can access the Verify Disk feature and find out if your disk contains errors. You can also attempt to repair it with the Repair Disk function. Repair Disk won't fix any physical errors but it can repair some data errors. You can also verify that the disk permissions are valid, repair disk permissions, and show detailed technical information.

You will not be able to repair the section of your drive that contains your main system files. If there is a problem with these files, you must shut down your computer and restart it with the original installation disc in the drive. You will then be able to select Utilities | Disk Utility and attempt to repair the disk.

- **Erase**   You can use the Erase tab to format a disk or a disk partition (see Figure 19-5). Select a volume and use the Erase Free Space button to prevent recovery of previously deleted files.

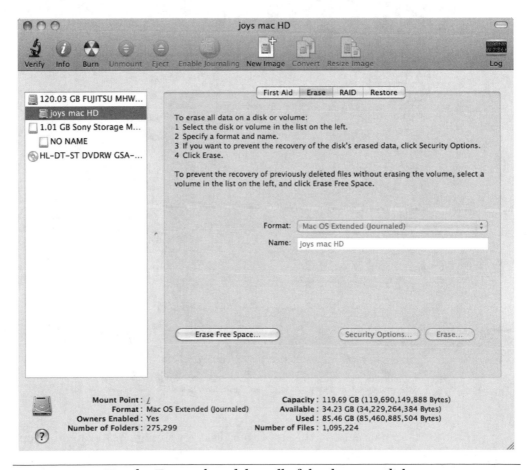

FIGURE 19-5   Use the Erase tab to delete all of the data on a disk.

- **Partition** When you select a drive from the list on the left, the Partition tab appears (see Figure 19-6). You can create partitions on your disk to install other operating system versions or just to create separate spaces (for an example of partitioning, see the discussion of Boot Camp in Chapter 13). Partitioning a disk, like formatting or erasing, removes all of the data on that disk.
- **RAID** RAID stands for redundant array of inexpensive (or independent) disks and allows you to create sets of multiple disks that act as one. If you don't know what RAID is, you will not need to use this feature (see Figure 19-7).
- **Restore** This tab enables you to copy or restore a disk or disk image to another disk (see Figure 19-8). Select the disk or disk image that you want to restore and then select a destination.

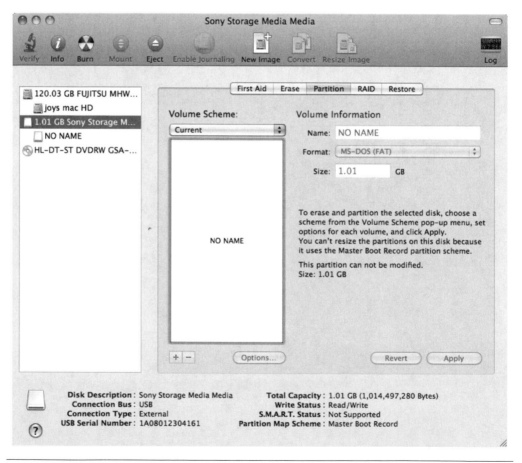

FIGURE 19-6 Create partitions of your disks for storage or to run other operating systems.

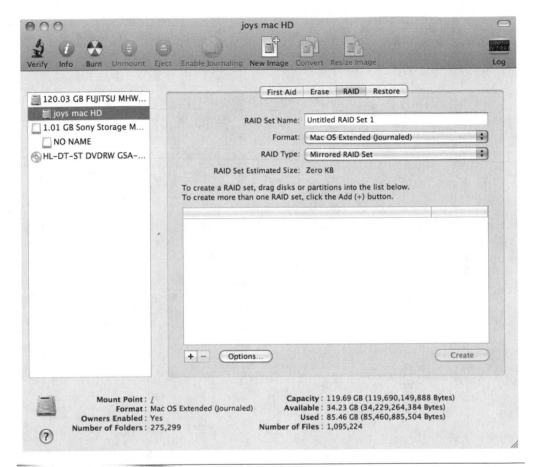

FIGURE 19-7   RAID is a data storage process that allows information to be split across multiple drives.

How to...   Check Your Hard Drive Space

Depending on how much data you collect and how large your drive is, you may need to keep abreast of how much free space you have available at any given time. To do this, select your disk's icon in the Finder. Press COMMAND-I on your keyboard to open the Get Info window. Information about your available and used space will be presented. To free up more space, empty Trash, uninstall programs that you no longer use, and archive files to another location, such as DVD/CD discs or an external drive (or MobileMe iDisk), and then delete them from your drive.

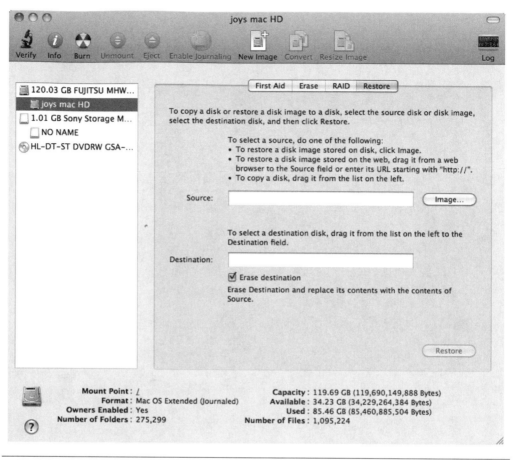

FIGURE 19-8 Restore a disk or disk image to another disk.

Back Up Your Data with Time Machine

Since you can't predict a system failure or an accident that disables your machine, it's important to know how to back up your data. How often you back up is up to you to decide, but it's generally a good idea to do so after you create or do something that you'd rather not (or can't) do again (such as downloading all of the pictures of the new baby from your camera or creating that special anniversary tribute video for grandma and grandpa). Of course, if you don't back up your data and something terrible happens to your system, in *some* cases you might be able to restore what you've lost, but it's sure to cause you some sleepless nights and a lot of money. You might as well just go ahead and back it up now...

Get Started with Time Machine

To use Time Machine, you need an external (preferable) or internal (won't help you much if you accidentally drive off with your laptop on the roof of your car) drive with enough space to contain your entire system. You can also use Time Machine with a server on your network.

You will be prompted to use Time Machine with a drive when you first connect the drive via USB or FireWire (assuming it's an external drive). If you choose to do so, your MacBook will handle everything else for you. The first backup will probably take a while, so be patient and don't interrupt until it is complete. After the initial backup, things will go faster in the future. Time Machine will also set a schedule for automatic backups so that you don't have to worry about backing up your system again (as long as the drive it needs is connected to your MacBook).

 Time Machine will keep hourly backups of your data for the past 24 hours, daily backups for the last month, and weekly backups until your drive is full. Once your drive is full, Time Machine will write over the oldest information first.

How to...   Change Your Backup Disk

Suppose you start backing up on one disk but decide later to change it to a new, larger disk. You can change the disk that Time Machine is using from System Preferences.

1. Click Apple | System Preferences | Time Machine to open the Time Machine preferences window.

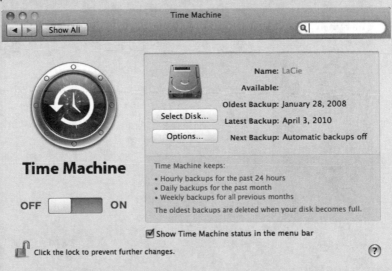

2. Click Select Disk.
3. Choose a disk where backups will be stored, then click Use for Backup.

Tip If you want to change which volumes Time Machine backs up, click the Options button in the Time Machine preferences window. This opens a dialog box that shows which volumes are *excluded* from being backed up. You can use the + and – buttons to remove volumes from this list. When you click Done, Time Machine will begin a backup in about two minutes.

Restore Files with Time Machine

So now that you have all your files backed up, what can you do with them? Well, you can access these restore points by using Time Machine! Launch Time Machine from the Applications folder.

A timeline appears on the right side of the screen that contains your update dates (see Figure 19-9). Use the arrows in the bottom-right corner to scroll through your backups. You can use the Finder windows in Time Machine to find files that you want to restore. Click the file to select it and then click the Restore button at the bottom of the screen to restore it to your computer. Click Cancel to leave Time Machine.

To restore an entire disk using Time Machine:

1. Make sure that your backup volume is connected to your MacBook.
2. Reboot your computer using your installation disc.
3. Select your language and continue.

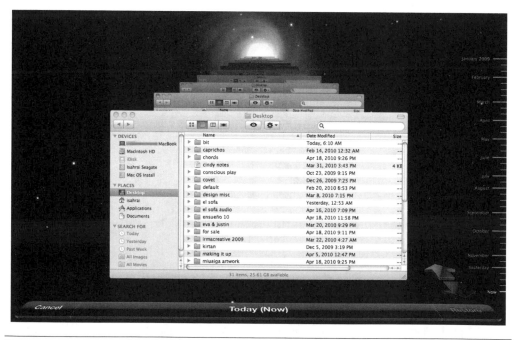

FIGURE 19-9 Travel back through time with Time Machine and restore deleted files.

4. Click Utilities | Restore System from Backup.
5. Select your backup disk. If you've chosen a username and password, enter that now.
6. Select the time and date of the backup up want to restore, click Restore, and Time Machine will do the rest.

Keep Your MacBook Clean

Regardless of brand, make, or model, computers have some common enemies: crumbs, water, and dust. Dust can damage sensitive electronic components, and crumbs can damage keyboard keys and stop them from working. Water, of course, is deadly when mixed with electronics.

Before you begin cleaning your MacBook, make sure it is unplugged and the battery is removed (if your MacBook has a user-removable battery). Wipe the exterior with a soft, lint-free cloth. You can purchase cloths made especially for computer cleaning from computer and office-supply stores. If you need to use a damp cloth, use fresh water and make sure the cloth is just barely damp, not wet!

You can wipe the screen with the same cloth, or you can buy antistatic, screen-cleaning cloths and kits. Never use any cleaning products on your screen or the computer body. You can use compressed air or cleaner made especially for computers to gently blow any crumbs from your keyboard and dust from any ports or fans. Do not take your computer apart; just a quick spurt from a few inches away will suffice. Do not place the pressurized air into a port or vent! Doing so could cause serious damage.

 To disinfect your keyboard, use Lysol wipes. Do not use any cleaning products on your computer screen that weren't specially formulated for that purpose!

Keeping your MacBook clean will not only keep it looking nice but prolong its life. Avoiding eating and drinking at your computer will also help keep your keyboard crumb free and avoid sticky keys.

Summary

By keeping up on routine updates, backing up your system, and keeping your computer clean, you will ensure that your MacBook runs problem free for a long time!

20

Troubleshooting and Finding Help

HOW TO...

- Perform basic troubleshooting procedures
- Force a restart when your screen is frozen
- Troubleshoot hardware and software issues
- Find additional help when you need it

Whether you are new to computers or just new to MacBooks, the first time something goes wrong with your computer is incredibly stressful! Performing some basic troubleshooting steps will usually resolve most computer problems. If these steps don't correct the issue, you will find additional detailed information in this chapter on troubleshooting common problems and finding extra help when you need it.

Basic Troubleshooting Steps

Even reliable computers like Macs experience hiccups from time to time. Sometimes you can perform the same task every day for months and then suddenly, for no reason at all, it just doesn't work. Well, there are reasons for these seemingly inexplicable events, but most of the time they are hidden way behind the scenes in your computer processes.

By performing the following simple steps, you will find that the majority of these little glitches, like frozen programs, crashing applications, or other anomalies, can be resolved quickly and without additional help. Just take a deep breath, follow these steps, and with some luck you'll be back up and running in no time at all.

Before performing any troubleshooting steps, it's a good idea to back up your important data to an external drive or onto CD/DVDs. If something goes terribly awry, you will still have the files that matter the most to you. See Chapter 19 for details on how to back up your system with Time Machine.

1. *Check the obvious.* When you call technical support, they often ask you almost insulting questions. Is your computer plugged in? Is it turned on? Are all of your cables and connections attached securely? They ask these questions because these are some of the most common reasons people call support. Save yourself the trouble and check all of these things before continuing. Sometimes plugs come loose from the wall or batteries aren't charged.

2. *Make a list of recent changes to your system.* Did you recently install a new program? Update your software? Maybe you connected a new device, like a printer or scanner? Think back on what you were doing just before the problem began. This might give you a clue as to where to start troubleshooting. If you have installed a new program or new hardware, uninstall it and see if that corrects the issue.

3. *Restart.* You'd be surprised at just how often this one works. Powering down your computer (especially if this is not a daily event for you) can help clear out any applications and processes that have been running in the background and perhaps contributing to your problem. You can get a fresh start and then see if the problem returns.

4. *Log out of your user account.* Log out of your user account and into your Guest account or another account. See if the problem still exists. If it doesn't, then you know that the issue is with your personal account and not the system software or your computer hardware.

5. *Run Software Update.* It could be that Apple has already released a fix for your problem. Run Software Update from Apple | Software Update to check for any new patches or fixes that are available for your system.

6. *Free up some space.* Computer applications tend to write a lot of temporary files that take up space when you are using them. If you do not have enough space on your hard drive, this can cause some issues. Delete unnecessary files, empty Trash, and remove any programs that you no longer use. After you've deleted your files and emptied the Trash, reboot to clear out any temporary files and see if the problem is resolved.

Common Problems and How to Fix Them

Some computer problems are incredibly common—so common that it's actually uncommon not to have experienced one or more of them at some point during your computer-owning lifetime. Examples of these problems include not being able to turn on or turn off your MacBook, becoming stuck in a frozen application, and experiencing graphics problems. This section discusses some of the most common issues and the steps you can take to correct them.

Your MacBook Won't Turn On or Won't Boot Properly

You should try these steps if your MacBook doesn't seem to be receiving any power and will not turn on, or if it does turn on but you experience display problems and/or do not hear any hard drive/fan activity:

1. Check your battery. If you are attempting to run your MacBook on battery power, you should check to see if the battery is charged. On MacBook and MacBook Pro models, there is a small button near the battery on the left side or bottom of your computer. Press it and green lights will appear to indicate your battery's charge. If only one light appears, you need to charge the battery. If that doesn't work, try running the computer on AC power.

 If you have the MacBook model that includes a battery that you can remove and replace yourself, try removing the battery for several minutes. Reinsert the battery and then try to turn the computer on.

2. Disconnect any external devices, such as a display, printer, scanner, keyboard, mouse, and so on. If you are connecting to the Internet through a wired connection, disconnect that as well. Attempt to start your computer when everything has been removed.
3. Check the outlet and your MagSafe port. Plug in another device to your wall outlet to make sure that it is receiving power. If you use a surge protector, make sure that the breaker has not been tripped and that it is active and receiving power. If it is, check that the prongs on your adapter are not damaged or dirty. Additionally, check your MagSafe port to ensure that it is clean and free of lint or other debris.
4. Make sure that you are using the correct power adapter. Do not use adapters that were not made for your computer's make and model.
5. Press the CTRL-COMMAND keys and the power button simultaneously to attempt to restart the computer.
6. Reset your PRAM. Press the power button and hold down all four of these keys: COMMAND-OPTION-P-R. Continue to hold them until you hear your MacBook's startup sound twice.
7. Reset the System Management Controller (SMC), which regulates your power settings, including battery management. Resetting it could resolve some power issues. See the How To box for instructions on how to perform an SMC reset on the two MacBook models.

 If your MacBook won't shut down, press and hold the power button for about ten seconds. That should cause the computer to power down.

What Is PRAM?

PRAM stands for parameter random access memory and is where some very important information for operating your MacBook is stored. This memory contains data on your personalized settings and your startup disk and display settings, among other things. Resetting it restores it to the factory defaults and can resolve some power and display issues.

How to...

Reset the System Management Controller on Your MacBook

There are two MacBook models: those that have a battery that the end user can remove and replace, and those that have a battery the user can't remove. Here's how to perform an SMC reset for each type.

SMC Reset for MacBooks with a Nonremovable Battery

1. Shut down the computer.
2. Plug in the MagSafe power adapter to a power source and connect it to your MacBook.
3. Press the SHIFT-CONTROL-OPTION keys and the power button simultaneously. Use the keys on the *left* side of the built-in keyboard.
4. Release the keys and the power button at the same time.
5. Press the power button to turn on the computer.

SMC Reset for MacBooks with a Removable Battery

1. Ensure the computer is powered off.
2. Disconnect the MagSafe power adapter from the computer.
3. Remove the battery.
4. Press and hold the power button for five seconds.
5. Release the power button.
6. Reconnect the battery and MagSafe power adapter.
7. Press the power button to turn on the computer.

Your MacBook Won't Recognize External Devices

If you use external devices like printers, scanners, external drives, or displays, you might find that, upon occasion, your MacBook suddenly doesn't recognize the device. Here are some steps to take to help you identify and correct the situation:

1. Check that all of your cables are connected and that the device is receiving power. Is the device turned on and working properly on its own? Is the outlet the device is plugged into active? Are the cables connected securely? Check all of these basic (and all too common) problem causers before moving onto other steps.
2. Make sure the cable isn't at fault. If you have a replacement cable, try connecting your device with that. Sometimes damage to the cable can cause it to stop working.
3. Shut down and restart your computer. See if your device is recognized.
4. Update your drivers. If you are working with a third-party, non-Apple piece of hardware, check the manufacturer's website for any driver updates or patches. Install them according to the directions provided along with the driver file.
5. Check the System Profiler. If you're a converted Windows user, this is similar to the Device Manager, except a lot more detailed. Open the System Profiler by choosing Apple | About This Mac | More Info (see Figure 20-1). A list of

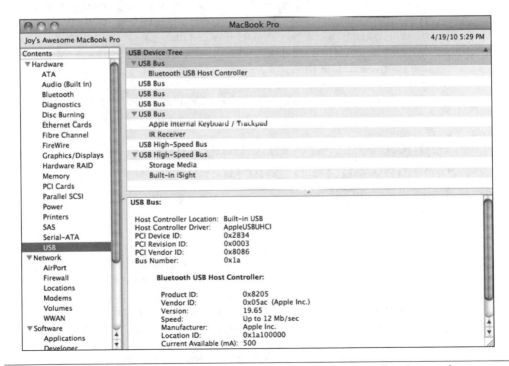

FIGURE 20-1   The System Profiler: more than you ever wanted to know about your MacBook

hardware and software appears in the left column. Click on USB and FireWire (MacBook Pro only) to see which devices your system recognizes as connected. If your device is listed there but doesn't work, then it's probably a software issue. Update your drivers or reinstall any software that came with the device. If your device is connected to the MacBook but doesn't appear, then it is a hardware problem.

6. Call the technical support number of the device manufacturer. You can usually find this on the Support page of the manufacturer's website.

Resolving Display Issues

If you turn on your MacBook and hear the fan and drives whirring but there's no video, you can take these steps to attempt to resolve the issue:

1. Check that the brightness of the screen is not set to zero. Increase the brightness by using the F2 key.
2. Reset your PRAM. Press the power button and hold down all four of these keys: COMMAND-OPTION-P-R. Continue to hold them until you hear your MacBook's startup sound twice.
3. Reset the SMC (see the "How To: Reset the System Management Controller on Your MacBook" sidebar earlier in this chapter).
4. Check whether your MacBook displays video when booting from a disk. Locate your installation/recovery disk and insert it into your optical drive. Shut down your MacBook and restart it while holding down the C key. This will cause your MacBook to boot from the disk. If you see video, your software may be corrupted. Use the Archive and Install function of the disk to create a new installation of your operating system without losing your personal data and files (but just in case, you already backed up your system, right? Right?).

Applications Are Crashing and Freezing on Your MacBook

Ah, the wonderful world of computer software glitches! Crashing applications! Frozen screens! Well, not to worry, there are a couple of steps you can try that will resolve the majority of your software problems.

1. *Reboot.* Yes, the numero uno problem solver! Shut down your computer and restart it. Relaunch the application and see if the problem persists.
2. *Check the system requirements.* Read the original packaging carefully. Check the system requirements against what you have running on your MacBook. Pay special attention to which operating system the software requires and the amount of memory it requires. Check the software developer's website in the Support section to see if there are known compatibility issues.

3. *Run Software Update.* Always run your Software Update utility to see if there are any system updates available that could address the problem.
4. *Remove and then reinstall the program.* This should remove any corrupted files.
5. *Repair disk permissions.* Permissions are what tell your MacBook who is able to access, read, and write to a file. Sometimes these files can get corrupted and need to be repaired. Open Disk Utility by choosing the Applications folder and then Utilities | Disk Utility. Click on your hard drive, then the First Aid tab, and finally the Repair Disk Permissions button (see Figure 20-2). Disk Utility will check your file permissions and repair any that require it.

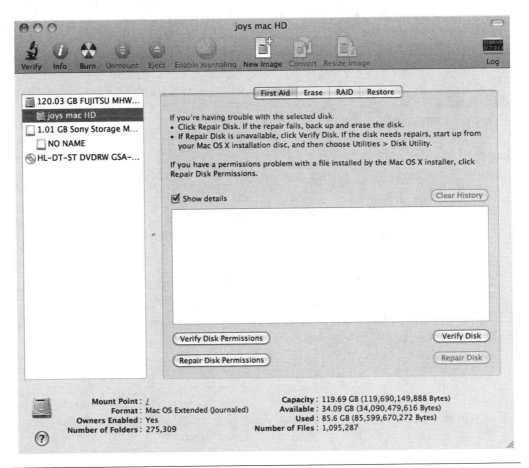

FIGURE 20-2 Check your disk permissions if you experience system slowdowns, permissions error messages, or software problems.

Boot into Safe Mode

Safe mode is a way to start your MacBook with only the minimum required processes and software running. This is a helpful tool for troubleshooting hardware and software issues. Shut down your computer and restart it. Press and hold the SHIFT key as soon as you hear the startup sound (not before). When you see the gray apple symbol, you can release the SHIFT key. Once in safe mode, your computer will scan its drives and directories, seeking out problems, and attempt to fix any that it finds. Once the MacBook is fully booted (and hopefully any issues are addressed), you can restart without holding down any keys to resume normal operations.

Tip If you experience a frozen application or process, try these two tricks to get moving again: stop a process by pressing COMMAND-period (.) or force an application to quit by pressing the COMMAND-OPTION-ESCAPE keys at the same time.

Find Additional Help

Whether you want additional help on working with an application or need help solving a problem that wasn't covered in this chapter, there are some resources available to you, both on your MacBook and online. You might be surprised at just how much information is available, if you know where to look!

The Mac OS X Help System

Even the most basic applications on your MacBook have their own help files included in Mac OS X. In the majority of cases, you will find the Help menu as the last entry in the menu bar. Figure 20-3 shows the iPhoto Help page. Figure 20-4 shows the iPhoto Help index, accessed by clicking Index in the upper-right corner of the main Help page. Depending on the application, you may be given a list of topics in the Help window or a brief overview of the application's main functions. It varies by program.

You can search Help through the search field or click the Index button to see all of the available topics. Click the Home menu button to choose Help for a different application or for help with the operating system.

Apple Online Support

Apple's website has a Support area that contains a wealth of detailed information to answer almost any question that you might have. Open your browser and head to www.apple.com/support to see what's available (see Figure 20-5).

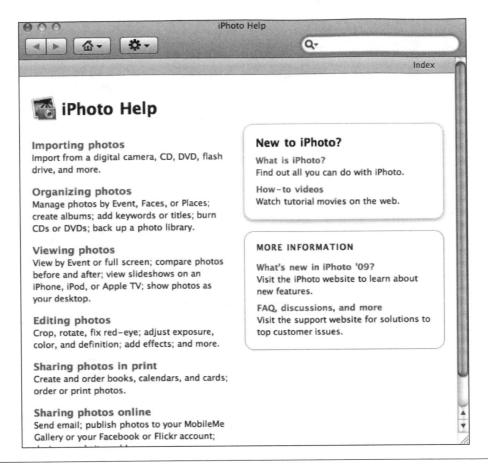

FIGURE 20-3   Select iPhoto Help and you'll be taken to the Help page.

Use the search box to seek product information or look for your product under the Browse Support heading in the left sidebar. Under Browse Support you will see Contact Us, containing links to Apple Technical Support and other resources. Here you will find tech support phone numbers and other options for contacting technical support personnel.

In the center of the page are the highlighted support features as well as links to product manuals (see Figure 20-6), technical specifications, and the Apple community. If you can't find an answer in the thousands of pages of Apple's support library, you can probably find an experienced Mac user in the community area who will answer a question or two.

In the right sidebar you will find the Self Service section, where you can check your product's warranty, check the status of a repair, or see your repair options for your MacBook.

FIGURE 20-4 Clicking Index shows all of the topics available in alphabetical order.

Additional Online Resources

Apple isn't the only website available with information on Macs. Check out these popular websites for tips, tricks, help, and Mac news.

News

- **Macworld** www.macworld.com, the official site of *Macworld* magazine
- **AppleInsider** www.appleinsider.com
- **MacInTouch** www.macintouch.com
- **MacLife** www.maclife.com

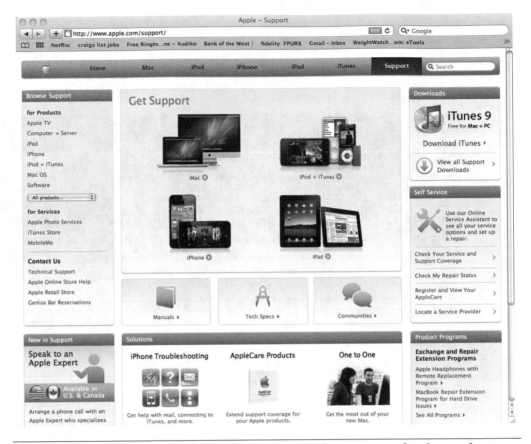

FIGURE 20-5 Apple's Support pages contain everything you need to know about your MacBook and its applications.

Tips and Tricks

- **Mac OS X Hints** www.macosxhints.com
- **MacYourself** www.macyourself.com
- **OS X Daily** www.osxdaily.com

Troubleshooting and Support

- **MacFixIt** http://reviews.cnet.com/macfixit
- **AllMac** http://allmac.com/
- **Macmend** www.macmend.com/

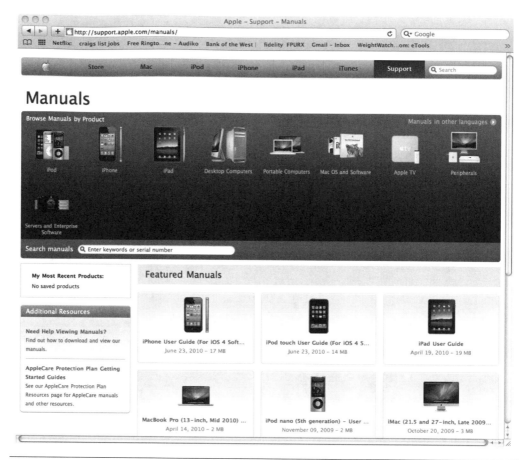

FIGURE 20-6 Lost your manual? You can probably find it online on the Apple Support site.

Summary

I hope this chapter has brought you some solace that all is not lost if your MacBook experiences some glitches. Computer problems happen to everyone, from the novice user to the expert. Using the steps in this chapter, you should be able to resolve many of the most common hardware and software problems that you might encounter. If not, you now have some great help resources at your fingertips and some new websites to check out for all things Mac!

Index

004.165
NOE